The Sikh Next Door

The Sikh Next Door

An Identity in Transition

MANPREET J. SINGH

BLOOMSBURY
NEW DELHI • LONDON • OXFORD • NEW YORK • SYDNEY

BLOOMSBURY INDIA
Bloomsbury Publishing India Pvt. Ltd
Second Floor, LSC Building No. 4, DDA Complex, Pocket C – 6 & 7,
Vasant Kunj, New Delhi 110070

BLOOMSBURY, BLOOMSBURY ACADEMIC INDIA and the Diana logo
are trademarks of Bloomsbury Publishing Plc

First published in India 2020
This edition published 2020
This paperback edition published 2023

Bloomsbury Academic India
An imprint of Bloomsbury Publishing Plc

ISBN: PB: 978-93-56404-67-0 eBook: 978-93-89165-58-6

2 4 6 8 10 9 7 5 3 1

Typeset in Minion Pro by Manipal Technologies Limited
Printed and bound in India by Thomson Press India Ltd

Bloomsbury Publishing Plc makes every effort to ensure that the papers used in the manufacture of our books are natural, recyclable products made from wood grown in well-managed forests. Our manufacturing processes conform to the environmental regulations of the country of origin.

FSC www.fsc.org MIX Paper from responsible sources FSC® C010615

To find out more about our authors and books visit www.bloomsbury.com and sign up for our newsletters

To Jai Jeet

His acute awareness of loss as a descendant of Sikh parents displaced during Partition, his alienation as the only turbaned boy in a school in Bihar, his early recognition that he did not belong in Punjab—the promised land, his discomfiture at being slotted into a type which he was not, his obsession with rooting himself through Gurmukhi language, Punjabi literature and music, are important strains underlying this work.

One way to avoid the hazards of rigidifying aspects of identity into a misleading categorical entity is to incorporate into the core conception of identity the categorically destabilising dimensions of time, space and relationality.

—Margaret R. Somers

Contents

Preface ix
Acknowledgements xii

Introduction
Beyond the Normative: Re-Contextualising Sikhs 1
1. Nudged Out of the Narrative: The Trader/Professional Sikh 15
2. Evolving Urban Profiles: From the Village to the City 49
3. They Are Not Like Us: Sikhs in Other Cultural Settings 71
4. Finding New Anchors: Sikh Identity in Foreign Lands 106
5. Process of Becoming: The Sikh Woman 144
6. Images and Stereotypes: Exploring the Impetus 176

Conclusion
Continuity in Change: A Centre that Holds 195

Glossary 203
Bibliography 208
Index 215
About the Author 229

Preface

When I talk of the Sikh next door, I mean one of the many you might encounter in everyday, normal, routine urban life. As individuals, they are different from the images associated with them—as obvious as the fact that those images still colour perceptions about them in stubborn ways. The purpose of this work is to look at the people behind those images by unhinging understanding from opinions already formed. It is to probe into who they are, how they are influenced by different pasts, and how that impacts their social stances in the present. It is to know the trajectories, which have broken and built them as a people, to discover the histories that have gone into the building of their identity and to understand the nuances of their engagement with the world around them.

Making this analysis has been a delicate process for it has involved a constant interplay between 'us' as the community understands itself, and the 'they' that is used to describe it from the outside. The baggage of the past continues to hang heavy at both ends, as do the very different narratives built on either side. There have been other factors too, like these narratives excluding important facets, or sustaining some despite their incongruence with lived reality. To make an analysis that fills these blanks, one that bridges the gaps with a story that remains true from either perspective, has been a challenging one.

The journey began with a senior fellowship from the Indo-Canadian Studies Centre, University of Mumbai, funded by the British Columbia province, through the University of Frazer Valley, British Columbia (Canada). The idea was to bring into focus the Sikh community in the centenary year of the *Komagata Maru* incident of 1914, when Indians, majorly Sikhs from British India, attempted to emigrate to Canada and were denied entry. For me, it was an unusual opportunity to make a concerted and academic analysis of an identity

I have personally lived. While that particular project dealt with Sikh identity in British Columbia, the research, once initiated was a roller-coaster ride leading to much more. One aspect which intrigued me was a heavy bent of the existing work towards the religious and political identity of the Sikhs. There was much lesser focus on their social identities or the shifts in them. Although one cannot dissociate one from the other, a lack of balance does create a stilted view.

As someone placed at a vantage point which has given me access to otherwise disparate and isolated narratives within the Sikh social life, it seemed particularly so. As an offspring to parents from two very different groups within the 'homogenous' Sikh identity, as someone who has lived both within community hubs and outside and felt acutely the difference between the community self-image and the one constructed by others, I saw crucial bits missing. During my research, I delved into socio-historical trajectories and broader community patterns within which these personal experiences are rooted. It helped scratch amnesiac patches in community narratives and those generated outside it. It also revealed gaps in understanding arising from perceptions caught in inertia and a people changing with time.

My apprehensions before venturing into this study were real. There was the oft-repeated danger of an insider's view. Would I lose objectivity while working on areas that have had a bearing on my own life? Or would my training as a researcher help me maintain a distance and allow an overview? It has been a journey through the unwieldy terrain of memories, observations, emotions, losses woven into the mental make-up, apprehensions inherited and experienced. It has also been one of pitting all this against research validated through systems and intellectual scrutiny, of using it to question narratives, and of resisting the pressure of expectation. This work has passed through innumerable revisions, till I found the blanks filling with cogent answers. Retrospectively, I feel that it is the insider perspective that has helped identify many of these blanks lying dormant within the folds of community experience.

The prospect of making the leap from literature, my core field, to a topic which flirted with history, sociology and even psychology, had seemed daunting too. However, as I proceeded, I realised that it is human stories which make the foundation of all disciplines. A background in literature has helped me to process data and theory into a lived human experience. As I have traced trajectories to the many facets of contemporary Sikh identity, an anchoring in literature has helped me construct the present as an organic outgrowth of the past. It has also made it easier to analyse Sikh experience as it emerges through works of fiction, popular culture, music and the stories these tell.

I have been lucky to have been working at a point preceded by significant primary research on different facets of Sikh identity. To be able to use that as a foundation has been a special privilege and I am thankful to all those whose work helped in formulating opinions and insights. Besides, one is also lucky to be equipped with other tools of analysis that have emerged from broader studies of social patterns across demographic and cultural spaces. These tools have helped in contextualising the Sikh experience within social anxieties, homing desires and identity shifts common to people and communities across the world. This, in turn, helps in rethinking the community responses in terms of underlying psychological patterns, rather than structuring them as exotic, heroic or even mock-heroic.

Although academic, the work deliberately avoids jargon to make it coherent to the general reader too. Questions about Sikhs as a people persist not only outside the community but also within it. This pertains more to the younger generation whose curiosity has not been blunted by stereotypes, in-group accounts or uncontextualised glimpses into the past. I hope this work provides some of the answers and creates the desire to know more.

Acknowledgements

The making of a book is attributed to the author only by default. It belongs to many others, who contribute to it in different ways. I would like to thank the people and the institutions that aided the process.

My thanks are due to Dr Nilufer E. Bharucha, former HOD, Department of English, and coordinator of the Indo-Canadian Studies Centre (ICSC), University of Mumbai. She not only helped begin the journey with a fellowship from ICSC but also shared her vast understanding of postcolonial and diaspora studies, prompting me to look beyond the focus I initially started with. Handling a canvas as big as the present one involves occasional slipping into directions which veer off the focus. She kept me on track with her incisive observations, at times leading to entire chapters being deleted. I hope the vast amount of work not included in this book will find a way into another one, for she has maintained that I had two books in making while working on one.

For my work on the Sikh diaspora, I am indebted to various people and institutions. Foremost among these is the Centre for Indo-Canadian Studies (CICS, now South Asian Studies Institute), University of Fraser Valley, British Columbia, Canada. The CICS provided the opportunity and logistical help for fieldwork in Canada. I thank Dr Satwinder Bains, Director CICS, who with her indefatigable energy, not only helped me connect to the community but also provided significant insights herself. I also thank Sharanjit Sandhra, Kusum Soni, Anju Dhindsa Gill and Ruby Rana for their nuanced perspectives. For insights into the lives of Sikhs in South East Asia, I thank Mr Ajeet Singh, Consul General of Singapore in Mumbai and a second-generation Sikh from Singapore. He was kind enough to connect me to others from Singapore and also helped source research material on Sikh diaspora in South East Asia.

For research on Sikhs in India, my thanks are due to members of the community across urban India who shared their memories, experiences and opinions. I am grateful to more than 90 people who took out time to reply to questionnaires. Their considered responses provided clues to the shifting dynamics within the community. I would also like to acknowledge internet bloggers, social-media enthusiasts and those associated with popular culture, whose work I used to gauge contemporary trends. My special gratitude to Dr Himadri Banerjee and Dr Birinder Pal Singh, who allowed me extensive use of their ground-breaking research on Sikhs in Bihar, in the North East and the Deccan. I thank Dr Pritpal Singh Anand and Mr Jagjot Singh who helped my understanding of Sikhs in Bihar. I also thank many elders, including my parents and mother-in-law, who through the labyrinths of memory, narrated little incidents, making interesting revelations on the shifts which the community has undergone.

My daughters, Harnidh and Sukhnidh, have been particularly potent triggers in the direction this work has taken. Living away from community hubs, they have posed difficult questions to which I have not always had convincing answers. Their curiosity about contexts to their lived experiences was not satisfied with distant histories or in-group narratives. As young adults with moorings in social sciences, they demanded a more nuanced understanding of their identity. I also saw their curiosity mirrored in others of their generation, who observed keenly and wished to know more. Their questions provided leads to many of the areas covered in the book.

If there is one person who has travelled every step of the journey with me, it is my husband Jai Jeet. The fact that a person as meticulous as him has lived with the chaos of lost files and crashed computers in a room cluttered with books and papers without complaining is reason enough to have his name in the acknowledgements. But he did more. From sourcing readings to hunting for material and arranging for interviews, going through my innumerable drafts to providing honest feedback, he has been there always, helping me through all the doubts.

Finally, my heartfelt thanks to Chandra Sekhar at Bloomsbury who has trusted me with creating a fresh, contemporary perspective on the Sikh community. Special thanks to Shreya Chakraborti at Bloomsbury and Nilanjana Dey, both of whom showed infinite patience as they helped me fine-tune the work.

Introduction

Beyond the Normative: Re-Contextualising Sikhs

There is a tendency to see people in unidimensional terms, ossifying them into types and stereotypes, thereby dismissing the dynamics operating within what is constructed as a closed category. This has been true of communities and the people within them. Ignoring their many constituent identities and the shifts these undergo through time and space results in perceptions incongruent to their lived realities. This results in images collated from points in history getting embedded in social memory, which then refuse to give way to more relevant ones. The collective image built around such identities forces those within them to negotiate with perceptions that are at odds with their lived experiences. It also confuses those looking at them from the outside, trying unsuccessfully to dismiss the differences as aberrations. Sikhs, as a community, have lived with such impositions, resulting in a tunnel view of their identity.

There could be many reasons for this, the most important being a lack of information and context. Being a minority, there have been no structured means of dissemination, which could have led to awareness regarding the community. Perhaps there has also not been an adequate emphasis on collating information through well-documented aspects and making it available to an interested readership. In recent times, there has been a spurt of research on diverse topics like the theological constructs of Sikhism, the evolution of Sikh identity through historical processes, specific events in the past and selective upheavals in recent times. These varied focuses document crucial aspects of Sikh experience, each providing significant insights. However, for these insights to become tools for constructing a more comprehensive understanding of the community, they need to be brought together as parts of a larger story, a continuum which offers links to the present. They need to be merged into one common background to create an understanding of the complexity and diversity of the way the community has evolved. This, moreover, needs to be structured in a language and syntax which makes it comprehensible to the average reader.

Gaps in understanding have also been created due to an imbalance of focus. What is ostensible is not always the whole; neither is the opportunity to construct knowledge always equitable. As a result, greater attention has been paid to particular aspects of the community relegating others to relative obscurity. The Sikh community, contrary to popular perception, is an accumulation of heterogeneous people under a homogenous identity. The different constituents of the community have come together through separate backgrounds, with different world views and have been differently impacted by diverse experiences of displacements, class and caste shifts, etc. Many of these experiences have not been fully integrated into the construction of the community identity. For instance, interest in Sikh identity has been largely focused on its agrarian and martial aspects, which pertain to particular sets of its people. There is hardly any focus on the trajectories of others from different occupational backgrounds. As a result, their stories have become peripheral to the dominant narrative, resulting in a lack of understanding of a substantial part of the community. The same is true of Sikhs in areas far away from Punjab, tethered to different pasts and influenced by cultural shifts. They too do not fit into the narratives constructed around the community and remain outside its purview. In the present context, even the so-called normative identities are in the process of changing, thus leading to new identity patterns, which do not fit the existing tropes. There, thus, needs to be a reallocation of space to bring in those who are different from the prevailing notions of Sikh identity or are in the process of transitioning to different ones. One needs to forcefully draw into the picture what has been pushed outside the frame or what no longer fits in. The narratives structured around the community must be rewritten with due place given to its various actors, for an authentic construction of its contemporary identity.

There is also an overarching tendency to construct the Sikh community primarily in terms of the politics surrounding their religious identity. Though significant, it does not preclude the necessity of looking into other important aspects of their lives. Surinder S. Jodhka says, 'The changing nature of social and economic life of the Sikhs, their internal dynamics and divisions, their experience of development over the last five or six decades, or the effects of globalisation and migration on the social well-being of the community have mostly remained marginal concerns…'(2009). These are crucial to the understanding of their changing profiles and shifting priorities. There is a concomitant lack of focus on how this new identity negotiates with the broader social milieus in which the community exists. How it struggles to reorient itself within new contexts or why this attempt faces resistance from certain quarters is not being given adequate attention. Identity has to be rooted within the 'change in the surrounding contexts – changes in the groups and networks in which people and their identities are embedded and in the societal structures and practices in which those networks themselves are embedded'(Howard 2000). There is a need to contextualise the community's shifts within its social surroundings. This includes, among other things, analysing the responses of the people they live amidst, probing the dynamics these involve and revaluating the shapes this takes. This is imperative to stepping out of old paradigms into new ones.

Meanwhile, the community remains caught in the web of limiting and anachronistic images deriving from unresolved historical anxieties tethered to the past. Intellectual inertia filters into social perceptions, preventing any outlook except the one garnered through a pre-set lens. The result is a skewed perception of the community. Vacillating between images of men in bhangra regalia dancing in mustard fields and the obtuse Santa–Banta stereotype, between the dichotomous images of valorous soldiers and hated terrorists, the blingy sardar of Bollywood movies and the exotic Nihang, the average Sikhs find no adequate representation of who they are. Many of them, living normal urban lives and pursuing the same goals as others in similar circumstances, are left to grapple with images, which do not resonate with their lives. The stereotypes foisted on them are not just amusing social irrationalities. They create difficult undercurrents because of the power paradigms underlining them. They also prevent a nuanced comprehension of the community and its shifts.

This work is an attempt to push aside such images to make way for more relevant ones. It focuses on real-life people to see how they have evolved through the complex shifts of time. It also broadens the frame of reference to create a more comprehensive community profile. It probes neglected histories, marginalised identities and shifting profiles within the community. It also contextualises these within broader social milieus. In tracing these evolutions through old and new contexts, it establishes the centrality of these identities to the understanding of the Sikh community as it exists today. Among these are sections with histories of displacement and minority positioning. There are those, whose profiles have been changing through processes of urbanisation. There are also Sikhs whose interactions with other cultures, at home and abroad, are changing them in fundamental ways. There are shifting gender paradigms evolving through contestations of a progressive religion and a not-so-progressive social system. Within this spectrum also lie the many subaltern identities, some of whom have broken through their caste and economic disadvantages and some who continue to be caught in them, within the new environments.

By contextualising these disparate facets of Sikh identity within their pasts and linking that to their present, this work hopes to situate them squarely within an understanding of the contemporary Sikh profile. This leads towards creating a more nuanced comprehension of behaviours otherwise susceptible to stock portrayals. It would explain, for example, the street-smart attitude of the Delhi Sikh whose tendency to hoard and display is rooted in a history of displacement. It hopes to bring an understanding of the aggressive young Chandigarh Sikh flaunting his Hummer, pit bulls and guns or the Dalit Sikh whose brash assertion of identity deflects off a barely concealed hurt. It hopes to explain more about the Bihari Sikh whose peculiar accent makes him susceptible to double 'othering'. The study of staggered diasporic identities could explain the difference between the Surrey Jack with a *khanda* tattooed on his arm and the turbaned student in a university campus—just as it would provide a perspective on the Sikh woman who writes Kaur against her name with elan, even as she pushes the boundary of the culture that usurped the right to define the identity it entails.

The book traces how these varied profiles have formulated and mutated over time. It begins by bringing into focus the non-rural trader Sikh, who over time has been constructed as an anomaly to what has come to be seen as the real Sikh identity. There is often the misconception that Sikhs necessarily have an agricultural background, and that in their association or disassociation with that rural past lies their awkward relationship with contemporary urban life. To go beyond this frame of reference, the study creates a broader identity base. It considers the intra-community differences, which have characterised the community profile since the time of its inception and continue to influence its internal dynamics. 'Nudged Out of the Narrative: The Trader/Professional

Sikh' provides a background to this by focusing on the Khatris and the Jats, most starkly representing backgrounds in trading and agriculture, their very different socio-cultural orientations, and their respective integral places within the community identity. The discussion tries to place the two groups in their respective historical contexts to show how the less recognised of the two has evolved as a people, and why their difference needs to be recognised as a reality for a reconstruction of a more inclusive community identity.

It attempts to show how historical turns have led to the repeated displacement of the traditionally urban traders and professional Sikhs and a concomitant rise in the power of the agriculturist Sikhs. Over time, the community has come to be identified with the cultural tropes of the latter, leaving the former stuck with images that clash with their real identities. Under focus are Sikhs living in North Indian cities, particularly New Delhi and adjoining areas, who contribute substantially to Sikh visibility outside Punjab. Most of them are descendants of Partition refugees who came from West Punjab. On one hand, their peculiar positioning in East Punjab, now the Indian Punjab, renders them as 'others' within their community. On the other hand, their attempts at relocating within a diffident majority outside Punjab has resulted in a mutated and diluted identity. There has been a failure to recognise their awkwardly positioned identity as one with its distinct focuses and interests, many times different from those of the agriculturist Sikhs. Contextualisation of their contemporary identity within Partition and the second setback in 1984 following the political upheavals in Punjab, shows how this class has suffered due to a thwarted identity entrenchment. Woven within these contexts are new ones, created by the opportunities of liberalisation and globalisation. The second and third generations of those impacted are now tiding over many of the earlier disadvantages. This has also helped close the gap between them and others from the community drawn into similar shifts.

A steadily growing Sikh urban middle-class with rural backgrounds is another new facet demanding individual attention. 'Evolving Urban Profiles: From the Village to the City' focuses on those Sikhs, who over time have shifted base from villages to cities in Punjab and other places in the country. These transitions, propelled by both historical factors and recent developments, involve not just the Jats but also other rural groups such as the Mazhabis and Ramgarhias. The Green Revolution in Punjab, economic liberalisation and the desire to avail the growing opportunities of urban life, have led to a sharp spurt in their numbers. However, the shift from a rural to an urban life entails a complex interplay of psychological adjustments that is not always a smooth process. This has been further complicated by the fact that the new opportunities and the levelling inherent in urban life have led to different shifts for different groups within the community. For some, it has demanded the relinquishing of an ego-enhancing identity rooted in the rural past, while for others it has brought greater empowerment than what that old life afforded. Attempts at maintaining old hierarchies within new surroundings and counter-attempts have led to complex undercurrents. This work sifts through these shifting identity paradigms to show the evolution of new dimensions within Sikh social identity.

There is a substantial Sikh community in places like Bihar, Bengal, Assam, Meghalaya, Nanded in Maharashtra and Hyderabad in Andhra Pradesh. Many among them are quite unlike the Sikhs in the North, who despite their differences, do form a part of the recognised Sikh identity. Among their staggered identities lie histories of people who followed the gurus to distant places and stayed on as bearers of legacies, of locals who converted to the faith but continued old cultural practices, of those who came in search of work and stayed on, gradually adopting local customs. The fact that they look and sound different due to cultural assimilation, makes them less acceptable within the community in the northern hubs. There are also the more recent migrants who might have preserved their language and culture but do not fit into the ego-enhancing image of the exuberant, successful and powerful Sikh community. In either case, it has led to a convenient overlooking of their peripheral existence by the community and others. 'They Are Not Like Us: Sikhs in Other Cultural Settings', explores the fluidities inherent in identities which are difficult to comprehend unless one acknowledges a Sikh history broader, bigger and more inclusive in intent. It also points to the need to draw these identities within the construction of an inclusive community identity.

Sikhs, particularly from East Punjab, have also had a history of migration to countries beyond their own. The trend was initiated by the British recruitment of Sikhs from rural areas into their army and paramilitary forces, who were then deputed to various British colonies, areas of economic interest and arenas of war. Many more from home followed them in the hope of being absorbed within similar positions and when that was not possible, to find other occupations which were financially more lucrative than the opportunities back home. The fascinating trail of Sikh arrival in South East Asia, their movement as British subjects to other British colonies, and the different trajectories these led to provide a background to the substantial Sikh diaspora in places as diverse as Singapore, Australia, Canada, US and UK, etc. In more recent times, Sikh communities are also establishing themselves in various European countries. Meanwhile, the trend to migrate from Punjab continues unabatedly as people move out for better opportunities and living standards. Defined by the different contexts of their departure and arrival in host countries, these Sikhs have undergone different processes of adjustment, with responses shifting over time.

'Finding New Anchors: Sikh Identity in Foreign Lands' focuses on the different forms these overtures have assumed and how these have influenced the Sikh profile over time. While identity formations persist at different levels for the old and the new migrants, these reveal the broad evolving patterns indicating the direction Sikh diasporic identities are taking. The shift in focus from nostalgia for the old life to a better entrenchment in current homes is evident. This, in turn, has involved recalibrating how cultural and religious identities are reinforced in adopted homes. It has also involved establishing new transcultural networks and practices. The importance of analysing these shifts lies in tracing the gradual breakdown of previous selves and the tentative formulation of new ones, which leads to social behaviours that cannot be slotted in old community tropes. This work attempts to integrate these shifts into old perceptions about the diaspora Sikhs for a better understanding of their contemporary identities.

Within these stories of different Sikh groups also lie the stories of their women. While sharing the histories of their men, they have also been going through their own journeys of becoming. Constructed within the liberal intellectual tradition of their religion and the patriarchal bent of the social culture within which it has operated, Sikh women have negotiated their positioning within the community in peculiar ways. The public and private narratives about the place accorded to them within the community have at times been inimical to each other. These contradictions have interplayed differently within the socio-cultural legacies, community power structures, inter-community power paradigms and new social modalities. 'Process of Becoming: The Sikh Woman' looks at this journey through past trajectories and a slowly changing present. It also traces it through other variables like class and caste dynamics, demographic shifts and processes of urbanisation. The advantage of the liberal religious foundation, which has forced inroads into an otherwise conservative socio-cultural structure, has had interesting implications. At one level, it has allowed processes of empowerment like education for girls, which are bringing shifts within the community. At another level, it has not disallowed little everyday subversions of patriarchal mandates that have traditionally created gender disparities. This does not, however, veer the focus away from larger issues like sex selection and economic disadvantage that the Sikh women continue to face but are conditioned not to verbalise.

An analysis of these varied constituent identities and the pasts through which their contemporary stances and behaviours have evolved is important to reframe contemporary Sikh identity. Equally important, however, is an analysis of its locus in broader social milieus to see how others respond to it. 'Images and Stereotypes: Exploring the Impetus' focuses on this. The response to the community, within the country and outside, varies in the undercurrents in which it is rooted. Within the home country, it is shaped by the cleaving of one identity into two through social and political upheavals. Hence, the majority's response swings between claiming the community as its own and also 'othering' it through socially acceptable mediums. Sardar jokes and Sikh representation in cinema are some examples. An analysis of the stereotypes constructed around the Sikh and the reluctance to let him step out of these tropes reveals the anxieties underlining the responses and the reservations in accepting his difference. These anxieties have also manifested in open hostility and serious harms in times of crises, as during the 1984 carnage. Outside the country, the response to the community is rooted in peculiar histories of arrival and settlement in different places. For instance, in South East Asia, historical circumstances have aided the evolution of an educated and culturally acceptable community profile, thus influencing perceptions of the people they live amongst. In the West, Sikhs continue to be associated with a working-class immigrant identity, constantly connected to the home culture. This, in turn, holds threatening connotations for the locals in terms of jobs taken and their culture infiltrated. Whether in the home country or abroad, the responses to the community seem to be hinged to the past and many times out of sync with its shifting profile. A focus on these issues probes into the disjunct between the community's self-image and the images constructed from the outside, keeping in mind the importance of bridging the gap.

How the community responds to these varied experiences has its own stories of resistance and accommodation. The mixed responses include an emerging emphasis on a proactive attempt to explain and consolidate their identity, instead of being limited by constructions from outside. The impact is reflected in the gradual change in the images constructed around the Sikhs. The power of social media as a medium of outreach and greater availability of education, language and expression is helping the young among the community in creating a more comprehensive and inclusive image of the Sikhs. The reciprocity from outside, influenced by the growing emphasis on respecting difference, of the need to understand minority identities and a more nuanced mapping of Sikh identity is also helping the process. 'Continuity in Change: A Centre that Holds' reflects on these trends while also focusing on the different ways in which Sikhs are consolidating their core collective identity within the shifting parameters. The younger generations of Sikhs are negotiating with many more identities than the linear ones of an earlier time. The apprehension that this might relegate religious and community identities to a less significant place is a concern within the community. On the contrary, despite the movement away from closed in-groups and the changes brought by new influences, young Sikhs are eager to maintain their religious and community identities. They are redefining the ways in which they do so, some of which might not always find favour with the conservative sections, but do ensure continuity of practice and commitment to identity. Moreover, the many convergences that urban life entails bring different constituents of the community closer than they have been before. The work concludes by showcasing some of these new trends within the community.

By bringing together these different threads, one hopes to adequately emphasise that identities are neither insular nor static. They are impacted by internal heterogeneities as well as shifting contexts of the larger worlds in which these operate. While this work tries to provide a window to a broader and more relevant understanding of Sikhs, it does not claim to be exhaustive. The vastness of the subject at hand has necessitated a selective approach. While dealing with each of the areas, selected strains have been focused on for their overarching impact on the evolution of the identities under consideration. For instance, the analysis of the traditionally non-rural component of the community focuses primarily on the Khatri Sikh leaving out many more subgroups. The analysis of the urban Sikh's experience of Partition and events of the eighties does not minimise the impacts of the two situations on the rural Sikh or the Sikh in Punjab but leaves that for another study. The lack of focus on contemporary rural Sikh identity only pre-supposes that adequate attention has been paid to it in works with a different focus. The many other identities pushed out of the Sikh fold in course of its evolution into the present form also do not find a mention in this work. The urban Sikh identity evolving outside the country leaves out a lesser number of Sikhs living in many other parts of the world, whose experiences are as important as those residing within bigger groups. The analyses of the stereotypes perpetuated through jokes and stilted representations in Indian cinema can be extended to a much vaster study. These selective focuses in no way reduce the significance of what has been left out, and one hopes they will be explored at greater length in future studies.

I would like to express gratitude to those whose critical works have formed the foundation of this work. These have helped in creating well-researched backgrounds, allowing me to draw trajectories and provide links to contemporary stances. Without the threads provided by them, it would not have been possible to weave the tapestry that reveals bigger patterns. McLeod's crucial insights into the institutionalisation of Sikh religion, Harjot Oberoi's work on the processes of identity construction within the community and Pashaura Singh's collation of work on different facets of Sikh life have offered important clues. So have Anshu Malhotra's insights into social diversities within the Sikh community and Giorgio Shani's analyses of the construction of Sikh political identity. Nicola Mooney's work on Jat Sikhs in India and abroad, and Priya Khanna Mahajani's work on the shift from rural to urban identities in India have provided crucial insights. Veena Das's focus on the experiences of Partition and the underlying trends in violence against the Sikhs in 1984 has provided insights not always revealed through statistics. Surinder S. Jodhka's focus on caste within Sikhism, marginalised Sikh identities explored by Himadri Banerjee and Birinder Pal Singh are important steps towards exploring peripheral stories in the community. Darshan Singh Tatla's work on Sikh diaspora, A.P.S Mandair's painstaking collation of patterns of Sikh migration outside India, Gwar Kristina Myrvold's focus on Sikh diaspora in Europe, Arunajeet Kaur's collation of Sikh experiences in South East Asia, Cao Yin's work on Sikhs in China, Rory G. McCarthy's research on Sikhs in Australia are among those, which have helped in constructing the many facets of Sikh diasporic identity. Insights have also been garnered from scholars of diaspora studies like Avtar Brah, Verne Dusenbury, Martin Sokefield, Robert Cohen, Khachig Tololyan and others. Focus on Sikh women owes to the contributions of Karamjit K. Malhotra, Doris Jakobsh, Anshu Malhotra and Purnima Dhavan. Natasha Behl's research has provided important leads, particularly in introducing the theories of Margaret Somers and Linda Martin Alcoff. Insights on stereotypes surrounding Sikhs have derived from the work of Parvinder Mehta, Harleen Kaur, Jawaharlal Handoo.

Insightful analysis of humour surrounding ethnic identities in the works of Christie Davies, Melissa Hughes, Joseph Boskin and Joseph Dorinson, Gislinde Kuipers and many more have helped in the analysis of power paradigms underlying them. The insights provided by these researchers are the building blocks that have gone into structuring this work. The overview, which I have tried to create, owes itself to each one of them and others who might not be mentioned here.

References

Jodhka, Surinder S. 2009. 'Sikhs in contemporary times: Religious identities and discourses of development'. In *Sikh Formations*, June, 5(1): 1–22.

Howard, Judith A. 2000. *Social Psychology of Identities*. In *Annual Review of Sociology*: 367–368. Seattle, Washington.

1

Nudged Out of the Narrative: The Trader/Professional Sikh

Community identities are deceptive in their display of homogeneity for they are multitudinous assimilations, holding subgroup schemas and stratification statuses. This is true of the Sikh community too and derives from the fact that Sikhism emerged out of a fluid social order. The religion attracted followers from diverse backgrounds and occupations that sometimes included people with conflicting interests and attitudes. This resulted in divergent strands within the community with different trajectories and cultural focuses. Two such strands, with fundamentally different worldviews, are the trader/professionals and the agriculturists. The former represents the mercantile and service class. The latter, apart from being the face of the Sikh agricultural community, also represents its martial identity. Bound by a common faith but fundamentally different from each other, the two groups have often presented confusing and contradictory stances in behaviour, attitude and priorities. Through historical and political twists, as the numerically stronger agriculturists have gained advantage, the narrative centred around Sikhs as an agricultural community has overshadowed the story of the trader/professional class. This has been exacerbated by the tragic displacements and losses of the latter during Partition and its aftermath. A growing marginalisation within the community as well as national narratives has also resulted in their distinct identity being subsumed within the dominant community identity. This, in turn, has led to a tendency to measure them by false normatives creating misleading attributions with crucial implications ranging from the banal to the serious. The undocumented history of these experiences holds within itself more than just material losses. It carries within it a story of an identity compromised, of a position repeatedly thwarted and also a resilience, which has seen them through it all.

A reconstruction of this history vis-à-vis the contemporary positioning of the Sikh trading community is important for many reasons. Apart from allowing an understanding of their distinct group schema, it helps trace the sequence of events that led to their once-dominant position within the community being compromised. Shifts in power paradigms can become 'explanatory devices and justification of social relationships' (Howard 2000). These contexts, therefore, also help analyse subsequent evaluations created around their difference from those who replaced them in the hierarchy. It shows how, while on one hand it constructed them as anomalies within the highly masculinised community identity, on the other hand, outside that identity, it also made them susceptible to being identified with the views not necessarily their own. Theirs thus became an identity doubly challenged within the community and the nation. An understanding of these backgrounds helps re-situate them within a frame of reference allowing greater cognisance of their identity. It also provides better understanding of the behavioural stances and attitudinal patterns of the group.

The trading community among the Sikhs is identified, among others, with two important subgroups called the Khatris and the Aroras. Among these, it is the Khatris who assume a greater significance because of their once-powerful position within the evolving Sikh identity, which gradually shifted to the Jats or the agriculturists. An understanding of the dynamics this involved and how it impacted future perceptions of the community, requires contextualisation within the past. Both the traders and agriculturists were integral parts of Punjabi society before they came into the Sikh fold. Historically, the Khatris had been concentrated in the central and western parts of Punjab. Their observance of upper-caste social codes and better financial position gave them a privileged place in the social hierarchy. Broadly speaking, they were categorised into four main subsections called the Bahris, Bunjahis, Sarins and Khokhran. Within these were various *zats* which were endogamous groups. Within the *zats* were *got*s or exogamous groups with lineages tracing common descent through male progeny. The Khatris distinguished themselves from other mercantile castes like the Aroras. They spread to areas of Pothowar, Gujranwala, Rawalpindi, Lahore etc. of present-day Pakistan, and beyond that to Hazara and the Western Hill states. Some of them were also located in places like Baluchistan, Iran, Afghanistan because of business opportunities and due to their appointments by the ruling powers. Some among them also served in non-combative civil and petty administrative positions. Their occupations, caste and cultural patterns distinguished them from the agriculturists in the central and eastern parts of Punjab whose identities were rooted in the land. These agriculturists, mainly Jats, were closely bound to the demographics they evolved through, and the areas and villages they belonged to. Demarcations based on common descent were more important to them than caste (Malhotra 2002: 30). A hardworking and physically robust people, they resisted authority, could make good allies and bad enemies. Within the larger Punjabi social order, however, the Jats were placed at the lower rungs of the caste hierarchy due to their agricultural background and the socio-cultural patterns prevalent therein (P. Singh 2010).

Khatri Pre-dominance in the Early Phase of Sikh Evolution

In the 15th century, people from different occupations had started following Guru Nanak, the founder of Sikhism. Nanak himself came from a Hindu Khatri family from Talwandi near Lahore. His father Mehta Kalo was the *patwari* (the official land record keeper) of his village. As Nanak grew up, his inclination for the spiritual manifested in a negation of the upper-caste social codes followed by his family. Nanak's understanding of spirituality was personal and did not concede any importance to dogma and ritual. Rather, he propagated its outer manifestation in the form of a righteous engagement with social existence. This righteousness involved egalitarianism and compassion while dispensing with superstitions and ritualism. In a way, Guru Nanak's teachings offered a middle path between asceticism and worldly life, which could still lead to spiritual fulfilment. His practical philosophy attracted followers from all walks of life and caste hierarchies. For the Khatris, it provided a way to spiritual connection, more fulfilling than mere ritualism, while carrying on with the business of life. For the Jats, who seem to have been drawn to spiritual groups that condemned rigid caste hierarchies, it provided a sense of dignity. Just as some among them had been drawn in large numbers to Sufi shrines like those of Baba Farid, others were now drawn to the new Sikh faith.

Guruship in Sikh faith did not necessarily pass from father to son, at least in the early phases. However, it did continue being passed on to members of different *gots* of the Khatri group. While Guru Nanak belonged to the Bedi *got*, Guru Angad, the second in line, came from the Trehan *got*, Guru Amar Das, the third guru, belonged to the Bhalla *got*. All the gurus who followed came from the Sodhi *got*. This led to an increase in Khatri influence among the gradually evolving religion. The process of the entry of the rural people had already begun during the period of Guru Nanak and continued with the successive gurus. As the son of a land-owning *patwari*, Guru Nanak's association with the peasantry was not new. In the later years of his life, he chose to settle down in Kartarpur, a village largely populated by the cultivators. This was the first step towards bridging the gap between the urban culture of the Khatris and the rural lives of the agriculturists (P. Singh 2010).

While in due course, an increasing number of followers of Sikhism began to come from the rural background, the leadership role remained in Khatri hands. The primacy of the Khatris is reflected in the fact that all Sikh gurus were Khatris. Moreover, in the early stages of Sikh formation, all leading members came from among the Khatris while the agriculturists existed at a less significant level of membership (McLeod 2000: 60).

The fourth guru, Guru Ramdas, conceived the idea of digging a tank in village Tung in the Majha region of Punjab hoping that people from all professions would settle around it. This came to be called Ramdaspur and would emerge later as the holy city of Amritsar. The fifth guru, Guru Arjan Dev, got a centre of worship built in the centre of this tank and called it the Harmandar. In 1604, he had the Adi Granth installed in it making it the most important Sikh spiritual centre. While the Khatri dominance in the *guru ghar* continued, Guru Arjan Dev's focus on the well-being of the agriculturists of the area reflects the growing connection of the Sikh gurus with the rural population. Among the many measures he took, one was the excavation of a well with six Persian wheels (*chheharta*), an irrigation technology for which the Mughals had extracted a huge revenue from the Jats. This had caused discontent and uprisings against the Mughal officials. Such measures brought many more from the proud and loyal Jat class into the Sikh fold, a shift already causing unease among the Mughals. Akbar, in fact, sought cordial diplomatic relations with Guru Arjan Dev as an indirect means of controlling these otherwise turbulent people.

The rising Sikh influence was in itself a cause of concern for the Mughal emperors. The growing presence of the belligerent and not-easily-cowed-down Jats within its fold was an added reason for apprehension. Guru Arjan Dev's blessings to Khusrau, the rebellious son of Jehangir, became the last straw. In a rapid escalation of tension, Guru Arjan Dev was captured by the Mughal forces, tortured and killed in Lahore. To consolidate power against Mughal hostility in

1634, Guru Hargobind, the next guru, decided to shift base from Amritsar to Kiratpur, a village in the Shivalik Hills, which separated the plains of Punjab from the Himalayas and was on the fringe of the Mughal empire. Guru Tegh Bahadur, the ninth guru, shifted base from Kiratpur to nearby Anandpur. Constant skirmishes with the combined forces of the Hill Rajas and the Mughal forces required military upkeep. From the time of Guru Hargobind to the time of the last living guru, Guru Gobind Singh, the gurus took upon themselves the mantle of political as well as spiritual leadership. Defending the right to their faith became as important as practising it.

The Rising Jat Influence within the Sikh Fold

As the gurus aggregated power, they also required men, money and weapons to establish armies. This made way for the rise of the Jats to a more prominent position within the Sikh fold. Most of them were *khud kasht* or self-cultivating farmers. Some, who had ventured into ploughing uncultivated tracts along the rivers in Punjab, settled down permanently in those areas, aggregating clout. They eventually got rights to collect taxes from the people who came later. As their economic influence increased, they also aspired for upward social mobility. One means to such aspirations, worldwide, has been affiliation with socio-religious groups which have an already established standing (Dhavan 2014: 51). The Sikh gurus came from upper castes but negated the distinctions made by caste hierarchies, which made Sikhism a favourable option. Moreover, as a fiercely independent people, they were frequently in cudgels with Mughal authority. Aligning themselves with the increasingly militarised Sikh sect gave them a better standing and made them a part of an organised group gearing to fight Mughal authority. They started contributing lavishly to the Sikh gurus by way of cash, arms, horses and military manpower. Letters of the gurus testify that in due course they became critically important in the Punjab Hills (Dhavan 2014). By the 17th century, a substantial proportion of the *panth*'s membership was already Jat, and as a group, they were steadily gaining greater influence (McLeod 2000: 61).

As the 18th century began, Guru Gobind Singh, then Guru Gobind Rai, the last of the living Sikh gurus, found his position in Punjab reaching a crisis. Repeated attacks by Rajput rulers ruling other hill areas of Punjab, along with the existent threat from the Mughals, made his position vulnerable. Adding to his troubles was the reluctance of the influential Khatri members to pay attention to these disturbances (61). Having traditionally worked for the Mughal kings, they did not wish to be seen as standing against them. This was a challenge to the guru's authority. Added to it was the misuse of their clout deriving from some of their traditional roles. The Khatris till then had also wielded considerable power as the links between the guru and his followers. As per the practice started by the fourth guru, Sikh followers in places other than the one where the guru resided followed the directives of the *masands* appointed by the gurus. The *masands*, generally from the Khatri class, collected the offerings made by the faithful and sent it to the gurus for the upkeep of the Sikh administrative, military and religious establishments. There were, however, increasing instances of the *masand*s creating power centres in this role. In cognisance of the undue power aggregated by the Khatris and their dwindling allegiance in the fight against the Mughals, Guru Gobind Singh abolished the *masand* system and did away with their authority as mediators. Instead, he ordered a direct connect with his followers. In 1699, he created the Khalsa fold. Those who partook initiation into the fold were given a new identity, which dismissed all previous power hierarchies. It recognised no caste or class differences, only allegiance to the teachings of the gurus and a zeal to fight oppression under the leadership of the guru. Some accounts indicate that a section among the Khatris was even wary of adopting the Khalsa identity, for fear of being othered within their existing Khatri kinship networks in which caste identity and the practices it entailed remained crucial. While the ending of the caste hierarchies was a setback to their traditionally superior status, their dithering over adopting a clear position in the new power paradigm adversely impacted their place within the community as well.

Meanwhile, the Jats gained further influence when in 1705, the joint forces of the Mughals, Rajput and Hill Rajas tried to destabilise Guru Gobind Singh. He shifted his seat from Anandpur and moved to a region of Punjab called Malwa. Here, he made important contacts with Jat groups, and they joined the Khalsa in huge numbers (Dhavan 2014: 50). This gradually shifted the character of the Sikh following, particularly those directly involved in fighting for the Sikh faith and position. There remained Khatri leaders within the fighting force but their numbers were far exceeded by the Jats. McLeod feels that from here on, powerful Jat influences in some measure influenced the changing character and philosophy of the developing *panth* (2000: 61). Many critics have questioned McLeod's presumption, pointing out that it was the guru's decision to militarise the Sikh order rather than the influence of the Jats, which further militarised the Sikh faith. In a way, it was the logical progression of Guru Nanak's emphasis on the necessity of combining spiritual righteousness with social life that now emerged as the same righteousness merging with political life. In either case, it brought the more aggressive component of the community to the forefront. The Jat temperament was better suited to the emerging focus of the Sikh faith. It is to be remembered, however, that despite the growing influence of the Jats within the military culture of Guru Gobind Singh's time, the other prominent sections of the Sikh *panth* continued to survive in the non-militarised social and spiritual spheres (2000: 63).

The Rise of the Sikh Kingdom, Divided Areas of Influence

After the death of Guru Gobind Singh in 1708, the Sikhs were led by Banda Bahadur for a short while. He was arrested by the Mughals a few years later and the armies of the Khalsa—now leaderless and divided into groups—were involved in constant infighting and skirmishes even though they acknowledged a common Khalsa identity. This period also coincided with repeated attacks by Afghans under Ahmad Shah Abdali, who also desecrated the Golden Temple in Amritsar. The need to fight a common enemy led to the organisation of Sikh *misl*s or units with independent leaders and defined territories. A majority of these *misl*s were led by Jat leaders. Once the Afghans withdrew, the leaders of the *misl*s started fighting among themselves in a bid to gain ascendancy within the Khalsa fold. Many of them established independent states. The 18th century thus proved to be a phase of survival and struggle for them. Eventually, Ranjit Singh—the Jat Sikh leader of the powerful Sukerchakia *misl*—consolidated power by bringing many other *misl*s under his leadership. He expanded his kingdom and went on to occupy Lahore to become the most powerful Sikh ruler. This gave further impetus to Jat ascendancy among the Sikh fold.

While the pride in the formation of the Sikh kingdom was common to the entire community, there were subterraneous apprehensions. The shift in the power paradigm was apparent and was causing apprehensions. It is reflected in voices from the era, even though not specifically in response to a particular event. For instance, Waris Shah, the well-known poet from Punjab, wrote of a social order falling apart. He refers to men of menial birth and peasants flourishing, the Jats taking over as the masters and creating new modes of government while the nobles were reduced to a pitiable situation (Malhotra 2002: 21).

As a ruling class, martial identity became more significant for the Sikhs. Although there were Khatris, Muslims as well as French in

Ranjit Singh's army, the dominant warrior identity was Jat. The fact that the reigning king belonged to the same group, probably further bolstered the status of the group despite Ranjit Singh's democratic practices. Paintings of the time portray Sikh soldiers and generals as spectacular and awe-inspiring. The Jats were eulogised for their bravery, which in turn translated to pride in that warrior identity. By virtue of their association with the martial aspect of Sikh life, they were also more closely identified with the exclusive Khalsa identity bestowed by Guru Gobind Singh. Jat Sikh boys were reared with a great emphasis on physical fitness, specifically with a view to their recruitment as soldiers. The rise in self-esteem among the Jats was accentuated by recognition and compensation by the ruling power.

While the Jats gathered both political and military power, prominent Khatris were still accorded special status, particularly in the spiritual spheres. They continued to be credited for spreading the words of the gurus within Punjab and outside, of aggregating their teachings in written forms, of creating literary works about Sikh traditions and of providing direction to the Sikhs following the death of the last guru. Some among them were elites in the late 18th and 19th centuries. This was particularly true of those who belonged to the guru lineages. Harjot Oberoi points out that the Sodhis of Anandpur controlled most of the shrines in the area, performed ritual duties and were venerated by the Sikh masses. They lived grandly through the vast revenue-free land grants from the Lahore state and the other Sikh kingdoms like those of Patiala and Faridkot. Exercising considerable clout were also the Sodhis of Harsahai in Ferozepur and the Sodhis of Kartarpur, both in possession of relics and parts of the writings of the gurus. They too had huge followings.

The Bedis, as direct descendants of the founder of the faith, had a special position in the eyes of the ruling classes. Sikh chiefs and *jagirdars* acknowledged their superior spiritual status and granted them revenue-free lands and important positions. Many times, they were called upon to settle disputes among the Jat chieftains. Sahib

Singh Bedi, a descendant of Guru Nanak's family, held so much clout that he not only accompanied Ranjit Singh on military expeditions but also influenced his decisions in crucial ways. After he seized Lahore from other Sikh chiefs, the ceremony for his assumption of the title of Maharaja of Punjab in 1801 was performed by Sahib Singh Bedi. This was considered important for bestowing religious sanction on the new ruler. Sahib Singh Bedi and others of the line were so powerful because of the combination of ritual authority and economic resources invested in them, that they could be placed at the apex of the Sikh *panth* (Oberoi 1994: 111–115). They also wielded considerable influence among the Jat peasantry in the capacity of babas and bhais. The illiterate Jat peasantry flocked to hear their discourses on Sikh religion and its tenets.

Colonial Preference for Jats Sikhs, Frayed Community Dynamics

Colonial influence in Punjab proved to be a major accelerator in further defining the Jats and Khatris into two very different identities, which was also to further tilt the power axis in favour of the Jats. It was also to construct images and stereotypes for both the Jats and the Khatris, which would determine how they would be perceived by others in the decades to come. Much of it began with the writings of orientalist scholars, who wrote their images for the two, informed by British observations. The British perspective of ethnicities in Punjab was influenced by their limited understanding of the local social ethos and defined by their interests. Denzil Ibbestson's ethnographical survey of Punjab in 1881 is the beginning of the colonial gaze on Punjabi society. The British divided the people of Punjab into identifiable religious communities and as agriculturists and non-agriculturists. For them, the primary concern was to establish a stable rural base for revenue collection for the Raj. This automatically made the Jats an important factor in the equation. The colonial accounts described them as the ethnologically prominent people of the area who had also held political power before the arrival of the British. They were also described as crucial from the economic and administrative point for they were good taxpayers, generating revenue for the British through agriculture.

Significantly, Jats also provided the much-needed supply of soldiers to the British army (Malhotra 2002: 28). After Ranjit Singh died in 1839, the two Anglo-Sikh wars (1845–1846 and 1848–1849) led to the dissolution of the Sikh kingdom. The British, having seen the Sikh army in action, knew of their military prowess. After the initial phase of disarming them and forcing them to go back to their villages, Sikh soldiers began to be recruited in the British army. The British policy of respecting their religious identity and fully supporting the Sikh form was one of the primary reasons for Jat reciprocation. Many of these Jats soldiers brought in more kinsmen, thus starting a chain, which over the next few decades would lead to a huge Sikh presence in the British army. By the beginning of the first world war in 1914, Sikhs formed nearly 40 per cent of the British combat troops. Most of them were from rural backgrounds, mostly Jats, and some others like Ramgarhias too. The British, aware of the need to keep them loyal, hyped their bravery and dedication, and portrayed them as the 'lions of Punjab'. While portraying the Jats as an independent, powerful and manly race, whose martial capabilities stemmed from their religious background and political past, the British also portrayed them as the only true Sikhs. Thanks to the British, 'the quintessential Jat merged with the quintessential Sikh to yield the ideal Punjabi native'(Malhotra 2002: 28).

British magnanimity towards the Jats included grants of land at nominal prices for those who served the British army. This served the dual purpose of rewarding the Jats for their association with the British and populating the colonies of the once-barren parts of Punjab, which were being developed through a network of canals. The divide established by the British between Jat Sikhs and others from the community was aggravated with the passing of the Punjab Land Alienation Act of 1900. Sikhs, other than Jats, were forbidden from purchasing any agricultural land. This led to a phenomenal rise in the financial as well as social status of the Jats. From being looked at as inferior in terms of their agricultural background, they became the celebrated face of Sikh identity in British India. Their aggressive pride in their agricultural and military identity set in motion the construction of traits which gradually become synonymous with their community characterisation. On the other hand, the Khatri Sikhs were portrayed as less favourable natives, who still followed backward practices like caste and exploited the more favoured agriculturists. They were also more closely associated with the Hindu Khatris, traditionally the literate classes, who could create problems for the British (Malhotra 2002: 35). Eventually, these distinctions took the form of social value judgements. The identity constructions built during this period have deeply influenced the way Jats perceive themselves and the behaviour patterns they continue to reiterate even today. Nicola Mooney, in her work on Jat Sikhs, points out that colonial descriptions of the Jats were the foundations of many 'stereotypical' and even 'essentialist characterisations' that Jats hold true of themselves as a people even today (2011: 48). They also determined the not-so-flattering Jat attitude towards the Khatris and other trading groups among Sikhs, which too has filtered through to the present.

This did not, however, dent into the eminence of Khatris in social spheres, especially in the upper strata of the times. Hindu and Khatri Sikhs still held control over trade. Many of the Khatri Sikhs were also city elites with prosperous businesses. They were at the helm of literary and cultural activities too (Malhotra 2002: 32). Some among them, particularly in urban centres like Lahore, wielded considerable influence among their people and were even placated with honorary land grants and titles by the British. Old havelis like the Sujan Singh Haveli in Rawalpindi, the Bakshi Ram Singh Haveli in Kontrilla, Gujarkhan, the Khem Singh Bedi Haveli in Kallar Syedan are silent reminders of positions of eminence.

There is also evidence of works of charities, of Khalsa schools established by them and the gurdwaras financed by them. Many of these, now in Pakistan, have been captured in a rare photographic composition by Amardeep Singh, and are a testimony to the deep entrenchment of the trading classes, particularly Khatris, in non-military, social spheres (2016).

They also continued to harbour a sense of superiority based on caste positioning. Khatri Sikhs preferred sharing religious and cultural practices with the Hindus of their caste, rather than with Jats of their religion. Many Hindu families made their firstborn a Sikh. Daughters were married into Hindu and Sikh households according to the Khatri sub-hierarchies. The implicit differentiation from the Jats was palpable in social undercurrents. They asserted their pride in their urban roots and were highly conscious of their higher status and standard as city dwellers. A popular saying among them was: *Khani kanak bhavein ghuggi hove/rehna sheher bhavein jhuggi hove* (One must eat wheat, even if it is infested with pests/and live in a city even if in a hutment). They looked condescendingly at the Jat peasants and often referred to them as *Jat Boot*, a term used to refer not only to their naivety as a peasant class but also as an implicit reference to their rural lifestyle with all its associated lack of privileges. Even their choice of colours and clothes were described as *jatka* by the Khatris, who perceived themselves as refined and urbane

Jats, on the other hand, were increasingly contesting this sense of superiority and breaking through the once-rigid social codes. Anshu Malhotra refers to the writing of a poet from Amritsar, Sondhe Ram, later Sondhe Singh, who wrote verses in the local genre called *jhagra*, (translates into 'fight' and tells the story of an altercation). In his composition, *Jhagra jatti te Khatrani da* ('The fight between the Jat and the Khatri Woman'), he reveals the often-belligerent stands between the two groups. The Khatri woman in the *jhagra* speaks of the highly precious honour of the Khatris, their high-born status and high-class living, and speaks of the Jats as people lacking in honour and at the receiving end of the Muslim government's anger. The Jatti, on the other hand, speaks with pride of the Jats as agriculturists who feed everyone and because of whom Khatris become rich *sahukar*s (moneylenders). She calls the Khatrani *kirarr* (derogatory term used for petty shopkeepers and moneylenders). The Khatrani, in turn, tries to show the Jatti her place by referring to marriage customs among the Jats, which the Khatris considered disreputable. Her condescending tone in describing *chaddar pana* (the Jat custom of marriage with the brother of the dead husband), considered disreputable among the higher castes, reflects her superior airs (Malhotra 2002: 22). While these representations in popular culture indicate the continuing consciousness of a higher status among the Khatris, they also portray the growing confidence in the Jat class, their pride in their own way of life and their refusal to be slotted as secondary in the hierarchies of the past.

Reform Movement and Leadership Roles from Trader/Professional Groups

Within these many shifts were undercurrents of another kind, stirrings of a movement that was to bridge the distance between the two groups, at least for a while. It was also to provide a fillip to the urban Sikh's role within the larger community, bringing sections among them into leadership roles once again. With the British annexation of Punjab in 1849, the subsequent increase in missionary activity and conversions among the Sikh royal families as well as lower castes, there was deepening concern among the community. At the forefront in the brainstorming to stem the tide were Sikhs from the non-agricultural classes, who had the benefit of education, unlike the rural Sikhs. Their initiatives led to the formation of the Singh Sabha (Assembly of the Sikhs) in Amritsar in 1873, and later in Lahore in 1879. Khem Singh Bedi, a descendant of Sahib Singh Bedi, with a committed following in the Potohar region in North West Punjab was an important presence in the Amritsar Sabha. He was in the good books of the British for the help he offered to them in suppressing the 1857 uprising for which he had been conferred membership of the legislative council. He was aided by powerful people from the landed gentry and royal houses among the Jats. However, he was in favour of continuing the existing class and caste differences within Sikhism, in keeping with the Sanatan Sikh tradition with its proximity to Hindu traditions. The Lahore Singh Sabha, on the other hand, was in the hands of people like Gurmukh Singh, Jawahar Singh and Ditt Singh, all of them non-Jats. They represented those educated in the Western tradition, who apart from propounding the necessity of a distinct Khalsa identity also wanted to give it a modern democratic thrust and an egalitarian outlook, which adequately countered the British narrative of the need to convert to a more accepting religion. In 1890, both groups were merged under the umbrella organisation called the Khalsa Diwan Society and came under the sway of the Lahore school.

Their stress on a new, differentiated Sikh identity gained further impetus due to the growing exclusivity of other Hindu and Muslim organisations of the time. The call for a separate Sikh identity cutting across internal differences became stronger under the new leadership. The need for this consolidation gained impetus from other subsidiary reasons too. For example, elections to municipal boards were opened to Indians, and in 1892, members of municipal boards also became voters for candidates to provincial councils. In representational politics, this entailed the possibility of getting substantial funds for the improvement of their community. Lack of education among the rural Sikhs was a solid reason for getting educational funds. But the ordinary Jats, despite general allegiance to Sikh faith, followed fluid cultural practices like worshipping local deities, visiting pirs and following babas from across faiths (Oberoi 1994: 369–370). It was important to bring them together under one exclusive identity to achieve the numbers required for representation and the benefits it entailed. The movement gained momentum, and with it, people from all sections of the Sikh community were encouraged to adopt practices as well as ostensible articles of faith, which differentiated them from other communities. Many from among western Punjab began to adhere to this new exclusive identity. Influential people from central and eastern Punjab with following among the Jats joined them too and actively participated in the movement. In the first half of the 20th century, Master Tara Singh, a Khatri Sikh from Rawalpindi, emerged as the most important leader of this new consolidated Sikh identity. He helped establish the Shiromani Gurdwara Prabandhak Committee and led its political wing the Akali Dal. In the 1920s, he spearheaded the gurdwara reform movement, which demanded Sikh control over gurdwaras in the hands of *mahants* (ascetic Hindu priests appointed as heads of temples). He was also successful in mobilising Sikhs from rural as well as urban areas from all walks of life. Akalis, now consisting of Khatris, others from the trading community, Jats as well as Mazhabi Sikhs, gained immense clout and even toyed with the idea of a separate Sikh state in the event of partition when the British finally left.

The Trading Communities and the Irretrievable Losses of Partition

When Partition eventually happened, it came with very different tidings. Master Tara Singh was close to the Congress leadership, which had sided the Sikhs in an attempt to draw the Gurdwara Reform movement within the larger national movement. It made him believe that Sikh interests were part of the larger focus of the Congress. To prevent further bifurcation of the country, Congress leaders had also promised Master Tara Singh and the Akalis that they would not finalise a constitution for India without consulting the Sikhs. He was sure that Sikh assets would be safeguarded in any division of India that might occur during British withdrawal. However, when Radcliff drew a line cleaving Punjab into two, most of the land and properties belonging to Sikhs went to Pakistan. Although rumours about this had been rife, Sikhs in western Punjab had refused to believe that citadels of Sikh life like Lahore, Rawalpindi, Sargodha, Lyallpur and other areas could ever be given away in the terms of a settlement. Unfortunately, the Akalis, under Master Tara Singh, failed to negotiate for Sikh interests with the political leaders. The brunt of this was to be borne by his huge following among Khatri and other trading classes in western Punjab.

Many Sikhs, mostly from the prosperous trading class, settled since generations in central and western Punjab, found themselves torn away from their homes and lives. It is not as if only the trading class suffered in the shift. Many from the Jat community, who had shifted to the canal colonies in western Punjab, after disposing of their land in eastern Punjab, also found themselves displaced with nothing to go back to. Many with land in central Punjab lost their fields, families and homes in the mayhem. The movement back to East Punjab was a difficult re-migration for them too. Many, who could afford, migrated to other countries rather than go back to East Punjab and begin anew. For those who did return, life was not easy. Many came back to divided landholdings, while others were given compensatory lands which needed much hard work to begin yielding produce. It took them time to establish themselves too. The difference between them and the Sikhs who originally belonged to the other side, however, was that they could come back to an area where kinship networks still existed, where the little nuances of their everyday lives could be relocated in the world that they had once moved out of. Much of the rural life of East Punjab and the cultural patterns emanating from it had carried on without being impacted in an elementary manner. These were an anchor for those who returned to an earlier home.

Unlike them, the trading/professional class had no roots, no familiar environment to come back to. Partition destroyed not just their homes but also the only way of life that they knew. People left behind homes they were sure they would return to. Many left their jewellery buried in the *kutchha vehras* their valuables stuffed into water tanks, their belongings locked in rooms, hoping to find these when they returned. It was difficult for them to comprehend that they were being asked to leave their livelihoods, the neighbourhoods where generations of their families had lived, homes which held in themselves innumerable little things which make up life. The Sikhs of West Punjab, mostly the trading/professional classes had lost not only businesses and properties but also their anchoring to a life which would never be replicated again. Within the turmoil of ruptured lives, abandoned homes, raped women, lynched men, they also lost their sense of belonging. Relocated to urban spaces and trading markets along the Yamuna–Ganges plains, they were also driven to live among a people who remembered their bold assertion of being a different identity. This exposed them to tropes of 'otherness' as they struggled to retrieve their shattered lives. Khatris, the one-time power bearers of the Sikh faith, did not just lose influence within the community power paradigms, but also in the broader social milieu. Once the custodians of culture and the intelligentsia of the community, they were reduced to a people deprived of both history and culture.

For those in North Indian cities, who first saw the Sikhs from west Punjab as refugees, it was difficult to locate their previous selves, buried as they were under the emotional baggage and the lost dignity of an uprooted people. The dichotomy between what they were and what they came to be, was never bridged by an understanding of their pasts. With no context to the evolution of their identity, it was perhaps difficult for the people among whom they came to live, to envision a world where they had been the centre of a milieu composed of their very own language, culture and way of life. Among one of their biggest losses was that of their religious sites, the gurdwaras, which anchored them to a past they comprehended and through which they derived their identity. For the Sikh community from West Punjab, the loss of their homes and institutions and with it a permanent loss of a sense of rootedness could never really be erased. For decades after the Partition, whenever people inflicted by it met, the first inevitable question was '*Pichhon kithon de hon?*' (Where are you originally from). Shauna Singh Baldwin, in her fictionalised rendition of the Sikh experience of partition, *What the Body Remembers,* points out that colours on a map dividing land cannot show anything of what a man feels when he talks of home, even when he is told that home is elsewhere now. That sense of loss and the rootlessness that accompanied it has been handed down from one generation to another (2011: 498).

Nehru's promises to the Sikh community, particularly to those who had no semblance of a home to return to, of compensating the losses with a glow of freedom in independent India got lost in the chaos which followed Partition. After being huddled in camps at the mercy of others, many were gradually allotted plots and houses left behind by Muslim refugees or were given spaces at low rates and financial assistance to set up shops or build houses. Those in government service got their jobs back after some waiting, but the majority who left their businesses had to start from scratch. People got thrown into areas of which they knew nothing. Some reached bigger cities like Delhi, Mumbai, Kanpur, Jamshedpur, Kolkata, Lucknow. Others found themselves in smaller towns like Jabalpur, Indore, Muzaffarpur, etc., many times through sheer chance of being disembarked at one of those stations by the trains, which brought them in. In Delhi, people shifted into the tiny areas allotted to them in newly sprung refugee colonies such as Lajpat Nagar, Patel Nagar, Rajendra Nagar, Jangpura, etc. The displaced Sikhs had no established networks through which to route their work and in many cases not much cash to begin anew. Many had to set up makeshift shops on *patris* or footpaths to sustain themselves. Dealing with the loss of status was a challenge as was the resentment by the local people, whose livelihoods were being encroached upon. Life was beginning at the lowest juncture and they found themselves at a psychological threshold which would determine many of their future attitudes.

The brutal separation from home now rendered a different and threatening country, awareness of terrible compromises made in the course of survival and a loss of trust in the normalcy of life, made the displaced community a breeding ground for insecurity. It led to mutations of identity, determining their subsequent attitudes. In a race to grab scarce resources, resorting to heckling and shouldering their way through a crowd composed of equally desperate people, Sikhs as a community began to be seen as aggressive. The sudden lapse of a secure life introduced an acquisitiveness, a tendency to horde, one to aggregate. There emerged an obvious tendency towards ghettoisation in places with large refugee populations as in Delhi. Large areas of West Delhi still hold the tag of refugee colonies. Social memories carry within them the association of these places with a desperate, deprived community huddled together, making others wary of its intentions and inclinations. The lack of structure and a loss of security also gave rise to a growing convergence to a rigid religious and community identity. This was, to an extent, the result of a loss of so many other identities. It became the only common one available, providing an anchor, a point of bonding in times of a wild scattering of other variables. This accounted for the huge congregation of Sikhs on every religious occasion. The fact that a lot of refugee relief work was organised out of gurdwaras also made these the focal points of community identity and camaraderie.

There was anger too. The acute feeling of being sacrificed in the hurried acquisition of power and freedom stayed with the people for a long time. Many among the uprooted have heard their elders wonder why they should be celebrating the day of their destruction as Independence Day. The discontent increased when Master Tara Singh's proposal for a 'Punjabi Suba'—an area within Punjab, to preserve their culture, language and religion—was dismissed as unfeasible by the government. This dismissal was perceived by the dislocated community as a betrayal of the promise of respectable settlement in the free nation. Unfortunately, the agitational strategies of the movement which used Sikh traditions of martyrdom to create mass support in the 1950s also created a wedge in Hindu–Sikhs relations across the country. This was further exacerbated by the government's portrayal of the same as an anti-national agenda. It also created fissures with a section of Jat leadership who were not in favour of dividing the bigger Punjab into smaller segments for creating the Punjabi Suba.

Negotiating a Crisis of Identity

Ironically, by the time the Punjabi Suba did come into existence in 1966, the displaced Sikhs of Partition discovered that the land of their supposed resettlement, one where they were to preserve their culture, language and life, was not only a place reflecting an ethos very different from their own but also one where they would be outsiders. Two things which contributed to this was the change in Akali leadership and the success of the Green Revolution. By 1966, the power praxis within the Akali Dal had changed from being Khatri-centric to Jat-centric. The focus of their interest too had shifted from the displaced trading community of West Punjab to the larger Jat population of East Punjab. The Akali leadership had passed from Master Tara Singh, the leader of the urban Khatri Sikhs, to Sant Fateh Singh, who was more concerned with the interests of the land-owning Jat community of East Punjab. This shift in the paradigm had the blessings of the Congress government, who in course of time had begun seeing and painting Tara Singh, with his base among the urban Khatri refugees from West Punjab, as communal. The faction led by Sant Fateh Singh was posited as more 'secular' and favourable for the bigger numbers of the agricultural community (Shani 2008: 33–36).

The 1960s were also witnessing the success of government-led campaigns to provide high-yielding seeds and other technological resources to convert Punjab into the granary of the nation, making the country self-sufficient in grains. The Green Revolution not only brought untold prosperity to sections of Jat society but also made the Jats the symbol of the nation's celebratory mood. Mainstream media romanticised their proud land-owning identity and its cultural referents. By default, Sikh culture began to be represented by the Jat culture. Concepts of *pind, khet, makki di roti, sarson da saag,* bhangra, *giddha, phulkari*s and Patiala turbans were all beginning to be identified with Sikhs at large. Jats became the centre of Punjabi traditions and symbols of their identity became 'symbols of wider Indian nation's understanding of the region' (Mooney: 2011). Within this celebrated 'Sikh identity', the trader community of Sikhs, with no landed property, no claims to a culture defined through its agrarian life, were outsiders. They were the Bhapas, the mercantile lot, looked at with condescension by the locals. There was not much incentive for them to uproot their fledgling businesses in North Indian cities and relocate to a place which did not even feel like home.

Even though most of the trader professional class of Sikhs continued to stay outside Punjab, they did not escape comparison with the Jats and were confused with the latter in ways difficult to counter. City-bred, physically attuned to urban life, with a temperament more suited to business negotiations than to driving a tractor through fields, the Sikhs of western Punjab found themselves at odds with what was expected of them in terms of their interests and attitudes. Thanks to mainstream media projecting the 'Sikh' as the 'Jat', they often felt challenged to live up to the valorous, ego-enhancing Jat image. This included negotiating with social expectations demanding from them many secondary identities associated with the Jats. Many outside the community assumed that they had lands tucked away in Punjab, that they were sportsmen or soldiers—identities very different from their lived reality. Their inability to live up to these images also led to ridicule, many times couched in the benign covering of humour, jokes and caricaturing. While on one hand, these expected tropes clashed with their lived reality, on the other, the constraints of adjusting within a majority community outside Punjab led to a dilution of their original cultural identity. This, over time, has been reflected in the dilution of its cultural referents. The printed turbans of the Sikhs of Rawalpindi and Lahore have given way to the solid colours worn by Sikhs in East Punjab. Dialects of Punjabi like Pothwari and Saraiki have gradually disappeared as an increasing number of families in North Indian cities have shifted to Hindi as the language of everyday communication. Punjabi, as it is spoken, is heavily influenced by the shift in location. It is only in Pakistani YouTube videos or in Punjabi folk songs sung by the likes of Surinder Kaur, Prakash Kaur and Asa Singh Mastana that nostalgic connections with a once-thriving culture and language remain.

For the Sikhs in North Indian cities, particularly in Delhi, which gradually became the hub of the Sikhs from western Punjab, the next decade was spent re-establishing themselves. The small- and medium-sized auto part, textile, chemical and furniture businesses among others gradually picked up. Some became flourishing business houses leading to an enviable status in a short time. Sikh professionals could be found in academics, medicine, engineering and all the other fields open to anyone else in the country. Delhi Sikhs took control of the management of their gurdwaras. In 1971, instead of the Sikh Gurdwara Prabandhak Committee (SGPC) with its headquarter in Punjab, the Delhi Sikh Gurdwara Management Committee (DSGMC) with headquarters in the city was given government approval to establish a committee through elections by Sikh vote. It was invested with power to look after the affairs of historical gurdwaras like Sisganj Sahib, Rakabganj Sahib and Bangla Sahib, once again constructing their religious and historical anchors in the new home.

Just as things seemed to be falling in place, political situations dissociated with the lives of the trading community but pertaining to the larger community were building up to new points of tension. In the 1980s, Prime Minister Indira Gandhi, having been out of power post the Emergency debacle and in need of a political revival, used Punjab as a playing field. In trying to displace the now overly powerful, Jat-led Akali party, she created an alternative power centre under Jarnail Singh Bhindranwale. In doing so, she unwittingly unleashed a militant discourse over which she soon lost control. Punjab was plunged into an era where radical, separatist voices sounded louder than the saner, moderate ones. Having barely found their bearings with no real association with the separatist movement in Punjab and spectators like the rest of the country to the bloodletting happening there, the trader/service class Sikhs nevertheless found themselves being swept into the web of events which followed.

Bhindrawale's call for a resurrection of a militarised and hyper-masculine Sikh image had serious repercussions for them. On one hand, their unwillingness to join the aggressive militant chorus to avoid jeopardising their own precariously poised lives within the majority community, portrayed them as diminutive and timid within the larger Sikh community. On the other hand, this did not prevent them from being seen by the majority as belonging to the community espousing the militant cause. For those outside the community, their bearded and turbaned bearing identified them with those espousing radicalism. The undercurrent of tension being created was palpable even though no one spoke of it openly yet. Wary and anxious each time there was news of bus passengers being killed, Hindu leaders being gunned down, police officers being attacked in Punjab, they could only watch and wait. Each news increased their discomfiture among their neighbours, colleagues and friends from the majority community.

In 1984, Operation Blue Star, wherein the government took the inexplicable decision of sending the army into the Golden Temple to flush out Bhindranwale and his followers on a day when people from across the country had congregated to celebrate *gurupurab*, drew the

Delhi Sikhs into the web of anger being woven over the past years. The desecration of the Darbar Sahib, demolition of the *Akal Takht*, destruction of the *toshakhana*, above all the horrific killing of innocent pilgrims left the Sikhs outside Punjab as stunned and angry as those within. Delhi Sikhs verbalised their anguish and anger, even as many from the Jat community left their posts in army and police and many among the younger generation of Sikhs turned to radicalisation. The resulting increase in the militant discourse and the anxiety over the possible backlash by the community sent the state apparatus into overdrive. State-controlled TV and print media became the ruling government's mouthpieces. They constructed not just a section, but the entire Sikh community as terrorists. In Punjab, the average Jat not involved in militancy too became a target of police paranoia.

In Delhi and other areas of North India, Sikhs were humiliated by being singled out for police questioning in trains and buses, their work bags rummaged through, their turbans removed in public to check for hidden arms. This exercise, carried on in the presence of the majority community, became part of the state ideological apparatus to show them in the image of the 'other', a process which painted this 'other' as a threat and elicited silent consent to physical and psychological excesses on them. Raymond Williams says, 'What is decisive is not only the conscious system of ideas and beliefs, but the whole lived social process as practically organised by specific and dominant meanings and values (1977: 109). The public was beginning to identify its security with these coercive tactics and choosing to support them. The entire exercise created an atmosphere of distrust in which the Sikh on the road, in the office and the neighbourhood, began to be seen as someone with the potential identification of a dangerous separatist. Images constructed by media superimposed themselves upon real people with whom the majority community had lived and shared their lives for half a decade. These were the same people who over the last 34 years had entrenched themselves into a new home, learnt lessons of patriotism structured within its systems of knowledge and internalised a sense of belonging to the only place they now knew as home.

The fact that the trading community had neither the inclination to endorse the terror nor the means to curb it was overlooked by all those perceiving them as threats. Veena Das, in her book *Life and Words: Violence and the Descent into the Ordinary*, talks of rumours fuelled in the absence of this understanding. It was reflected in the Hindu readiness to believe that Sikhs in Delhi were taking oaths to avenge the desecration of Harmandar Sahib, that they were hoarding weapons in gurdwaras and preparing to demolish the state structure through the help of outside agencies. The average Sikh in North Indian areas was not even aware of these rumours, let alone be a party to the dangerous agendas enumerated in them. Sentiments had been running high since operation Blue Star but to attribute an organised backlash by Sikhs in urban areas outside Punjab was far-fetched by any measure (Das 2007: 110).

When Prime Minister Indira Gandhi was shot dead in her official residence at point-blank range by her Sikh bodyguards on 31 October 1984, anxieties generated over a period came to the fore. Like in times of uncrystallised fears, scattered pieces of information were combined to construct things already believed. Images of Sikhs distributing sweets in England were taken as proof of Sikhs in Delhi doing the same. There were rumours of the Delhi water supply being poisoned by Sikhs. A decade of militant discourse, which had portrayed the majority community as emasculated in contrast to the macho Sikh image generated by militancy, now rebounded. There was selective blindness in the associations being created, a refusal to acknowledge that the Sikhs one encountered were real people with normal lives, not embodiments of the images that had been created about them in the course of militancy and its aftermath (Das 2007). Responses among Sikhs to Mrs Gandhi's assassination varied from endorsement to distancing to condemnation, but this variation was given no recognition in the stabilisation of the attributes. There seemed to be no cognisance of different kinds of persons who make up a community even though it 'was clearly articulated in social practices' (Das 2007: 132).

A people who had spent two generations constructing a home found themselves ravaged within it. The three days following the assassination were complete mayhem. Mobs, most rabid in the capital, attacked Sikh homes with voter lists in hands and dragged out male members irrespective of their age. Sikh men were humiliated, their hair and beards cut off. Shops and establishments belonging to the Sikhs were selectively burnt down. Police watched, at times colluded in different manners. Police stations refused to take complaints. At the end of the carnage, there were innumerable families left with no male member, only little children who had witnessed their fathers and uncles being killed and women left with the guilt of having survived. There was similar arson, looting and killing in Kanpur, Bokaro and other centres with a substantial Sikh population. In a chilling prologue to the events, the ruling party drew mileage out of the situation by spending crores on ad campaigns, insinuating that the planned pogrom against the Sikhs was a natural, spontaneous, legitimate outburst of inevitable anger. Jaspreet Singh, in his novel *Helium* patterned on the events of 1984, rightly points out that the ruling party also milked the pogrom to win the election that followed by using the media to portray Sikhs as terrorists. The image of the Sikh holding a gun on the other side of the barbed-wire fence constructed him as an enemy to be wary of (J. Singh 2013: 222).

Past Reflections, Contemporary Trends

The events of 1984 left an entire generation of the Sikh trading/professional community with memories of a numbing fear. It was a generation which was to retract its limbs into the foetal position from which an earlier generation had braved spreading out to build connections with a new life. The consensual silence, which surrounded the happenings of 1984, has been a palpable presence for the community. Nobody seems willing to find what it had been like for this group of people to be left standing amid bits of stone and rubble after the very structure of their life had been demolished (Das 2007: 6). Added to it was the awareness that the same inconvenient wounds could be prodded at selective intervals for political gains by those who perpetrated the crimes, and also by those who professed concern over it. For the relocated Sikh community, this has had a lasting impact. Veena Das sums it up when she says, 'The fragility of the social becomes embedded in the temporality of anticipation since one ceases to trust that context is in place'(9). While most of the community has moved on, there remains a second generation in homes without fathers, with memories of bloodshed, grappling with unemployment, drug addiction and anti-social behaviour. Their lives remain like the unstructured ugliness of illegal houses among structured edifices, which best remain hidden for the ungainly sentiments they evoke.

Since then, many Sikh trading families from Delhi, Uttar Pradesh, Bihar have shifted base to urban centres in Punjab. They have struggled not only to re-establish businesses but also to adjust to a culture and worldview different from their own. Despite all the help proffered by the Jats, the traditional differences between the two underline their social interactions. Even as common urban lives break down many of the old schisms, it is taking time to relinquish the value judgements surrounding them. Popular culture reflects the Jat desire to appropriate the cultural hegemony even today. This is best reflected in contemporary Punjabi cinema with a largely Jat viewership. *Jatt and Juliet 1* (2012) and *Jatt and Juliet 2* (2013), two hugely popular films in recent years, have a subplot which throws an interesting light on this. Here, Shampy, the petty businessman is pitted against Fateh, the Jat policeman. While Fateh's antics are constructed as swagger, Shampy is perpetually perplexed and unable to grasp the nuances of the 'dominant' culture. Fateh's thundering motorcycle is offset by Shampy's little moped. Fateh with all his fallibilities is a fully-grown character while Shampy as the *raja beta* to his similarly caricatured father is at best a child-man. With their printed turbans and caricatured accents, father and son are outsiders in the setting. Though exaggerated in intent, the portrayals capture the intracommunity dynamic in Punjab and the trading class's place within it. While the growing numbers of the trading Sikh community in Punjab have led to a consolidation of their community structures, the underlying differences between the groups continue to survive, though in less blatant forms.

The majority of the trading community continues to live in North Indian cities, with a big concentration in the capital city of Delhi. The general impression of the twice-routed Sikhs of western Pakistan, continues to be associated with loud, glossy and over-the-top culture, often looked down upon by the more refined elite. West Delhi markets spilling over with shiny clothes and electronic gadgets, jewellery shops and car showrooms are reflective of the general trend. It is as if a people having repeatedly lost all that they had are out to aggregate and do it to no reasonable limit. Ostentatious Sikh weddings and social gatherings, many times flashy and gaudy, seem to reflect a self-reiteration of reconstructed lives. The unapologetic display of wealth seems to have its roots in all that was once lost, including a sense of satiety. The show of strength at *nagar kirtan*s and *gurupurab*s is a similar reiteration of an identity arrived at. This preoccupation with money, property and outward display is very different from the sense of expansiveness and plenitude that at one time defined the same people and which they remember with nostalgia and regret (Dasgupta 2014: 191). It is as if the trauma of losing a life already built twice over has structured itself into their very DNA. There is also an unconscious tendency among the community to quick belligerence, particularly in response to underhand reminders of the setbacks they have suffered. Ridicule for the same coming in covert practices, underhand comments, humour loaded with a latent deprecation and 'othering' leads to sharp responses. Their losses at some level have induced an emotional fragility which translates into a tendency to be confrontational, as though to assert that they have not been broken yet. Running parallel to it is their persistent attempt at staking a claim, of rooting and entrenching themselves, of fighting to retrieve bits of history. Litigations over land for gurdwaras, possession of historical Sikh sites, proposals for the establishment of memorials relating to their recent histories are some of the ways in which they do so.

However, this does not overshadow the fact that in recent years things have improved for the trader/professional Sikhs. It has now been 72 years since the displacement of partition and 35 years since the Sikh massacre in Delhi. The cordiality between a vast section of the majority community and the Sikhs in North Indian cities has withstood the tests of time. Much has changed in the socio-political and economic dimensions of Indian life with many new factors influencing the people in question. The militant movement in Punjab has fizzled out and with it the focus on the turbaned identity as one associated with terrorism. Since then, India has also had a distinguished Sikh economist as a Prime Minister, ironically representing the party, which is alleged to have engineered the genocide. Liberalisation initiated by him has impacted the Sikhs in the same way as it has impacted the rest of the country, opening new opportunities and avenues. Like any other group, they are distributed in social classes ranging from the richest to the poor but rarely falling into destitution. The trader/professional class of Sikhs spread over North Indian cities, in Delhi and outside, has been doing well for itself. They have shown an intrinsic capacity to rebuild their lives even though the scars of the past remain.

The work done over the years by the DSGMC has strengthened the Sikh presence in areas of literacy, charity and culture. Delhi is today marked by many Sikh historical sites and gurdwaras. Sikh educational institutions—both schools and colleges—have contributed to the growing rate of literacy among the community. Minority status conferred on them has ensured seat reservations for children from the community creating an impetus for educating both boys and girls from every social stratum. This, in turn, has seen a huge rise in literacy levels. Still majorly a middle-level business class, many among the community are visible as academicians, scientists, economists, bureaucrats and more. The private sector, particularly in the post-liberalisation era, has opened new opportunities and many among the new generation are shifting occupations, cities, even countries. From being majorly associated with auto parts, fabrics and other small businesses, they have ventured into many new fields. This has also led to movement out of Sikh clusters created after Partition and 1984, leading to greater integration within the larger cosmopolitan urban milieu. The new urban culture reflective of global trends and tastes has impacted them as others, bridging gaps created by earlier paradigms.

The trading/professional class of Sikhs is today a visible and prominent section of the community. It has had a difficult trajectory, marked by a dwindling status, displacements and violent disruptions. Their smaller numbers, against the big majority of the agriculturists, their progressively dwindling place within the broader political structures, their marginalisation through historical processes, have collectively impacted not only their original status and identity but also perceptions within the community and outside. They have rebuilt themselves repeatedly, but each reconstructed phase carries within it distilled memories reflected in new behaviour patterns and group attributes. The evolution to their contemporary identity needs revisiting—as do the stories of loss and compromise, of mutation of identity, of misplaced retribution and how they have dealt with all of these. As a people, they might never recover their original identity but they have processed a new one, constructing it with what remained of an earlier life and that which has been available in the new one. What is important is their being recognized for who they are. A cognisance of their past helps reconstruct them as a distinct facet of the community identity, one different in attributes from the established normative. As they come into their own, they seem to be gradually shrugging off the many diminutive images they have had to contend with. The changing socio-economic situations and the shifting prerequisites of success are helping too. This is further accelerated by the fact that an increasingly urbanising Sikh profile in broader terms, is leading to convergences within and outside the community, which might in due course break through the earlier contentions.

References

Das, Veena. 2007. 'In the Region of Rumour'. In *Life and Words: Violence and the Descent into the Ordinary*. New Delhi: Oxford University Press.

———. 'The Event and the Everyday'. In *Life and Words: Violence and the Descent into the Ordinary*. New Delhi: Oxford University Press.

Dasgupta, Rana. 2014. '1947'. *Capital: A Portrait of Twenty-First Century Delhi*. Noida: Fourth Estate, Harper Collins.

Dhavan, Purnima. 2014. 'Sikhism in the Eighteenth Century'. In *The Oxford Handbook of Sikh Studies*, edited by Pashaura Singh and Louis E. Fenech. UK: Oxford University Press.

Howard, Judith. 2000. 'Social Psychology of Identities'. In *Annual Review of Sociology*, August, 26: 367–393.

Malhotra, Anshu. 2002. 'Gender, Caste and Religious Identities in Punjab'. In *Gender Caste and Religious Identities: Restructuring Class in Colonial Punjab*. New Delhi: Oxford University Press.

———. 1994. 'A New Social Imagination'. In *The Construction of Religious Boundaries: Culture, Identity, and Diversity in the Sikh Tradition*. Oxford: Oxford University Press.

McLeod, W.H. 2000. 'The Development of the Sikh Panth'. In *Exploring Sikhism: Aspects of Sikh Identity, Culture and Thought*. New Delhi: Oxford University Press.

Mooney, Nicola. 2011. *Rural Nostalgias and Transnational Dreams: Identity and Modernity Among Jat Sikhs*. Canada: University of Toronto.

Oberoi, Harjot. 1994. 'Sanatan Tradition and its Transmission'. In *The Construction of Religious Boundaries: Culture, Identity, and Diversity in the Sikh Tradition*. Oxford University Press.

Shani, Giorgio. 2008. 'The Territorialisation of the Quam'. In *Sikh Nationalism and Identity in a Global Age*. New York: Routledge.

Singh, Amardeep Singh. 2016. *Lost Heritage, The Sikh Legacy in Pakistan*. New Delhi: Nagaara Trust in Association with Himalayan Books.

Singh, Jaspreet. 2013. *Helium*. Great Britain: Bloomsbury.

Singh, Pashaura. 2010. 'Revisiting the "Evolution of the Sikh Community"'. In *Journal of Punjab Studies*, Special Issue, *W.H. McLeod: Assessing his Legacy*, Spring–Fall, 17(1&2).

Singh, Shauna Baldwin. 2011. *What the Body Remembers*. New Delhi: Rupa Publications.

William, Raymond. 1977. 'Hegemony'. In *Marxism and Literature*. Oxford: Oxford University Press.

Films:

Jatt and Juliet 1. Directed by Anurag Singh. Produced by Darshan Singh Grewal and Gunbir Singh Sidhu. Released in June 2012.

Jatt and Juliet 2. Directed by Anurag Singh. Produced by Darshan Singh Grewal, Gunbir Singh Sidhu and Manmord Sidhu. Released in 2013.

2

Evolving Urban Profiles: From the Village to the City

Social identity is a process continuously leading to new formations. Just as it has been shaped by the past, it also has the potential to be influenced by the future. The way we see it at a particular point of time in the present is itself the result of an amalgamation of social, economic and political transitions. These transitions continue in every age constantly introducing shifts, which demand cognitive assimilation. The once clearly slotted identities of rural Punjab, deriving their structures through the occupational and socio-hierarchical patterns embedded in that life, have undergone many shifts through history. They are once again experiencing changes resulting from the peculiar factors of their own age. Not just agriculturists but also non-agricultural community groups from villages are finding their way into cities and towns. This, in turn, is entailing a breakdown of occupational boundaries, the resulting economic distribution and the entailing social hierarchies. While each subgroup carries with it old identity tropes, these are inexorably impacted by the new requirements of urban living. The confusing process of relinquishing old identities and assimilating new ones is accompanied by the complex process of resistance and assertion. It is also entwined with adjusting to the requirements of a new ecosystem, which slowly and inexorably dents into old reservations. Much of this complexity arises from the fact that moving from the village to the city is not just a spatial shift. It is a shift into a different life, which operates in tandem with the workings of a larger world. It is also one, which demands adherence to its working.

To understand the old structure of rural Punjab, it has to be contextualised within the larger Indian village structure. For centuries it had been composed of a few powerful landowners, landless labour, the prevalence of caste-based division of work and social stratification based on the same. The lopsided control over land had been abetted by subsequent ruling powers. Power to control the rights to cultivation and collection of produce was vested in a few by the rulers. As long back as the Mughal times, the rulers classified large landlords in a system where they helped in revenue collection but paid less per unit. The British too organised systems of revenue collection but only to their advantage, continuing the existing feudal structures, making preferred groups even more powerful. The unstructured lending sector and the powerful position of the traditional moneylender were also harder on the lower classes and castes, many times binding them in perpetual debts. Caste and the distribution of work based on it ensured clear power hierarchies. The myth of the self-sufficient Indian village system built on reciprocal and mutually sustaining relations was underlined by exploitative patterns. The fact is that 'the hierarchy on the ground was not an outcome of ideological acquiescence but an outcome of unequal distribution of wealth and power in a closed agrarian economy' (Gupta 2012: 199). These unequal structures saw a gradual change in the socialist thrust of independent India. Steps were introduced to regulate rent and tenancy rights, impose ceilings on holdings, distribute the surplus land among the rural poor and facilitate the consolidation of holdings. These were significant measures but they suffered from loopholes and policy glitches leading to a slow trickle down. However, they did succeed in breaking the monopoly of the large landowners, and in creating a class of small landlords and substantial peasants as new relevant groups (Jodhka 2012: 10–11). The creation of credit through institutionalised sources like banks and credit cooperatives has allowed the disadvantaged sections to move out of a state of constant debt. The introduction of adult franchise and the abolition of the caste system have also dented into the once invincible barriers of caste and class.

Within these old and new patterns, lies the stratified profile of the Sikh in rural Punjab. Land ownership and the lack of it has been the biggest signifier of status or the lack of it. Within this lie differences based on caste and group hierarchies, working somewhat differently due to the reformative intent of Sikhism. The differences between the agriculturists and the trader/professionals have been one of culture, language, occupation as well as of demography. However, the social hierarchies within rural Punjabi life have existed within the same cultural and demographic zones. Among the land-owning classes, Jats have been the most numerous, constituting nearly two-thirds of the total population (Judge: 9). Through their sheer numbers, the historical ascendency to power discussed earlier, ownership of land and the consequent control over economic and political spheres, they have enjoyed the most prominent position in rural areas. Despite the many ongoing changes initiated by the governments in free India, they have continued to hold the maximum land and were made more powerful due to the post-Independence requirement of self sufficiency with regards to food. Other agricultural groups like the Sainis, Mahtons, Kambohs and Lobanas remain below the much more numerous and powerful Jats. Some among them, like the Kambohs and Lobanas, have also been classified as other backward classes. Next in the hierarchy to the agriculturists have been the Thokas or Tarkhans, who have been traditionally the village carpenters, but have also performed other artisan occupations, like masonry and smith work. Many of them have moved out of their traditional occupations. Kalals or the traditional brewers and distillers too have experienced occupational and demographic changes. Next in status have been the service/artisan castes like the Suniars, Lohars, Chhimbas, Nais, Jheers, Kumhars, etc. The other important and substantial component of rural Punjab has been the so-called lower castes or the Dalits within the Sikh fold. These mainly consist of the Chamars (leatherworking castes) and Churhas (sweepers). Broadly speaking, the Chamar caste group includes Ad Dharmis, Jatiachamars, Ramdasias, Ravidasias and a few others. The Churha group includes the Balmiki, Bhangi and Mazhabi castes. Apart from their traditional work, they have also worked as *siris* or labourers in the fields of the Jats (Ram 2011: 387). Traditionally, every class within the village structure has been dependent on the Jats for survival. Over centuries, many of these groups have experienced shifts out of villages due to respective advantages and disadvantages. These urban trajectories are important for the social and economic changes these have involved and continue to do in contemporary times.

Jat Migration to Urban Areas

For Jats, the shift from the rural to the urban sphere probably began when from an exclusively agrarian community they diverged into a martial one too. The creation of a fighting force in the times of the later gurus and the increasing induction of Jats into the Khalsa force by the tenth guru saw their movement out of the villages. After him, they organised themselves into *misls* based on old kinships and village networks. Some became mercenaries, who extended services in the military markets for feudal landlords as was the practice of the times. Some among them took employment with native rajas and others worked for zamindars. By the middle of the 18th century, many among this mercenary fighting class had spread out to areas around the Yamuna-Ganga-Brahmaputra watershed (Banerjee 2014). The *misl*s came to be consolidated under Ranjit Singh who eventually became the king of the largest Sikh kingdom and began an era of expansion of the kingdom. As Ranjit Singh's kingdom expanded, Khalsa soldiers began to be seen in areas outside Punjab. Many of them were also deputed to kingdoms already taken over by the Sikh rule. Others were sent on missions to aid rulers who asked for armed help against their enemies. In some situations, these soldiers settled down in the places of deputation. Even today, their descendants continue to live in areas like Hyderabad, Secunderabad, Nizamabad and Karimnagar.

The colonial era was the next trigger for Jat Sikhs and many others to move out of villages and go to even remoter areas. Many joined the British army. Families stayed back in villages while the men moved from place to place. As the favoured recruits of the British army and with no reservations about crossing the sea—something seen as problematic by many other Indians—they were not only deputed to British cantonments in India but also to British military missions abroad. During the two world wars, they were exposed to various parts of the world as they fought for the British army. Many were also recruited in paramilitary and police forces and were sent to British colonies like Singapore, Malaysia, Hong Kong, China, etc., opening new worlds and opportunities for them. From there, they moved further to countries like Australia, New Zealand, Canada, US and the UK. Some returned to their villages while others did not. They settled in new lands, far removed from their lives in rural Punjab, taking up occupations different from traditional ones and gradually settling into different sociocultural atmospheres. They also drew others from the villages with promises of work, money and a better life. Gradually, their wives and children joined them too. Their evolution into a different identity will be discussed in a separate chapter.

Within India, land fragmentation also led Jats out of villages to places which could offer other occupations. Calcutta was one such destination. With Sikhs soldiers embarking for foreign travel from the Calcutta port, Calcutta became a familiar place for their kith and kin. This was also the time when modern vehicular traffic was first introduced in India, opening scope for new occupations for a people strained under land fragmentation in an arid countryside. Jat Sikhs arrived in Calcutta and worked as bus and taxi drivers, cleaners and conductors. In course of time, they gained control over different transport bodies. Gradually, they brought their families from villages, and over a few generations got fully entrenched into city life. About a decade after Partition, when the city and local government took control of transport bodies, these Jat transporters, instead of returning to villages, found new avenues in transport business towards areas in Arunachal Pradesh, Mizoram, Meghalaya, Manipur and Nagaland. Raipur, Indore, Jabalpur and Bhopal became new centres of trade and commerce in the post-Independence era, providing more opportunities for transport-related works.

After the initial Jat migration as part of the colonial influence, there have been more recent impetuses for the Jats to move out into urban spaces. Government initiatives to kickstart the Green Revolution pumped money, knowhow and technology into the agriculture sector in Punjab. This resulted in the big landlords gaining even more influence and increasing their clout in the religious and political institutions of Punjab. They used their growing financial power to further improve their agricultural base leading to a cycle of gains. Over the years, as they became richer and more powerful, they started looking beyond villages and the possibility of shifting their children to better lives than that afforded by agriculture (Jodhka 2009). While parts of families remained in villages, others diversified into different occupations. In many cases, the father stayed back to look after the farm while the sons moved to urban areas. Many rural households began to have occupations other than only agriculture to depend upon. Many of these were related to the agricultural sector. Agricultural surpluses led to the growth of subsidiary industries like agricultural implements, insecticides, etc. It also led to the growth of trading towns with opportunities for marketing, trading, processing and so on. These provided new avenues to those who wished to expand into different directions.

The eighties were a period of political turmoil and missed opportunities for the people of Punjab. Many among the younger generation were caught, willingly and unwillingly, in the unfolding chaos. The Sikh agriculturist, particularly vulnerable to the sordid drama being played out, was caught between the militants and the police. Police crackdowns implicated innocents along with the accused leading to a cycle of retribution and payback. While agriculture no longer looked as promising as it had in the days of the Green Revolution, many other avenues seemed more profitable. As the 1990s revealed the benefits of a liberalised economy, the service sector in Punjab grew much beyond the primary and secondary sectors. The tertiary sector became the most important part of the Punjab economy. While the higher-income group of rural localities moved towards urban areas for better investment opportunities, the lower-income groups hoped to find better employment opportunities to raise their standard of living. The trend is corroborated by figures, which show that the growth of urban population in Punjab during 1991–2001 reached 37.86 per cent, that is, three times higher than the growth of population in rural Punjab (P. Singh and B. Singh 2014: 69–84). The trend was clear. The Sikh farmer was moving towards the city.

Those who shifted out of rural Punjab to pursue agriculture elsewhere in the country have shown similar patterns of transition. Examples are Jat Sikhs who moved to Ganganagar in Rajasthan, where canal construction had offered fertile land for cultivation. There are also those among them who shifted to the Terai region of Uttar Pradesh soon after Partition due to easy availability of land at low prices. Some of these areas are now in Uttarakhand. Despite the hard work it took for the first generation to convert these jungles into successful farmlands, the second and third generations have moved to urban centres in the vicinity. Their lives continue to be connected to their lands but the distancing is apparent. The trajectory of a family—originally from Nangalan village in Punjab, which shifted to Pilibhit—shows that out of the 13 male offspring of the five brothers, there is only one who is still actively an agriculturist. The others have either sublet land or manage it from their city homes through contracted labour. Most of them are settled in bigger UP towns like Lucknow and Bareilly, still visiting their farm to manage affairs but primarily occupied with city occupations including businesses, petrol pumps, etc. Their children, many of them educated in the best boarding schools of the country, some from universities abroad, have moved to bigger cities like Delhi. Many of them have chosen professional compatibility over caste, in their choice of life partners. There are similar trajectories in Ganganagar, where a substantial number of Jats now form the educated, urban middle-class, fully entrenched into city life. Their priorities rest on having all the amenities of modern life. Their aspirations include good education for their children, urban housing, modern gadgets and so on. Instances of return to farms are rare, particularly in the younger generation.

Within Punjab too, the trend to shift to urban areas continues. Division of land holdings generation after generation has largely ended the era of big landlords. Smaller portions of land do not yield attractive profits. Traditional labour is no longer willing to work for them. To procure labour from other places is a constant problem and does not afford the traditional feudal authority which they once enjoyed. The pressure on Jats to move out of the village has been accentuated by these cracks in a structure, which ensured their higher place within it. Even those still in possession of substantial land and equipment are perpetually at a risk of loss with the threat of erratic rains and electricity supply. If they have the resources, they prefer to move to the more reliable structures of urban life. Landowners with land in proximity to extending townships have been selling parts of their agricultural land at a high profit to builders. While some invest part of it in agricultural land elsewhere, most of them use substantial amounts for buying residential and business properties in urban areas. This is generally followed by a part of the family shifting to urban areas, with the education of children in city schools and colleges as their top priority. Those who shift rarely want to go back to villages or agriculture. Many, who themselves cannot shift, wish to send their children out. The drug menace in villages of Punjab has become an added reason for shifting to cities.

Considering the shifting focus, Jats are increasingly attracted to skill-building suitable to an urban rather than to a rural milieu. This has led to attempts by the community to create infrastructures and resources in the direction. The Jat-dominated Akali Dal government has designated three professional colleges being run by the Shiromani Gurdwara Prabandhak Committee (SGPC) in Punjab as 'minority institutions' in a bid to provide an advantage to the community in skill-building. These include an engineering college in Anandpur Sahib, and a medical and a dental college in Amritsar. For those with bigger aspirations, jobs in the bureaucracy are high on the priority list too. They are now well entrenched into government structures and professional fields. Education and exposure to employment opportunities available in the new age have led many to alternate professions. Recent research found that the once-preferred occupations like armed forces, the legal profession and politics have been giving way to others more suited to a stable life. Medicine, engineering, research and technology are the aspirations of most of the educated class.

For the Jats, this transition to urban spaces has been accompanied by a slow-moving shift in attitudes which is beginning to transmute into new orientations. At one time, even when they had ventured into other occupations, their connection to the land was never severed. It was kept alive and formed the basis of their primary identification.

Whether a Jat was in the army or academics, he was first a Jat and a landowner. His status within his kinship networks and social spaces depended on his possession of land. The more the acres, the greater the respect accrued to him. His integrity stemmed from his identity as an agriculturist, and he shared his contempt for the Bania (trader) with the rest of his kin. Today, the Jat Sikhs have a new-found inclination for a sector they have traditionally looked down upon. According to data collected from Chandigarh regarding the aspirational destination of those migrating from rural to urban life, business in a city is the priority among the urban Jats. Those with available cash have been investing money in showrooms, plots, transport, petrol pumps, liquor vends, cold storage, cinema houses, etc. Most of them do not want to go back to settle down in the village anytime in the future. Almost all cited a lack of basic amenities, less progressive attitude, politics, casteism and a lack of awareness as causes for not wishing to return. Instead of wanting to be identified as rural, they prefer to be identified based on class and caste in the urban context. Their social interactions depend largely on status, similar professional backgrounds and class compatibility which accounts for a social circle from diverse backgrounds (Mahajani 2014: 100).

Yet, Jats continue to reiterate their difference from others persistently. Even outside the rural life, they are economically the most powerful. Their clout extends deep and pervades many spheres of life. Influential Jat families with extensive familial links dominate the major political parties in Punjab as well. This includes the Akali Dal, which also controls the SGPC, hence bringing that under the Jat influence too. This indicates their continuing hold on the most important facets of Sikh life. Concomitant to it is a desire to carry over the rural power paradigm to the urban settings. Hence, despite the demographic and occupational shifts, it is not easy for them to let go of the earlier persona. Although settled in urban areas, they resist settling into urban anonymity or identifying with the urban behavioural codes. They insist on claiming the stereotypes associated with the rural Jat identity as the defining ones, even though the life from which those emerged is on the wane. Even those whose shift to cities is almost complete claim links with extended families in villages irrespective of the fact that schisms in lifestyles do not always make the rural kin welcome into their own lives. Bravado, honour, kinship loyalties—all that has defined the Jat identity in the past—are still held up as the intrinsic Jat characteristics. Within closed groups, affiliation and behaviour endorsements are often related to an earlier Jat identity. Jat boys are constantly reminded of their Jat roots and even encouraged to pick up macho traits of aggression. Most among the Jats, particularly those within Punjab, practise a great degree of exclusivity. There is resistance to the mixing of castes, particularly through marriages. Holding on to an identity rooted in a different environment manifests in behaviour patterns too.

The transition throes are most blatant in those who shift to cities with a sudden influx of money from land deals and hope to carry forward their dominant position to urban areas. Hard drinking, expensive vehicles, possession of weapons, having ferocious Pit Bulls for pets are some examples of their aggressive posturing. The continued attempts to reinvent the old image of authority and power in urban spaces sometimes becomes more aggravated under the apprehensions of dilution of identity. As the Jats find themselves drawn into the modalities of urban life, there seems to be a greater need to prove to themselves and to others that they are different from the timid Bania, whom they have always looked upon condescendingly. The shift from quiet confidence in their powerful rural identity to a a need for repeatedly proclaiming it is reflected in popular culture. The most interesting among these are trends in Punjabi music. The Punjabi music-video industry, cashing in on the new money from land sales and the need for an assertion of identity, is churning out songs which are loaded with references to Jat machismo. Repeated references to the Jat and his *bandook*, the Jat and his land reiterate an identity, which is actually on the wane. Examples of this forced swagger are lyrics like '*Jithe hondi hai pabandi hathyaran di, Uthe Jat fire karda*' (Wherever the use of weapons is restricted, the son of Jat fires), or '*Leopard de wargi ae chaal soniye, Pit Bull chale jih de naal soniye, Landlord munda land naal judeya, Bas hawa vich udd'de ne waal soniye*' (His gait is like a leopard's, Pit Bulls walk alongside him, he is a landlord forever associated with his lands, only his hair flies with the wind).

Nicola Mooney analyses these contradictory impulses of affinity for rural attachments and a concomitant dissociation with the life it represents. She looks at the 'assertions of the inauthenticity of Jat urban lives as a means of marking a nostalgia or of signifying a deep, immediate and emotionally gratifying lived memory for the caste-based, agricultural life whose practices and beliefs urban Jats consider to be more genuinely a measure of their Jat selves' (2011: 11). Caught between the ego-enhancing identity of the past and the practical requirements of the changing times, Jat Sikhs are in the process of an identity revamp. Perhaps, other traits born out of their connection to elementary life will hold them in good stead. Straightforwardness and value for tradition, a capacity for enterprise and hard work, will continue to be their strength under new circumstances.

Movement of Non-Jats from Rural to Urban Areas

Among the non-Jat rural groups, who have seen a major shift from the rural to the urban areas, are the Ramgarhias. They were carpenters by occupation but given the egalitarian nature of the Khalsa forces, many of them had converted to a martial identity under the tenth guru. They also formed one of the *misls* led by Jassa Singh Thoka. Thoka came to be called Ramgarhia after he retrieved the Ram Rauni fort near Amritsar (McLeod 2000: 217). This martial identity has continued to flourish with the Ramgarhias remaining integral parts of the British army and later of the Indian army too. This has led to their entrenchment into urban culture and also afforded them a respectability earlier reserved for the Jats. For the Ramgarhias, the movement out of villages has also been far more widespread and profitable because of their unique skill sets. The British, as they built railways and infrastructures for new administrative set-ups and cantonments in the areas they annexed, found their service indispensable. Ramgarhias began to travel from their rural homes in response to this demand for their services, particularly in areas of communications and industry. Carpentry in Shimla, railways in Eastern India, contracting in Assam, and a combination of the same opportunities in East Africa took them far and wide and also improved their financial position (McLeod 2000: 227). In Bihar, a place for the utilisation of their skills was the Tata Steel City set up Jamshedpur in 1907. The Tata Steel plant had the complete support of the British because much of the material for the world wars came from here. Over the years, more Ramgarhias flocked here and as their numbers grew, they also ventured into trade and contract business, started ancillary industries supporting the Tata Steel plant. Many of them also diversified into the furniture-making industry.

Today, there are established Ramgarhia communities in many parts of the country. They have been able to preserve their religious and cultural practices to quite an extent, without letting them be overly impacted by local cultures. Removed from the hierarchy of their rural lives, the Ramgarhias have established different hierarchies in places of settlement. In the urban North East, especially Assam, they have mobilised enough power to become the most important section of the Sikh community. They have also developed clout in other smaller towns where the earlier Sikh population had largely been composed of Sikh refugees from western Pakistan. As Sikhs outside Punjab, they have gained from the fact that those outside the community recognise them just as Sikhs and do not understand their lower position in the caste hierarchies of rural Punjab. Similarities in the language spoken, area-bound dialects, demographic background and their religious practices have led to their being conferred the same respect, which has generally been accrued to Jats for their valorous image. The common external symbols of Sikhism for all groups within it have contributed to this too (McLeod 2000: 230).

Largely aided by the profits gathered from their ventures outside the state, the Ramgarhias have also spread to urban areas within Punjab. Furniture, agriculture machinery, auto parts, etc., are some of the fields in which they are making good profits. This has also resulted in the consolidation of community identity in other manners. Establishment of *sabhas*, separate gurdwaras, educational trusts and institutions are some of these. As McLeod says, their political participation may still be at the nascent stage, but there is an interesting increase in the reach and numbers of the community. Others artisan castes from Punjab, like the Nais, prefer to be identified with the now-improved Ramgarhia status than with their own group identities on the lowest rungs of rural Punjabi society (McLeod 2000: 228).

Another group, which has moved out of the rural Punjabi structure to an improved stature in urban life, are the Kalals, the liquor brewers of the community. Like the Ramgarhias, in the distant past some of them had found their way into the Khalsa forces. They went on to become influential enough to be leading one of the Sikh *misls* under Jassa Singh Kalal. He earned an exalted status through military exploits, dropped the name Kalal and instead adopted the name of his village, Ahlua, thereafter Ahluwalia. Others adopted this more respectable identity too. The subsequent rise to power of the group is best indicated in the antecedents of the royal family of Kapurthala. Others from the Kalal community too adopted the name. Many in the traditional vocation were forced to move out of it during the colonial period when the British regulated the distilling and sale of spirits. They turned to commercial sectors avoided by the higher castes because of their association with menial work, like those dealing with footwear, bread and vegetables. As finances improved, some also purchased land. They gradually moved out of the lower status associated with their original vocation. The land-owning Ahluwalias in Punjab aspired for a Jat identity, or at least a Rajput identity, like the many other upwardly mobile groups did. However, Jat unwillingness to intermarry with the Ahluwalias put an end to that option. Their growing association with commerce, on the other hand, led to a movement out of villages and into the advantages of city life. Many among them went in for education, and some for higher education as well. Over time, many Sikh professionals and intellectuals emerged from this group. Many others joined the army and civil administration. This has also led to other interesting changes in the group's identity. Those living in cities have begun identifying themselves with Khatris and are increasingly marrying into the group too (McLeod 2000).

The Dalit Sikhs and the Impact of Urbanisation

An important shift to urban life, and with that a stark shift in status is that of sections of so-called lower castes within the Sikh community. Studies on Dalit Sikhs indicate that through the evolution of Sikhism and its stress on a casteless society, they had found a certain degree of acceptance within the Sikh social order. An oft-cited incident is that of Jaita, a descendant of a lower-caste Ranghretta family, which had served and risen under the various gurus. He took the severed head of Guru Tegh Bahadur to his young son Gobind Rai in Anandpur, putting his own life at risk. The group narrative claims that the guru embraced him and called Ranghrettas the sons of the guru. This special bond saw many other Dalits joining Guru Gobind Singh's army after the Khalsa was formed. It seems that after the death of the guru, one of the *misls* was largely composed of lower-caste Sikhs and led by one Bir Singh Ranghretta. The one-time presence of *Mazhabi Singhan da Bunga* (The abode of the Mazhabi Singhs) within the Harmandar Sahib precincts in Amritsar has been cited as proof of the same. It was later pulled down to incorporate the space in the langar hall (community kitchen), and the Mazhabis shifted their lodge to the gurdwara in Tarn Taran close to Amritsar.

Later developments dented into this special status. With Ranjit Singh's adoption of higher-caste customs and identification with Rajput identity, caste consciousness seemed to have made a comeback. Jats, with their rise in stature during the British period, started asserting superior caste status, which became an important part of their identification (Hans 2016: 147). The greatest thrust to finally cement caste hierarchies came with the Punjab Land Alienation Act of 1900, which not only denied possession of land to the lower castes but also declared them to be non-agricultural menials. Even the land where they had lived was no longer their own. They were left with no other option but to do menial jobs or work in the fields of the Jats on the terms dictated by them. If the Dalits continued living within these discriminatory rural practices, it was largely because they had no options. Punjab has not seen the kind of untouchability found in other parts of the country based on purity and pollution. However, in an agricultural society, aggregation of land with one class leads to a deeply skewed power dynamic keeping other classes completely dependent and subordinated. It also leads to a concerted effort by the powerful class to prevent the less powerful ones from aspiring for land ownership and the economic and political power which comes with it. This has been reflected in the many debilitating and discriminatory practices to keep the Dalits in place. Relegating them to separate living areas, denying them access to gurdwaras and maintaining a superior distance have been some of these.

Anger against these practices has been a subterraneous reality with the Dalit Sikhs. There has been a gradual build-up of awareness and consciousness about these discriminations through movements within Sikhism and outside too. The Ad-Dharmi movement, the communist phase in Punjab, Ambedkar's brush with Sikhism, the rise of the Dalit movement across India, all built up a growing awareness and resentment in the lower-caste landless Sikhs of Punjab. This restlessness came to the fore during the shifts which Punjab economy witnessed during the years of the Green Revolution. The state policies geared to equip the land-owning Jats with the latest technology and financial help made them more prosperous and powerful. It also implied a greater edging out of social as well as political spheres for the Dalit Sikhs.

Various factors at this point of time led to the movement of the Dalit Sikhs to urban areas. Among these was the reduced need for manual labour due to mechanisation of agriculture. The development of the industrial corridor along the Ludhiana, Jalandhar and Amritsar highways facilitated their movement to cities to look for work opportunities outside the villages. As Punjab emerged out of the phase of militancy and into one of a liberalised economy, the tertiary sector in the state became higher than the secondary and primary sectors. This created new job opportunities in urban areas, outside the traditional caste-based ones that had existed in rural Punjab. It provided Dalits with avenues to a changed professional and consequently social profile (P. Singh and B. Singh 2014: 69–84). Over the years, Dalits have increasingly distanced themselves from the works, which slotted them as low menials in the rural hierarchies. The gap between the legal status of their new position of equality and the continuing prejudices rooted in tradition makes living in villages an unattractive proposition. Opportunity for education aided by reservations and quota policies has allowed Dalits entry into professional fields, bureaucracy, academics and many more fields.

Political rallying too has become a means of some representation although Punjab politics remains dominated by the Jats.

This has simultaneously led to movement out of caste hierarchy based on occupations. Today, there is a minuscule percentage of Mazhabis working for the Jats. Most of the labourers in Punjab come from Bihar and Uttar Pradesh. Menial tasks of scavenging and cleaning are now being done by professionals not belonging to any particular caste. Migration from villages to cities among the Jats has also resulted from disenchantment with the dilution of the superior position they had once held in rural Punjab. It has also led to cycles of resistance and retribution based on new economic changes and old power structures. Jodhka rightly describes new schisms with caste as an 'axis of social conflict and competition' (Jodhka 2014: 590). The macro- and micro-practices of subordination, once used by the Jats over other groups as instruments of hierarchical superiority, are becoming less effective in the new landscape.

Many among the Chamars have at least one family member abroad. Unfettered by the biases of their society, availing the same opportunities as the privileged sections of their society, they have made sharp rises. An important factor accelerating their growing economic well-being is the money coming from abroad. Trends show that they either come back with the money they have earned or send it back to their families with a keen desire to see it used for upwards mobility. Signs of prosperity are loud and clear. In acts of defiance and assertions of having arrived, many purchase properties specifically in areas once occupied by upper classes. They also flaunt jewellery, cars, weapons and all that was once the domain of the Jats. Economic mobility has not only brought new confidence, but also led to an aggressive repudiation of the structures, which have pushed them to the margins for ages. Not as many Mazhabis have seen a similar rise and there remains a big chunk among them, still caught in the circle of poverty and deprivation. Yet, most of them prefer to work as coolies, construction labourers and rickshaw pullers in cities rather than work in the fields of Jat landowners. Even if they get lower wages, it helps them move out of the humiliation of being treated as lesser beings and also the uncertainty of what and when they will be paid by the landowners (Gupta 2012: 200).

Urbanisation, the consequent improvement in economic status and the concomitant shrugging off of traditional forms of persecution among the Sikh Dalits is further reflected in their assertion within religious spheres. Despite Sikh religion prohibiting caste discriminations, gurdwaras have been the site of caste-based persecution. Earlier discriminations such as Dalits not being allowed into the gurdwaras, or being discouraged to have langar with others have gradually ended after the Sikh reform movement. However, they have continued to be denied positions in gurdwara managements which remain dominated by Jats. The Dalit Sikhs are in the process of dissociation from the lop-sided arrangement by building their own places of worship. Many among them are increasingly identifying themselves with Sant Ravidas, one of the many lower-caste saints whose writings are included in Guru Granth Sahib. Instead of calling themselves Sikhs, they call themselves Ravidasias even though they continue to follow Sikh practices. Their affluence has been directed into the construction of impressive Ravidasia gurdwaras. By moving out of the paradigm which forced them to exist on the margins of their religious identity and constructing one where they are the centre, they have restructured themselves in their own consciousness as well as that of others.

Just as Jat reiteration of their continuing power in the new urban culture is manifested in popular culture, Dalit defiance of that power is amply reflected in the same sphere too. There are a plethora of Punjabi songs, celebrating the Chamar identity, clearly reminiscent of Jats celebrating the Jat identity. Prominent singers like Ginni Mahi, Rajni Thakkarwal, Pamma Sunar and Jaswinder Rayya make no bones about the radical undercurrents in their music. The lyrics of the songs sung by them are aggressive and sometimes threatening.

The videos include a blatant display of new prosperity through expensive cars, houses and weapons. There are also allusions to tales of a better origin and more illustrious past upturned by vagaries of time. There is frequent reference to the community's readiness to fight back discrimination, particularly against the Jats. Mazhabi Sikh women too are constructed as warriors ready to strike back at the Jat fiefdom. *Putt Jatan de* (the sons of the Jats), traditionally the reflection of a usurpation of power in the Punjabi milieu by Jats, are now accompanied by *Putt Chamaran de* (the sons of the Chamars) in a new and daring confrontational stance adopted by the younger generation of the so-called lower castes. This resurgence of caste identity gives an optical illusion that the caste system is enjoying a fresh lease of life. In reality, it is an indication that caste as a system is on the wane in rural India because of which caste identities can afford to come into the limelight (Gupta 2012: 201).

The shift from the rural to the urban for the Sikhs of Punjab is thus proving to be a complicated one. It has led to new occupational structures and changing economic equations. The gradual dismantling of structures, which had earlier determined social relationships, has created uncertainties at many levels. It has induced anxieties, brought to the fore repressed anger and allowed a shifting out from once-static categories. It has led to evolving power shifts and the consolidation of new identities. Reconfiguration of relational paradigms in these new situations is a complex process. It involves difficult adjustments involving self-perceptions and new social positionings. This is particularly true for those for whom it entails a challenge to a position of dominance. For those gaining ground, it is equally difficult to keep their stances balanced as they counter stubborn resistance to a shift in relational paradigms. It is a slow change, but a consistent one. On one hand, social customs continue to police identities. On the other hand, urban identity-markers of success constructed around education, profession and social strata keep gaining strength. It is to be seen how these opposing pulls act on the generations to come. Future goals will perhaps change, as pluralised experiences put a question mark on the rigid differentiations.

References

Banerjee, Himadri. 2014. 'Sikhs Living Beyond Punjab in India'. In *The Oxford Handbook of Sikh Studies*, edited by Pashaura Singh and Louis E. Fenech. UK: Oxford University Press.

Gupta, Dipankar. 2012. 'Whither the Indian Village'. In *Village Society*, edited by Surinder S. Jodhka. Hyderabad: Orient Blackswan.

Hans, Raj Kumar. 2016. 'Making Sense of Dalit History'. In *Dalit Studies*, edited by Ramnarayan S. Rawat and K. Satyanarayana. Duke University Press.

Jodhka, Surinder S. 2009. 'What Makes Sikhs a Minority'. Available at: http://www.india-seminar.com/2009/602/602_surinder_jodhka.htm (accessed on 4 March).

———. 2012. 'Introduction'. In *Village Society*, edited by Surinder S. Jodhka. Hyderabad: Orient Blackswan.

———. 2014. 'Changing Manifestations of Caste in Sikh Panth'. In *The Oxford Handbook of Sikh Studies*, edited by Pashaura Singh and Louis E. Fenech. Oxford: Oxford University Press.

Judge, Paramjit S. *Changing Caste Relations and Emerging Contestations in Punjab*, 1–29. Available at: https://core.ac.uk/display/33336814 (accessed on 1 March 2020).

Mahajani, Priya Khanna. 2014. 'Conclusions and Inferences'. In *Mobility and Identity: A Study of Jat Sikhs in Chandigarh*. US: Xlibris.

McLeod, W.H. 2000. 'Ahluwalias and Ramgarhias: Two Sikh Castes'. In *Exploring Sikhism: Aspects of Sikh Identity, Culture, and Thought*. New Delhi: Oxford University Press.

Mooney, Nicola. 2011. 'Introduction'. In *Rural Nostalgias and Transnational Dreams: Identity and Modernity Among Jat Sikhs*. Canada: University of Toronto.

Ram, Ronski. 2011. 'Caste and Marginality in Punjab: Looking for Regional Specificities'. In *Rethinking State Politics in India: Regions within Regions*, edited by Ashutosh Kumar, first edition. India: Routledge.

Singh, Paramjit and Balwinder Singh. 2014. 'Structure and Pattern of Urbanization in Punjab – A Macro Level Analysis'. In *International Journal of Punjab Studies*, January, 21(1): 69–84.

Songs

Jithe hondi hai pabandi. 2015. Lyricist: Amrit Mann. Singer: Diljeet Dosanjh.

Leopard de wargi. 2018. Lyricist and singer: Jaswinder Singh Bains.

3

They Are Not Like Us: Sikhs in Other Cultural Settings

As the Sikh community has experienced demographic transitions, their trajectories have diversified in ways that have led to different shifts in identity. Some among them have evolved so differently from the community in Punjab that they do not fit into the current normative defining 'Sikh'. The spatial and the cultural differences within which their identities have shaped make them look, sound and even think differently. As Sikh identity has taken a specific form, these marginal identities have become increasingly 'othered' and alienated. Many of them have been relegated to the no-cognisance zone by the larger community. Some among them are the Sikhs of Bihar, Assam, Bengal, Maharashtra, Karnataka and Andhra Pradesh. Their arrival at these places has also been staggered over different time zones resulting in a greater diversity. Among them are Sikhs who accompanied the gurus to places with cultures completely different from their own and stayed back to look after the legacy. Some went for occupational reasons and settled down—among them were soldiers, traders and ancillary workers. Many among them merged with the local culture even as they upheld their religious identity. Some maintained their ethnic and religious identities but were caught in a cycle of deprivation, which led to the loss of connection with home. Some locals converted to Sikhism under the influence of the gurus but never relinquished their cultural practices.

History has evolved in different ways for these different people. Their stories involve traditions upheld, adaptations made, lives diversified. They reflect mutation of identity in the course of developing roots in the places where they arrived. For many, the changing political landscape has meant a loss of authority. Some of them, once secure in the importance of their missions, have been reduced to a whittled people, copies of their original selves. The shifts in identity incurred in integrating with local life and the increasing gap with Sikhism as it has evolved back home make them outsiders within their community. The focus on their difference has become sharper with the arrival in these places of Sikhs representing the normative identity. Conditioned to regard their own insular identity as the only real one, they have been condescending and disapproving of the many fluidities, which these Sikhs represent. Constant attempts to push them out of religious and social spaces have added to the many levels of 'othering' inherent within the community.

Sikhs in Bihar

Bihar, lying towards the northeast of India has a diverse Sikh population. For Punjabis, 'Biharis' are people who come to Punjab as agricultural labour and work in their fields. They represent a culture, language and life very different from their own, and one that is constructed as 'inferior'. The idea of their community being a part of that culture is not easily acceptable to them, more so, when they look and sound like the locals. However, an open and unbiased look at Bihari Sikhs opens a rich repository of history and tradition, which reminds one of the heterogeneity within Sikhism and the many forms it has taken.

Himadri Banerjee's ground-breaking work on Sikhs in Bihar has provided crucial insights into their origin and evolution and forms the basis of many of the details presented here. Sikh connection to Bihar seems to have been established right from the time of the first guru. The *sakhi* tradition mentions Guru Nanak's travel to Bihar and his stay at places like Patna, Rajgir and Gaya. Recorded evidence of the Sikh connection begins from the Persian–Mughal times, providing insights into the reasons for their arrival and the circumstances of their stay in Bihar. Sikh gurus encouraged disciples to expand business ventures in dissimilar directions, hence the first to reach Bihar were probably the Nanakpanthis through the eastern Indian trade network of Delhi, Agra, Allahabad and Benaras. Some also reached different commercial centres located on the banks of different rivers. The Mughal annexation of Bengal and Orissa in 1576, opened the road to Bengal via Bihar. This increased Sikh connections with places like Benaras, Patna and Dhaka. The imperial highway also led to various smaller routes through villages leading to economic zones in various parts of Bihar.

Apart from the Nanakpanthi traders, there were men of the Udasi order—founded by Guru Nanak's son, Siri Chand—on these Sikh travel routes. In the absence of an institutionalised religious structure and greater flexibility of approach, their methods of reaching out to the people were varied. Their adoption of local vocabulary is reflected in different nomenclatures like *sangat*s, *matha*s, *akhara*s, *dera*s and mandirs for places of Sikh worship they established in these places. Here, they propagated the teachings of Nanak. This included an emphasis on the concepts of one formless god and universal brotherhood. They also welcomed everyone, irrespective of caste or social status, encouraging people from diverse religious backgrounds to join them. They helped people both with material resources and spiritual succour. Since they provided aid and assistance to travellers, holy men, traders and others, wealthy people of the area exempted them from taxes so that they could continue their socially useful activities (Banerjee 2018: 167–168).

It was the direct interaction of the gurus with the Sikhs in Bihar that began the process of consolidation of identity. In the first half of the 17th century, Guru Hargobind, the sixth in line, sent *hukumnamas* to important Sikh members in Bihar and also to Sikhs settled elsewhere in the country, asking for contributions for the newly evolving martial tradition in Sikhism. The ninth guru, Guru Tegh Bahadur, personally visited Bihar on his way to Assam. It is said that he was tracing the footsteps of the first guru, Guru Nanak, and spreading his word among people of distant lands. Added to it was a goodwill gesture to a king who requested his company. This also began the process of local conversions, which were to later evolve into the Bihari–Sikh identity. Himadri Banerjee tells of local traditions, which trace the guru's journey through Sasaram in west Bihar, an area inhabited by a trading class called the Agraharis or Munrias, for they shaved their beard and cut their hair. They were of diverse castes and followed different petty business activities like those of the Suniars (goldsmiths), Telis (oil pressers), Halwais (sweetmeat makers) and Kaser Banias (manufacturers and traders of bell metal). Having grown prosperous over the years, they aspired for a higher social status, which was resented by the higher-caste Hindus. Sikhism, apart from being an inclusive faith, offered an opportunity for social mobility. Agraharis became Sikhs albeit without foregoing their Hindu beliefs and traditions, which included idol worship, depending on Brahmins for religious practices and continuing Hindu practices like *shradha* (Banerjee 2018: 175–177).

Guru Tegh Bahadur reached Patna in 1666, where his stay had been arranged by the existing Sikh community. Patna was a convenient place for a temporary home where his pregnant wife and old mother could be entrusted to an already existing Sikh *sangat* while he travelled further to Assam. During his stay there, the guru met the sizeable Sikh population whose ancestors had once travelled from Punjab and who were then deeply influenced by local culture, possibly through marriages with locals. They took care of his wife and young son, who was born when he was away in Assam. Even after the guru and his family went back to the North, Guru Tegh Bahadur maintained close ties with the Patna *sangat*, as is evident from the eight *hukumnama*s he sent to them. The *sangat* too kept the memories of the guru alive through archiving memorabilia, commemorating important places associated with his stay and creating a whole repertoire of stories which have been passed on from one generation to another, largely by word of mouth. These local Sikhs have taken care of the historical connections with the Sikh gurus, helped in the conduct of ceremonies at gurdwaras and passed on the ensuing traditions from generation to generation. It is because of them that many of the gurdwaras reflecting the history of the Sikh connection with the Sikh gurus survive and allow a glimpse into the past. Gurdwara Guru ka Bagh, where Guru Tegh Bahadur stayed for some time, Gurdwara Gobind Ghat and Gurdwara Bal Lila, where the young Gobind spent a part of his childhood playing with other children are some of these. The birthplace of Gobind Rai commemorated by the local *sangat*s is today known as Takht Sri, Harmandar Sahib, Patna.

After the martyrdom of Guru Tegh Bahadur, his son Gobind Rai assumed the guruship of the Sikhs. The tenth guru (1666–1708) continued the close contact with the Patna *sangat* through *hukumnama*s, keeping them involved and integrated with the shifts in the Sikh political processes. He communicated to them important changes like the disbanding of the *masand* system and the institution of the Khalsa in 1699. He also sent instructions for local Sikhs to meet him in Punjab in the martial Khalsa identity, on Diwali and Baisakhi, and to contribute to the needs of maintaining an army in terms of soldiers, weapons and arms. The Sikh connection with Patna continued even after the passing away of Guru Gobind Singh. Among those who seem to have made their way there were the Khalsa Nihangs. The Nihangs were the special forces of the Sikh army and have traditionally held an important position in the running of Takht Sri Harmandar Sahib. They have always claimed a higher position than the earlier Sanatani Sikhs but have not been able to take total control. Nirmalas are yet another strand and can be traced to the Sikhs sent by the tenth guru to Benaras to learn Sanskrit and Vedanta. These different strands of the community created diversity in the Sikh profile in Patna. It 'not only brought in fresh challenges but also offered opportunities for response and exchange. These relationships introduced emigrants to new life experiences and provided enough autonomy to redesign the message of the Sikh Gurus' (Banerjee 2018: 167). This has also led to differentiation among the community as is reflected in names given to gurdwaras like Gurdwara Badi Sangat (big congregation) and Gurdwara Choti Sangat (small congregation). These also followed different rituals even though adhering to the same faith.

Over the years, the various Sikh groups in Bihar have evolved in different manners leading to a diverse community profile, much of it quite different from the community in Punjab. Agrahari Sikhs, who had trade relations with the Patna Sikhs, most likely came to know of the guru's announcement of the constitution of the Khalsa from the Patna Sikhs and carried the news back to Sasaram. This led to a major part of the community adopting the five Ks through the *Khande ka Pahul* initiation and adopting the Singh Agrahari identity. This transformation gave them social superiority over the non-initiated Agrahari Sikhs. However, while their physical form now became one of the Khalsa, their cultural practices and religious beliefs continued to be rooted in their earlier traditions. Himadri Banerjee tells us that they continued to follow Hindu marriage rituals and celebrate festivals such as Sivaratri and Doljatra. They also kept images in their sacred space and went to Gaya to perform *pindadan.* For these reasons, they also came to be called the Sanatani Sikhs.

By the end of the 18th century, the Agraharis had moved beyond Sasaram to new places like Kedli Chatti—part of modern-day Jharkhand—rich in plants used in oil pressing, wood for commercial consumption and *mahua* flowers used for brewing liquor. From here, they also moved to mineral-rich Hazaribagh. Many of them procured these minerals and sold them in markets in Kolkata; this made a few of them rich and prompted others to become forest contractors under the British in the 19th century. Their repressive role as *thekedars* in the Santhal Pargana region even led to a rebellion by the local tribes in 1830. Some of them also moved to Benaras in UP and Aarah in Bihar. Religious symbols displayed outside their houses in Kedli Chatti indicate that over time, the Agrahari Singhs became a fully distinguishable Sikh identity. However, their customs and rituals remained heavily influenced by the local Bihari culture (Banerjee 2018: 175–177).

Like the Agraharis of Sasaram, the Sikhs of Katihar form another Bihari Sikh identity. There are different opinions on the background of this group, which is largely restricted only to Katihar. They call themselves Sodhis and claim that they followed Guru Tegh Bahadur to Bihar in the second half of the 17th century and took residence in areas where local Sikhs already resided. However, many believe that they were local Sikhs involved in different occupations like farming, grain trade and driving bullock carts. A significant number of them could have been Kalwars, who manufactured and sold liquor, acted as moneylenders of the area and were known for their enterprise and credibility. British restrictions on the production of local liquor led many to shift to other occupations like grain and oilseed trade. Many purchased agricultural lands and let them out on rent to assume the role of landlords.

Being travellers, they were in the know of the shifts occurring within the Sikh fold in Punjab and the reforms, which were leading to the formation of a distinctive Sikh identity. At a time, when news of these movements was not easily reaching other Bihari Sikhs, they used the information for upward mobility within the community. They claimed a difference from the local sanatani Sikhs by adopting strict Khalsa Sikh codes in the early 20th century. They also learnt Gurmukhi even though their mother tongue was Bihari, and adopted measures endorsed by the Singh Sabha movement in Punjab. Along with it, they actively established the narrative that they were originally inhabitants of Punjab who had arrived in Bihar with the ninth guru during the late 17th century. Like their counterparts in Punjab, these Sikhs have been ingenious in adopting modernity to suit their needs and climbing the social ladder. From among them have emerged *ragi*s, *granthi*s and *langri*s, furthering social respectability within the community (Banerjee 2018: 177–179).

The Sikhs who came to Bihar after Partition were mostly the trading professional class of Sikhs, including the Khatris and Aroras, who were displaced from Western Punjab. These Sikhs, too, were heavily influenced by the Singh Sabha movement preceding Partition, and their perception of Sikhism lacked the flexibility that had been the hallmark of Sikh identity in Bihar. These refugee settlers did not feel a cultural affinity with the Bihari Sikh population and others who had been settled in Bihar long enough to be influenced by the local culture. One of the significant reasons for the social divisions between the old and the new Sikh residents is the issue of language. The locals speak dialects of Bihari mixed with a broken mixture of Hindi and a smattering of Punjabi which is unacceptable to Punjabi-speaking Sikhs. The duality of their identity, which is Sikh as well as Bihari, has been unpalatable for the Punjabi Sikhs. They also question Hindu traditions like *aarti* followed by the Bihari Sikhs in the Patna Sahib gurdwara. They consider these practices deviations from the Sikh *rehit*s and strongly protest against them. However, despite their attempts, they have not been successful in dislodging the local Sikhs and their practices from the gurdwara. The Bhai Sahib at the Patna Sahib Gurdwara, even today, speaks in a language, which is a mixture of Hindi and Punjabi liberally sprinkled with local terms and heavily accented by the Bihari lilt. Daily rituals continue to reflect the fluidity that has been the mark of the Bihari Sikhs. Meanwhile, the differences between the two groups have led to legal wrangles for ensuring representation of all groups in the management.

Ironically, the chain of 'othering' continues in more ways than one. Punjabi Sikhs settled in Bihar, too, over a period have picked up local accents and mannerisms, which distinguish them from the Sikhs in Punjab, Delhi, etc. Their way of talking is heavily marked by a Bihari accent, almost like a mother-tongue interference. While they 'other' the local Sikhs over linguistic differences, they themselves have been 'othered' by Sikhs in the North. Many of them, who decided to move to Punjab after the 1984 Sikh massacre, found themselves treated like outsiders because of these influences. In recent times, many among the new generation are trying to use education to move out into metropolises in other parts of the country. There is a consensus among many respondents that those who leave never return. The Sikh population in Patna—the hub of Punjabi Sikhs—has dwindled significantly in recent times. The Bihari Sikhs, meanwhile, continue in their old occupations as petty traders, gurdwara workers, etc. while only some among them have managed to move up the social ladder.

Sikhs in Bengal

Oral traditions suggest that during his Eastern *udasi* (long journeys to propagate his teachings), Guru Nanak passed through Bengal, from where he went to Puri. Bengal's first association with Sikhs can be traced to the 18th century with the arrival of Sikh fighter groups. They were part of the *barkandaze*s, mercenary groups composed of Sikhs, Rajputs, Hindustanis, etc., who with their ready paraphernalia of weapons and horses were recruited by kings and nawabs. They were most probably unruly and were targeted by British military operations and left the Bengal frontier for Assam in the late 18th century. Many critics believe that it is these Sikhs, who were later employed on similar terms by powerful groups and ruling kings of the North East too.

The presence of Sikhs as a social group in Bengal can be traced to the Agrahari Sikhs of Bihar, who in the process of dispersal from Sasaram had also reached Calcutta. Their regional antecedents were clear in their naming the gurdwara they constructed after Patna's Harmandar Sahib. They brought with them the dual identity of being both Bihari and Sikh as it had evolved back in Bihar. Their Bihari roots were reflected in their sociocultural practices. Like in Bihar, they spoke in Bhojpuri, observed Bihari rituals, celebrated Bihari festivals and used symbols like the *tilak*, which is not usual among Sikhs. These fluid cultural practices were not considered strange by the Bengalis until the arrival of Sikhs from Punjab in the late 18th century. Jat Sikhs and Ramgarhias, as part of the British army and labour force for other colonised countries, had been coming to Calcutta port for embarking on journeys. Familiarity with the place made them aware of the employment opportunities there, which increased when Calcutta was made the colonial capital. Many settled there permanently.

Awareness about the new community increased when in 1849, the British annexed Punjab and took with them many Bengalis to run different branches of the British administration in Punjab. This brought Bengalis in touch with the Sikhs of Punjab. The Brahmo Samaj, impressed with the ideas of universal brotherhood, started including some of Nanak's *banis* in the daily prayer meetings. In the early 20th century, the Akali Morcha reverberated across the country for control over gurdwaras. Bengalis saw Sikhs as a persecuted people fighting for their religious rights. Subhash Chandra Bose was invited to one of their programmes. The rise of the radical groups against British rule also saw Sikh contribution to Subhash Chandra Bose's Indian National Army. Much before that, Jat Sikh boys had actively participated in many anti-British activities led by Bose. The Sikh community endorsed the Bengali point of view. They also used the community mediums, including Punjabi media, to aid the national movement in the 1940s. Those involved with these activities were the Sikhs from Punjab, not the Agrahari Sikhs. Meanwhile, the Bengali perception of Sikhs as a brave and patriotic people was also influenced by the narrative of Guru Gobind Singh as a nationalist hero along with figures like Maharana Pratap and Shivaji. Sikh participation in favour of the Bengali Hindus in the communal riots of 1946 furthered the positive perception of the community (Banerjee 2007: 222–224).

This new image of Sikhs differentiated other Sikhs from the Agrahari Sikhs, mostly retail traders, with an un-Sikh like appearance and demeanour. People from the trader and professional class, who arrived around the time of Partition, despite their cultural differences with the Jats followed the same religious practices. Both groups were influenced by the Singh Sabha's attempts at a restructured Sikh identity and they collectively showed antipathy towards the ritualism of the Agraharis. These dissensions have continued among the Sikh community in Bengal. It has, at times, led to clashes between the factions. There have been attempts, sometimes successful, to take away the control of gurdwaras from the Agrahari Sikhs. Patnaiya or Bihari Sikhs and the Punjabi Sikhs remain deeply divided. The former are not accepted as real or *pucca* Sikhs by the latter. The Bihari Sikhs in Bengal are also economically inferior to the Punjabi Sikhs. All these differences prevent social mingling between the two. These social and historical anomalies are being gradually understood as more research is being initiated on the Sikhs.

Sikhs in Assam and Meghalaya

Not many had been aware of the Sikh community in Assam and Meghalaya until recently. News of their clashes with the local Khasis in Shillong appeared in newspapers in June 2018 (*Times of India*; *Hindustan Times*). This suddenly brought them into community cognisance and drew attention to their presence in the North-Eastern states. Sikh association with this area is an old one with a chequered past. The result is a diverse community profile comprising the agriculturist Asomiya Sikh community settled in Assam for nearly 200 years, the Mazhabis Sikhs working as sanitation workers settled in both Assam and Meghalaya for nearly 100 years, and the Punjabi Sikhs, who arrived and settled there later.

The history of the Sikh connection with Assam goes back to the time of the Sikh gurus. In the Janamsakhi tradition, Guru Nanak is said to have visited Kamrup in Assam. His visit was commemorated with the construction of a gurdwara in Dhubri at Goalpara in Assam by the ninth guru, Guru Tegh Bahadur. Guru Tegh Bahadur's visit to Assam is more precisely catalogued in Assamese *bhuranji*s as well as in the *hukumnamas* issued by the guru. While there is no controversy regarding the veracity of his presence in Assam, there are different opinions about the reasons for his visit. Assamese historian, Surya Kumar Bhuyan feels that Guru Tegh Bahadur accompanied the Mughal general Raja Ram Singh in the capacity of a friend and a respected spiritual leader when the latter was deputed to the difficult area to subdue the local Ahom rulers. It is more likely that the guru's primary aim was to spread Sikh teachings in Assam. His presence in Assam is marked by Gurdwara Dumdama Sahib. This area also became a garrison for Sikh troops in later times.

The evolution of the Sikh community in Assam has had various trajectories. Himadri Banerjee's work traces the many stories surrounding the history of the Asomiya Sikhs, who made Assam their home in the 18th and the 19th centuries. More than historical works, he uses works of Assamese literature to reconstruct the past and understand the histories of their arrival and settlement. Among these are Lakshminath Bezbaroa's novel *Podum Kunwari* (1890) serialised in the periodical *Jonaki*, Daibachandra Talukdar's play *Hardatta* (1935) and Rajanikanta Bordoloi's novels *Manomati* (written in 1900, published in 1993 by Sahitya Prakash Publishers) and *Dandua Droh* (published in 1919, and again in 1988 by Sahitya Prakash Publishers). Some of these throw light on Sikh arrival in Assam in the 18th century within the context of local political upheavals related to the brewing discontent against the existing monarchy. Hardatta Chaudhary, a revolutionary leader fighting against the ruling Ahom king, seems to have requisitioned the help of mercenary Sikh soldiers. The story suggests that while the Sikh mercenaries under the leadership of Kumedan Singh fought for Hardatta initially, they turned against him when he failed to pay them the promised remuneration. Instead, they joined the Ahom king. Bezbarua and Daibachandra Talukdar depict these Sikhs as greedy outsiders, who ravaged the area of Kamrup for personal benefits. However, Bordoloi in his *Dandua Droh* tries to explain how their assault on the local peasantry could have been dictated by necessity (Banerjee 2007: 54–59). There are different opinions about the veracity of these representations. One common derivation is that after the revolution was suppressed, they were rewarded with land grants by the Ahom rulers and decided to settle down in Assam, pursuing agriculture for livelihood. They also seemed to have married locally, to have adopted the Assamese way of life and been deeply influenced by Assamese culture.

Another set of Sikh soldiers seem to have arrived in Assam in the early 19th century. It appears that in the Assamese imagination, the image of Sikhs vastly changed with the new arrivals. The Burmese had been consistently involved in Assam power struggles since 1817 and had helped the weak Ahom ruler, Chandrakant Singha, get back his throne twice after being overthrown by family members. However, the Burmese divested him of power when he started getting suspicious of their intentions. This was when he is said to have solicited help from Maharaja Ranjit Singh of Punjab. While local Asomiya legends corroborate the story that Maharaja Ranjit Singh sent about 300–500 soldiers to Assam on the request of the Ahom king to fight against the Burmese forces, critics are sceptical of the version. Birinder Pal Singh, for instance, feels that Ranjit Singh had good relations with the Burmese. Besides, a treaty with the British forbade him from sending his troops outside British-held territories. Hence, it seems that the forces commissioned by the Ahom ruler might actually have been part of the mercenary Sikh troops once in service of the nawabs of Bengal but later disbanded by them. Among them could also be the Bihari Sikhs, called Dumdamiyas, who had accompanied Guru Tegh Bahadur to Assam and whose descendants were headquartered at Gurdwara Dumdama Sahib at Dhubri. While the debate continues, folklore says that the Ahom rulers lost and Chaitanya Singh died in battle, bravely defending the Assamese king's claims to power against the Burmese. Local tales talk about the exceptional bravery of these Sikhs under their brave commander, Chaitanya Singh. This has been reinforced by the account in Bordolai's *Manomati* in which Sikh Subedar Chaitanya Singh is painted as a loyal ally who fought the Burmese 'outsiders' on behalf of the Assamese royalty. It is said that after his fall, his wife, respectfully addressed as *Mataji*, led the survivors into a hideout in dense forests, and they finally settled at Chaparmukh near Nagaon, taking up agriculture as a livelihood. The two places, where they settled, have since come to be known as Chaparmukh Sing Gaon and Barkola Sing Gaon. Chaparmukh Sing Gaon has the Mataji Gurdwara named after commander Chaitanya Singh's wife. Barkola Sing Gaon is about 20 kilometres from Chaparmukh and the Sikhs settled here are an agricultural community (B. Singh 2018: 68–69). These Asomiya Sikhs insist on tracing their descent from the army of Ranjit Singh.

How far these different portrayals of the Sikhs were influenced by other factors needs probing too. Himadri Banerjee rightly points out that the outsider, greedy and almost barbaric version of the first lot could have something to do with the rising angst against all outsiders in Assam in the wake of the large-scale Bengali inflow into the state. Outsiders, in general, were being seen as threats to Assamese culture and the economic interests of the locals at the time when many of these works were published. On the other hand, the 'insider' version of Sikhs as friends of Assam in the second novel could be inspired by the nationalistic narratives of pre-Independence days. In either case, over a while, both narratives seem to have been subsumed in the evolution of an Assamese Sikh identity which has so deeply entrenched itself in the local culture, that even the Assamese accept them as one of their own.

The next influx of Sikhs in the early 20th century was to bring a completely different community profile to Assam. Their circumstances of arrival were such that instead of assimilating into the local culture, they stood out as different from it. While their life gradually changed from the one they left behind, it failed to grow strong roots in the new environment. As the British established their clout in Assam, they also made arrangements for the new administration which was to take charge. To keep the city of Shillong clean, a British military regiment, once stationed in Punjab, brought with them members of the Churha (sweeper) caste among Sikhs. Most of them came from the districts of Amritsar and Gurdaspur. By 1910, a separate section of Sikh sweepers and scavengers were employed on the payrolls of the Shillong Municipal Corporation for solid waste management of the British wards. Their services were later extended to the entire city. They were given fixed salaries and houses in the area called Bara Bazaar, which was distanced from the rest of the city. Regular payment and availability of accommodation fuelled migration and more Sikhs started trickling into Shillong. Gradually, as the numbers increased, they were given accommodations in Gora Lines in the Laitumakhra area and employed in varied jobs in the municipality.

The work entrusted to the Sikh sweepers seems to have been unfit for humans from today's perspective. Every man had to pick night soil from dry latrines, carry it on his head to throw it into bigger containers. These were transported in bullock carts to a designated place. The bullocks and the carts were then parked close to their place of residence, where they also had to help wash them every day. There were added problems like heavy rains, landslides, water getting collected at these places that also led to diseases (Banerjee 2018). Meanwhile, there was anger building up among the locals in Assam against outsiders being brought into their land by the British. Around 1920, 'Line System Legislation' was implemented in Assam, which restricted all forms of permanent entry and settlement within the area brought under the act. The sweeper Sikhs were asked to provide domicile certificates, which most of them did not have. The result has been the ghettoisation of the Sikh community in restricted areas where they had been forced to settle in by the British. Even those who shifted to the Guwahati

Municipal Corporation after the formation of the separate state of Meghalaya in 1972 have lived under similar constraints in the Marakhali colony once inhabited by the Harijans from Bihar.

These two different Sikh streams have evolved very differently over time, and that has impacted their contemporary social profiles. In the Assamese imagination, the Asomiyas have been accepted as insiders but the sweeper Sikhs continue to be branded as outsiders. Their contemporary profiles reflect the reasons for the same too. The Asomiya Sikhs have completely integrated themselves into local life. While they have continued to follow Sikh religious practices and have maintained the Sikh appearance, they are deeply entrenched in local cultural practices. Intermarriages with locals among the early settlers and close social interaction with them through the decades has influenced every aspect of their life. The Asomiya Sikhs not only strongly reiterate their Assamese identity but also posit it as distinct from the Sikhs who arrived later. Those among them, who can articulate in languages other than Assamese, go to great lengths to emphasise their ethnicity to others. They insist that to be called an Asomiya Sikh requires an entrenchment in Assamese life for generations. It derives that they have to be Assamese in terms of culture, language and commitment to an Assamese identity.

All this is reflected in their life practices too. Asomiya Sikh women dress like the local women in *mekhala*s and follow the same rituals and customs as them. They also cook local cuisine and celebrate the local festivals. Men, as well as women, visit *namghars* as much as they visit gurdwaras. They generally cannot speak Punjabi or Hindi and proclaim Assamese to be their mother tongue. Even in their attitudes and orientations, they are more Assamese than Punjabi. Their agricultural practices reflect the Assamese agricultural focus on acquiring all necessities of life through cultivation and being satisfied with them instead of aggressively pursuing better living standards like the Punjabi agriculturist. Their status among the locals is a respectable one. Sikhs seem to have married into the local Keots, a respectable agricultural class, and Kalitas who are considered just lower to the Brahmins. However, they claim not to believe in caste distinctions in keeping with Sikh injunctions. A very small number avail the Scheduled Caste status, which others of the community insist is a ploy to obtain state-welfare provisions (B. Singh 2018: 71).

The veracity of their commitment to the Assamese identity can be gauged by the fact that they actively participated in the Assam movement from 1979–1985. The large-scale infiltration of Bangladeshi immigrants into Assam after the formation of Bangladesh in 1971 created a furore which led to a movement against all foreigners. Asomiya Sikhs actively participated in identifying outsiders and fought for the rights of the local and tribal population, which ironically would go against the other Sikhs of Assam, the *safai karamcharis*. They participated in the radical Assamese identity reconstruction through organisations like the All Assam Student's union, Assam Sahitya Sabha, All Assam Gana Sangram and many other such organisations. Among those who lost their lives for the movement, were two Sikhs from Barkola village, Chandan Singh (February 1983) and Karan Singh (March 1983). The recognition of their contribution to the cause is reflected in a memorial built on the road to Kamrup and Barkola. They are honoured along with a local who died for the same cause (B. Singh 2018: 96).

Unlike the Asomiya Sikhs, sweeper Sikhs have been constructed as outsiders by the locals. The life of these Sikhs continues to be markedly Punjabi in its orientation. Given their substantial numbers, they have not needed to marry into locals. As a result, their cultural practices stay rooted in the Punjabi way of life. Their most crucial difference from the Asomiya Sikhs is the preservation of the Punjabi language. They not only speak Punjabi as their primary means of communication but even sustain the dialects and pronunciation of the particular areas of Punjab they come from. They have also sustained connections with Punjab through relatives. Their alienation from the local people and the administration has grown due to other factors too. The colonial policy of keeping them out of sight of the civil population laid the foundation for their exclusion from the assimilatory process. Restricted within the prescribed quarters outside city areas has prevented them from settling in the city. Over time, this led to congested pockets of Sikhs, surrounded by other ethnic groups, which has only increased their differentiation from the local population.

While there are no attempts to improve their pathetic living conditions, there have been consistent attempts to dislodge them from their homes through legal and illegal means. The living conditions of the Sikhs, whether in Bara Bazaar sweeper lines in Shillong or Marhakali in Guwahati are equally bad. Even basic amenities like clean water and primary education are scarce. Narrow lanes, unhygienic conditions and people spilling out of homes due to lack of space are common features. Instead of improving the living conditions of the people here, the municipalities focus on making these areas, now centrally located due to urban expansion, aesthetically pleasing. There is constant talk of slum clearance and the need to build flyovers in both the cities. Government authorities would like to demolish these quarters, which are an embarrassment in the rapidly modernising area. On and off, there are instances of bulldozing which keep getting stalled with the interference of well-to-do Sikhs from other areas. Eviction, however, remains a perpetual possibility for the Sikhs living here.

While there is constant pressure on them to vacate the area that has been their home for decades, there is no feasible alternative being provided. Accommodation in lieu is on offer only for those who have legal documents to support their residence, which 90 per cent of them do not have. In British times, these houses came along with government jobs with sons replacing their fathers generation after generation. With the end of colonial rule, these privileges have dissipated and their right to ownership debated. Unfortunately, most have no voting right, no ration card or electricity bill in their names, and find themselves vulnerable to state persecution (Banerjee 2018). There are other reasons for their particularly vulnerable position. While the security of residence during British times led these Sikhs into believing that they did not need to invest in land outside colonies, new laws forbade them from buying property in later years. Hence, they are now in the unenviable position of being in constant threat of being forced out of homes with nowhere else to go. Added to it is the economic pressure. Government jobs, once taken for granted, are no longer available to their growing numbers. They have neither amenities nor resources, for education or vocational training. Lack of awareness deprives them of any welfare schemes they could be entitled to. The area where they live has become synonymous with petty crime, drugs and law-and-order problems.

Added to the ghettoisation, poverty and government pressure is the increasingly belligerent attitude of sections of local people. Anger against outsiders has festered in Assamese consciousness from the time the British brought Bengalis to run the state administration. After independence, this anger has mutated into political consciousness of their constitutionally protected rights and privileges. They have also become aware of the power they can wield with their voting numbers and the material benefits it can get for them. Among their stance is the demand for local resources for local people. Adoption of the 'sons of soil' theory has conveniently made all non-indigenous people 'outsiders' (*dhkar*) (B. Singh 2018). This movement is most blatantly visible in Shillong where the local tribes had lost considerable land to outside incursions. With the formation of the separate state of Meghalaya in 1972, the locals, particularly the Khasis have been pressurising the state government to declare anyone not a tribal, an outsider. The sweeper Sikhs are one of these and the Khasis want them evicted from their homes as well as jobs so that space and resources are made available to the locals. The pressure to safeguard the interests of the politically significant tribals has resulted in the local governments turning a blind eye to their aggressive posturing or the quandary in which it puts the others.

While the Asomiya Sikhs and the sweeper Sikhs have had these different responses from the local populations, their place within the larger Sikh community is another issue. Like in other places, the North East too has seen the influx of a Punjabi-speaking Sikh community post-Independence. Unlike Bihar and Bengal, here it was not only the cultural difference with the local converts to Sikhism but also the question of caste that defined the paradigms. The Ramgarhias of East Punjab and the Suniars (goldsmiths) of West Punjab, who came to Assam in the 20th century, brought with them the caste practices of Punjabi society that placed the sweepers at the lowest rung. The former as transporters and auto-part traders and the latter as retail businessmen have also been financially superior to the Mazhabi Sikhs. One after the other, they took control of local gurdwaras and refused to allow the Mazhabis to enter the premises or sit in langars. This kind of discrimination did not go down well with the Mazhabi Sikhs. Despite their precarious economic condition, this was one indignity of an earlier life they had escaped from, which was once again catching up with them. Many of them responded by relinquishing their Sikh identity for a Balmik identity, a trend catching on in Punjab as well. This involved becoming part of an order where they were not the peripheral outcastes. The result was a moving away from the religious identity they had held on to for so long. The Mazhabi Sikhs in Shillong and Guwahati set up Balmik ashrams along with the gurdwaras, adopted new practices and even started cutting their hair, a major departure from Sikh tenets. Some also converted to Christianity. This was used to further ostracise them and they were blamed for flouting Sikh codes of conduct. 'The Suniars also accused them of conspiring with Masihs (Christian), bringing disrepute to Sikhism on the streets of Shillong' (Banerjee 2018).

Jat arrival to these areas has led to a strong reversal of this alienation due to the integrative overtures by the Jat Sikh community in the North

East. In a departure from their caste practices in rural Punjab, Jats in Guwahati have worked to integrate the Mazhabis back into the Sikh fold, which includes bringing them back to the turbaned Sikh identity. Mutual interests seem to underlie the overture and the response. Jats have not only mobilised the Guwahati Municipal Corporation sweepers into a trade union but also used their support to gain control over the gurdwaras. They are now powerful in the management of the primary Sikh body with headquarters at Dhubri Sahib. They are also economically and politically resourceful in areas of settlement. Boys in the sweeper colonies know that maintaining a clear Sikh identity will get them support from powerful Jat Sikhs of the area.

They are also discovering that an aggressive Khalsa identity helps them challenge the Khasi unions more effectively. It is because of this growing consolidation that Sikhs have been able to stand up to Khasi attempts at bullying them to evict their homes. This, in turn, is begetting greater loyalty to visible Sikh identity and the confidence it brings to them. This consolidation is filtering into other community practices as well. Many among the younger generation have started taking *amrit* and are sporting flowing beards and turbans. The trend to marry outside the community has given way to marriages completely within the community. Religion has become a means of asserting power in public spaces. The *nagar kirtan*s have become occasions to assert their identity, sometimes a tad too aggressively. Birinder Pal Singh feels that at that some level, the powerful Jat Sikhs might also be using the sweeper Sikhs as *lathait*s or handymen as they did back home. Yet, the fact remains that the Mazhabi Sikhs are back in the community fold (Singh: 2018).

The Punjabi Sikhs' relationship with the Asomiya Sikhs, on the other hand, has been marked with the same tropes of 'otherness' as with the Agraharis of Bihar. The Asomiya Sikhs do not fit into the cultural or the religious normative of the Sikh identity. Their total entrenchment in local customs makes them seem like anomalies within the distinct Sikh religious practices as they have evolved over the last century. The Asomiya Sikhs' continuing affiliations to local traditions make them 'others' in the eyes of the community. Language as a carrier of culture and tradition is also something that the Asomiya Sikhs have lost over the years. Pressures of assimilating within new cultural contexts, including marriage among locals, perhaps made it imperative for them to adopt the local language. It is also possible that Punjabi might never have been the first language of Bihari Sikhs among them. For the Punjabi Sikhs, it is a sign of their diluted religious and cultural identity. The relatonship between the Punjabi and the Asomiya Sikhs has been a strained one. The Assamese Sikhs have often been belittled because they cannot speak or read Punjabi and are hence also referred to as spurious Sikhs or *kachche Sikh*. Asomiyas, on the other hand, believe that though they do not know the language, they follow *Sikhi* more sincerely than the Punjabi Sikhs, who are more concerned with ostentation than spiritual understanding. The socio-economic disparity among the rich Punjabi Sikhs and the not-so-rich Asomiya Sikhs is also a deterrent to social interaction. Due to their overbearing behaviour, the Punjabi Sikhs are perceived as rude and arrogant. Attempts at improving relations and encouraging cohesion in the community through joint celebrations of *gurupurab*s, etc. are therefore thwarted. Differences, instead of narrowing, have only widened.

Within these measures of redrawn identities, these Sikh groups in the North East are negotiating their way through existing situations and the possibility of new shifts. For the sweeper Sikhs, poverty, lack of resources and illiteracy are permanent constraints. Alcoholism and drug addiction among boys are aggravating the situation. There is a dire need for occupational diversification. Some of the boys from the community are trying to find jobs in the tourism sector, as taxi drivers etc., but their number is limited. Even as they put up a brave façade in the face of eviction, many among them are making alternate arrangements. Some have been sending part of their earnings to relatives in Punjab for buying land in villages. Others are seeking to marry daughters in Punjab to have a foothold in case of eviction. This demands cultural reversions that are not always successful. Despite preserving their language and cultural identity, the Mazhabi Sikhs too have been influenced by local culture in other manners. Girls brought up in the liberal North Eastern atmosphere, for instance, find it difficult to adjust to the conservative attitudes in Punjab (Singh 2018). The larger Sikh community meanwhile is unaware of their difficulties.

The Asomiya Sikhs are also dealing with new challenges. With growing numbers and land fragmentation, there is a growing trend towards urbanisation and the new lifestyles that entails. Luckily for them, the presence of a polytechnic, a degree college and library in the areas of their residence has helped the young generation in finding new avenues. Urbanisation is leading to better integrative practices in the community outside the village life. Learning Hindi and English is helping them to connect with others outside their limited circles. Many have spread out to towns like Nagoan and surrounding areas for education and employment. They also keep sending memorandums to the state government seeking a development council for the Asomiya Sikh community, seat reservations in medical and engineering colleges and government jobs for their children. They also seek political representation through nomination. Today, though few in numbers, one would find writers, academicians and professionals among Asomiya Sikhs. Hopefully, by articulating their experiences and affirming their community identity along with the Asomiya one, they will gradually be able to connect to the larger Sikh community outside Assam.

The Sikh community in Assam, along with many others, has recently been in the spotlight due to the nationwide debate on the government intent to introduce the Citizenship Amendment Act 2019 in Assam as in the rest of the country. While the rest of the states have been divided on the merit of granting or denying citizenship to Muslim immigrants on the basis of religion, Assam has been concerned with that citizenship being granted to any outsider. While Assam has been protesting the upturning of the existing NRC and the terms of the Assam Accord 1985 declaring all migrants since 2014 as illegal, the government has been trying to push the date to 1971 to save the non-Muslim migrants from being evicted. The fight, for the Assamese, is that of preservation of the linguistic and cultural identities of their indigenous communities.

For the Sikhs, who have adopted the Assamese culture and language, it is easy to identify with the Assamese cause. As one of them says, 'We follow the culture of this place despite being Sikhs and we are opposed to the Act as it will compromise the culture and language of the state'. The question is whether the Mazhabi Sikhs are going to be included in this claim of assimilation. Culturally different from the Assamese and looked at as outsiders in both Assam and Meghalaya, they are once again unsure of their position. As Sushant Talukdar from *Frontline* says, 'The CAA has added to the complexities of settling the question of who is an "illegal migrant" in the North Eastern region. Defining who is indigenous in each state there is expected to be a new political puzzle' (2020).

The Dakhani Sikhs

Just as the Sikhs in Bihar, Bengal, Assam and Guwahati have identities which stand in contrast to the normative Sikh identity in Punjab, there is a substantial part of the community in the central and southern parts of India called the Dakhani (southern) Sikhs, who have evolved into identities peculiar to the region. Like in other areas, here too, Sikhs have evolved into diverse groups. Among these are the Huzoori Sikhs or the descendants of the Sikhs, who came to Nanded with Guru Gobind Singh at the beginning of the 18th century and stayed back to carry forward his religious legacy. Then, there are descendants of the Lahori Fauj, the troops of Maharaja Ranjit Singh who were commissioned by Nizam Nasir-ud-daulah in the 19th century (1829–1857). With the linguistic restructuring of states, the Nizam's estate was divided among three states. Nanded, comprising five districts, went to Maharashtra, Bidar with three districts to Karnataka and the remaining substantial area to Andhra Pradesh. With it, the Dakhani Sikhs too were divided into these three states, now subject to sharper local influences. In conjunction with their past histories and present circumstances, they have developed into facets of Sikh identity not always incorporated in the dominant narratives of the community. Much light is thrown on their identity by the groundbreaking work by Birinder Pal Singh.

The history of the Huzoori Sikhs is different and older than that of the other Dakhani Sikhs and is related to Guru Gobind Singh's Deccan expedition. The tenth guru halted in Nanded on the banks of river Godavari, presently the south-eastern part of Maharashtra bordering Telangana. Birinder Pal's research tells us that the royal party was accompanied by warriors, maintenance groups like Sikligars and Lambada/Labanas, scribes, musicians, cooks and all else required for a lengthy expedition. Unfortunately, the guru was stabbed by two Pathan brothers in Nanded and died of his wounds in 1708. Before dying, he invested the Granth Sahib with the status of a permanent guru of the Sikh community and left it to his Sikhs to safeguard the tradition. Among the Sikhs who had accompanied him, some returned to Punjab with Banda Bahadur, the warrior-turned-ascetic whom Guru Gobind Singh inspired to return and work for the good of his people. The rest stayed back to carry forward the legacy left in their care. A small gurdwara was established in the memory of the guru.

Over the generations, these Sikhs have been acutely aware of their peculiar placement at a point in history and their duty towards conserving the new order left in their care. They feel it is their responsibility to sustain Sikhism against all odds (B. Singh 2014: 168). Interestingly, these Sikhs continue to owe their primary allegiance to Guru Gobind Singh rather than to all the ten gurus. Their traditions commemorate the guru's life in all its diversity, in ways which might seem odd to those raised on other versions of history. Within the gurdwara, which was raised by Maharaja Ranjit Singh between 1832 and 1837, many of the traditions followed are different from the ones prescribed by the Sikh Gurdwara Prabhandak Committee elsewhere. Guru Granth Sahib and the disputed Dasam Granth are both given a place of honour in the sanctum sanctorum, which is a violation of the

Singh Sabha rules. Dasam Granth has been the centre of controversy in Sikh circles with debates on some of its contents and differences over its authorship.

There are other practices and traditions too which are not only different but also in direct contravention to the codes currently espoused as the 'correct' Sikh practice. The head *granthi* of the gurdwara has to be a bachelor from among the Dakhani Sikhs, which is again a contested tradition, as Guru Nanak had emphasised the importance of *grihasta* (householder's life) for all Sikhs. The *ardaas* is also different from the one performed in the Singh Sabha gurdwaras. On Hola Mohalla and Baisakhi, a *bakra* (ram) is sacrificed within the precincts of the gurdwara, which many Sikhs find completely opposed to their beliefs. The tradition of *hallabol* on Hola Mohalla or Holi, with Sikhs running on the roads brandishing naked swords in remembrance of their martial identity, is one of these too. The military disposition of their identity in keeping with the martial identity bestowed by the tenth guru is reflected in their total demeanour. It is also reflected in their aggressive attitude towards other communities in the face of attempts at intimidation. Most of the skirmishes in the past have resulted from an altercation with local Muslims over the occupation of land and processions passing in front of the gurdwara. Celebrations in public areas or during parades can seem very aggressive to onlookers because of the enactment of *gatka* (martial drill) and posturing of their warrior identity.

The Huzoori traditions are not the only ones that survive in Nanded. There are also Sikligars—descendants of those who crafted knives, daggers, swords, and polished and sharpened metal weapons for the guru's army. They were of Rajput origin and had been converted to Sikh faith by the sixth Guru, Guru Hargobind (1594–1644), who first organised Sikhs into a military force. Nanded has a substantial population of Sikligar Sikhs. They too trace their history to Guru Gobind Singh's times and take pride in their role of polishing the guru's weapons on ceremonial occasions till date. Members of the

Sikligar community were on the British radar for making and selling weapons, which were being used for anti-government and other illegal activities. Originally, a nomadic people, they were forced to settle down following the Criminal Tribes Act of 1871 passed by the British. They could not venture beyond a prescribed area and had to periodically report to the local police.

After Independence, The Criminal Tribes Act was repealed in 1952. Through this, the tribes were denotified and henceforth came to be called Denotified Tribes. Today, they come under the larger group of DNTs. Most of them still make only temporary arrangements to stay in tents or shanties and travel to nearby areas on bicycles to sell their wares. From making and maintaining weapons, they have whittled down to collecting scrap from junkyards and converting it into rough knives and utensils or sharpening kitchen knives and repairing locks and keys. In Nanded, some of them have also found employment in Huzoor Sahib for cleaning and polishing Guru Gobind Singh's weapons. These Sikligars have had neither the resources nor the inclination to educate their children or to improve their status in life and can be counted amongst the poorest. In 2005, a national commission was set up to look into the poor living conditions and dismal levels of education among the denotified, nomadic and semi-nomadic tribes. Several subsequent commissions have worked towards improving their situation. In consideration of the recommendations, in 2014-2015 the central government implemented pre-and post-matric scholarships and arranged for the construction of hostels for DNT students. Since Sikligars fall within this category, some of them are using the facility for educating their children. However, lack of awareness is a drawback which prevents the full utilisation of the meagre facilities available.

Another lot which traces their history to Guru Gobind Singh's time are the Labana or the Banjara Sikhs, a class of travelling traders and carriers of merchandise, who carried food, ammunitions and armaments for the guru's marching army. Due to the British policy of disallowing floating populations, they eventually had to leave their traditional occupation and instead take up agriculture. Many of them were not Sikhs and have converted to Sikhism only recently. Traditionally close to music, they are being trained in Sikh seminaries in and around Nanded to do kirtan. Many of the *kirtaniya*s now come from the Banjara community. They are inspiring others from the community to make the shift too, for the respectability and financial security it begets them.

Unlike the descendants of Huzoori Sikhs in Nanded, Hyderabad is home to the descendants of the contingents of Maharaja Ranjit Singh's army, which arrived there around 1830–1832 to help with civil unrest in the Nizam's kingdom. Chandu Lal, an influential minister in the Nizam's kingdom, solicited a Sikh contingent from Punjab to consolidate his own power amidst the Arab and Rohilla troops in the Nizam's army. They were called the Lahori Fauj and numbered around 1,500 men. Since it was a goodwill mission, their salaries were paid by Maharaja Ranjit Singh himself. The Nizam gave them around 200 acres of land to establish a cantonment on the peripheries of Hyderabad. The Jamait-i-Sikhan, as the contingent eventually came to be called, gradually became so powerful that they replaced the elite Arab force in all the ceremonies and even in transporting the royal revenues to the treasuries. They also helped in establishing law and order in the area, thus earning the goodwill of both the local administration and the people. As stories go, one Sikh soldier in a village was enough to deter miscreants and criminals. These soldiers were also not afraid of the Nizam, or his other troops, as they owed allegiance to Maharaja Ranjit Singh. It is said that they once inserted a *farman* (royal edict) by the Nizam granting a *jagir* (fiefdom) to them, and pressed the trigger because they would not accept any favours from anybody other than their king.

Birinder Pal Singh provides insights into the lives of these Sikhs, who have remained outside the purview of the community for long. It appears that many of these Lahori Fauj Sikhs settled around the gurdwara they built in Barambaḷa in Hyderabad. Their descendants continue to stay here and a recent survey shows that there are nearly 550 households of these Dakhani Sikhs here. The Dakhani Sikhs have also settled in areas like Gowliguda, Ameerpet and Rahmat Nagar (Guru Ramdas Nagar). Among these, Gowliguda in the centre of the city has the biggest Dakhani Sikh settlement. A majority of these Sikhs are from the low-income strata living in clusters. Only a few have the preferred government jobs, while most of them are self-employed. Many of them work as drivers, either of self-owned three-wheelers or cabs or in the government or private-sector offices. Some hold lower-level positions in the police, work in offices or own petty businesses too. A secondary occupation for some is moneylending. Considering their low financial status, their clients are either people who take small loans for short periods or they act as moneylenders for other people. Some of them also mediate in property disputes, particularly in Hyderabad. Their old reputation of people who 'traditionally tamed marauders and miscreant comes in useful here'(Singh 2014).

Although many of the Sikhs from the Lahori Fauj married local women, the women were first baptised into Sikhism as a pre-condition for the Sikh marriage. Hence, a big majority of women in the community across generations are Sikhs by religion. This, however, does not reduce the local cultural influence on the community. Birinder Pal Singh's data reveals that most of the women do not know Punjabi and if they do try to speak, it is in combination with other languages like Hindi, Marathi, Kannada and Telugu depending on their place of residence. Most of the women wear sarees except while going to the gurdwara. Most families eat local cuisine. Despite these cultural dilutions, the men in the community keep hair and all the *kakars (the* five K's) even though all of them have not taken *amrit*. They are very proud of the fact that they are conserving the spirit of Sikhism which even people in Punjab do not do. A flowing beard and turban is their way of proclaiming their faith and most insist on the younger generation following the same. They are also keenly conscious of their past. 'The notion of living with respect and domineering effect (*dabdba*) is ever important to them in their day to day life. They still feel in them the element of the Nizam's Sikh force and tend to behave likewise'(Singh 2018: 203).

Unfortunately, these Dakhani Sikhs have not been able to avail the opportunities of the changing times. Used to the Nizam's rules, where their sons were provided schooling till the age of 18 and then recruited into service, they never gave any importance to education for children. As a result, they are not equipped for the new opportunities in the service sectors and cyber sectors coming up in Hyderabad. The same is true for the Sikligar community in Hyderabad, who came here with the Lahori Fauj. With their old work not much in demand, they have shifted to other metal works like making iron grills and gates. Some of them have been able to seek employment in the heavy metal industry as well. The Sikhs who came to Hyderabad after Partition are different from the Sikhs settled here since earlier. They too had to work their way up in Hyderabad but have gradually established prosperous businesses primarily in the automobile and finance sectors. Though most of them speak Punjabi at home, they are comfortable with local languages and dialects like Deccani Hindi and Telugu. Many of them started lives in old Hyderabad in areas like Begum Bazaar. The next generation is preferring to move out of the cramped old city, not only for better living standards but also because of better business prospects. In this manner, they are different from the Dakhani Sikhs, who stick together in the old residential areas.

A relatively lesser number of Sikhs are also found at Bidar and Bangalore in Karnataka; Bidar is known for Gurdwara Nanak Jheera. As per the *sakhi* tradition, Guru Nanak stayed here temporarily during his return journey from Sri Lanka in the second *udasi* to the South. He came to this Muslim-ruled Bahmani kingdom and is said to have stayed close to a monastery of ascetic Muslims. Sikh tradition believes that on coming to know from Pir Jalaluddin and the local congregations about the lack of drinking water in this place full of mineral springs, Guru Nanak lifted a stone in the barren land releasing fresh water, which exists even today and is called the Amrit Kund(Pond of Nectar). From this derives the name of Gurdwara Nanak Jheera. Over time the gurdwara has become a part of Sikh pilgrimage. This has created some employment opportunities for the few local Sikhs as *sewadar*s in the gurdwaras, or as auto-rickshaw and cab drivers catering to religious tourism. Another few run small businesses selling memorabilia associated with the history of the gurdwara. They too are deeply influenced by the local culture. Their women, in particular, display an interesting cross-cultural orientation where local customs and traditions are as much a part of their lives as going to the gurdwara.

Conclusion

Despite their affiliation to Sikh religious identity, sections of Sikhs from Bihar, Bengal and the Deccan seem to have been pushed to the peripheries of what has come to be perceived as normative Sikh identity. Demographically apart and culturally hybridised, their evolution has not been the same as the rest of the community. Sikhs in the mainstream, conditioned to believe in the validity of their version of Sikh identity, see them as oddities. There is a refusal to appreciate that histories tie these groups to a past different than their own, which does not invalidate their claim to community identity. There is also an unwillingness to contextualise the local Sikhs' fluid identity within a more flexible Sikh past.

Underlying these fundamental differences are more banal ones that the community finds hard to acknowledge. Economic status is perhaps one of these. The socio-economic status of most of the Sikhs on the peripheries is very different from that of the local Punjabi Sikhs or those from Punjab and North Indian cities. Sikhs are one of the most prosperous communities in India. A very small percentage of the community lives below the poverty line. A mere five per cent of rural Sikhs and six per cent of urban Sikhs could be categorised as poor (Jodhka quoted by Birinder Pal Singh 2018: 209–210). The result is that the Sikh community is constructed as an upbeat, prosperous people who like to live a good life. The poor Sikligars, the sweeper Sikhs living in slums or the Dakhani Sikhs on the lower rungs of social life do not gel with this image. To accept them as part of the identity is to acknowledge a less dynamic, underprivileged facet to the community which creates chinks in the existing narrative built around it.

The local Sikhs, whether Bihari, Assamese or Dakhani have also been caught in a time warp. Over time, cultural influences might even have created a fundamental attitudinal difference between them and others from the community. Those who came as refugees after Partition, for instance, have moved beyond their conditions through a certain grit. They have built up businesses from scratch. They have attempted to educate their children, equipping them with the skill sets required in the new economic shifts, thus opening new avenues of integration into the other financial and cultural spaces. On the other hand, a lack of desire to move out of their condition seems to mark many of the local Sikhs. They seem to have accepted their place and made no effort to move out of it. This could also have to do with lack of resources and economic drawbacks. Occupational diversification dependent on resources and education has eluded them, which in turn has inhibited their integration into the broader milieu. As a result, most among them have no option but to carry on with traditional work even though they resent the social marginalisation associated with it.

The Sikh community instead of othering them could take steps to improve their condition. This would involve efforts by Sikh intellectuals and Sikh religious organisations. There are people from the community who are working in this direction. Some attempts have been made by Sikhs in positions of influence. Eminent intellectuals, bureaucrats and business people from the community have prompted initiatives for the upliftment of the Sikligars. The Karnataka Sikh Welfare Society (KSWS) in Bangalore has started the Sikligar rehabilitation programme, which provides scholarships to Sikligar children to acquire formal education. Broader measures to improve economic upliftment and create support structures for the economically marginalised Sikhs have also been initiated through state measures pushed through by members of the community. Minority status given to Sikhs in Karnataka and Andhra Pradesh has helped the Sikhs, especially the Sikligar and Banjara Sikhs, with the education of their children and loans for housing and small businesses. There is a growing academic focus on them, which too is helping in generating more awareness regarding them.

Combined attempts by Sikh organisations and state governments to develop religious tourism around these places is also helping in retrieving these groups from relative oblivion. The 2008 Gurta Gaddi celebrations (commemoration of 300 years of the consecration of the Guru Granth Sahib) in Nanded, and the 2017 Prakash Purab celebrations (commemoration of the 350th birth anniversary of Guru Gobind Singh) in Patna, brought to light some of these groups. The fact that these occasions were supported by the respective state governments, brought in substantial funds for building infrastructures and initiating welfare schemes. This has also created ancillary works in construction, transport and food industries, giving diverse employment opportunities to the local Sikhs. Similar overtures in places like Assam, still not in the ambit of cognisance, could help Sikhs from across the world to understand more about the local Sikh populations, besides procuring state and central government help in improving facilities for them.

There remains the question of the feasibility of the assimilation of these 'other' Sikhs within the broader Sikh community. One view is that it is difficult to envisage such a convergence due to the socio-cultural differences and that these sections should resist being evaluated against a distant normative. In aspiring for liberation from the superior gaze of the Punjabi Sikhs, they would be following the core intent of the Sikh movement which worked to release the underprivileged from an inequitable social system (Chiranjiv Singh quoted by Gurdev Singh Panesar 2011). However, for the rest of the community to accede to that would be to let go of a part of themselves just because that part does not fit into their understanding of the normative. In assessing them through parameters of Sikh identity which have evolved over the last 100 years, the larger community might be missing out on the many different facets of Sikh past which they represent. Perhaps, delving into those pasts could help retrieve lost identities and create an appreciation for the heritage upheld by these groups. This might still not bridge the gap created by cultural differences but it could help create more respect for that difference. There is a big spectrum between assimilating and othering. A beginning could be made by reducing the distance between those two binaries.

References

Banerjee, Himadri. 2007. 'The Other Sikhs'. In *A View from Eastern India*, Vol 1: 225. New Delhi: Manohar Publishers.

———. 2018. '(Curfew-Read) Lives & Histories of Mazhabi Sikhs of Shillong and Guwahati'. Available at: https://www.raiot.in/curfew-read-lives-histories-of-mazhbi-sikhs-of-shillong-and-guwahati/ (accessed on 4 February 2020).

———. 2018. 'Sikhs and Sikhism in Bihar: Their Distinctiveness and Diversity'. In *Sikh Formations*, 14 (2): 167–187.

Jodhka, Surinder Singh. 2018. Quoted by Birinder Pal Singh, in *Sikhs in the Deccan and North –East India*, 209–210. Abingdon Oxon: Routledge.

Panesar, Gurdev Singh. 2011. 'Away From Punjab–the South Indian Sikhs'. Available at: https://www.speakingtree.in/blog/away-from-punjab-the-south-indian-sikhs (accessed on 25 February 2020).

Singh, Birinder Pal. 2014. 'Sikhs of the Hyderabad Deccan'. In *Economic and Political Weekly*, 26 July, XLIX (30).

———. 2018. 'Axomiya and Mazhabis Sikhs in North East'. In *Sikhs in the Deccan and North–East India*. Abingdon Oxon: Routledge.

———. 2018. 'Dilemmas of Shillong's Dalit Punjabis'. Available at: https://www.raiot.in/dilemmas-of-shillongs-dalit-punjabis/ (accessed on 1 February 2020).

———. 2018. 'In Lieu of Conclusion'. In *Sikhs in the Deccan and North–East India*. Abingdon Oxon: Routledge.

Hindustan Times. 2018. 'Dalit Sikhs on the edge as Khasi tribal anger rises in Shillong'.

Hindustan Times, 3 June. Available at: https://www.hindustantimes.com/india-news/dalit-sikhs-on-the-edge-as-khasi-tribal-anger-rises-in-shillong/story-tq0IVn10r4nys4BeyVwbvI.html (accessed on 17 February 2020).

Times of India. 2018. 'Violence flares up again in Shillong'. *Times of India*, epaper, 3 June. Available at: https://timesofindia.indiatimes.com/city/shillong/violence-flares-up-again-in-shillong/articleshow/64441074.cms (accessed on 4 February 2020).

4

Finding New Anchors: Sikh Identity in Foreign Lands

Community identity expands with an expansion of the ambit within which it operates. Exposure to alien cultures creates new facets to it. There is a huge component of the Sikh community, most of them from rural Punjab, who have diverged into urban spaces in continents, countries and faraway lands under socio-economic and political pressures. According to Darshan Singh Tatla, there are about 1.5–2 million Sikhs living in the diaspora today (2014: 499). Their experiences in the process of dislocation and relocation have created varied responses, more complex than they seem from the outside. A shifting environment, coupled with strong affiliations to their core identity, desire for a better life and the need to feel at home away from home have been crucial catalysts in the evolution of new identities. The tussle between retaining their original selves and inventing new ones, between guarding cultural boundaries and adopting assimilative practices has involved complex negotiations. This analysis is an attempt at exploring the demographic as well as the psychological trajectories that have gone into constructing the Sikh diaspora identity, in its multiple stages of formation, as it exists across the world.

Sikh migration to other countries has happened in waves beginning with the colonial times. Recruited from villages in Punjab, sepoys of British paramilitary forces were deployed in British colonies that included an array of South-East Asian countries, from where they also moved to Australia and the western coasts of Canada, US and UK. As soldiers in the British army, the First World War saw them deputed to East Africa, Mesopotamia and Egypt as soldiers and sometimes as officers too. In World War II, Sikhs went to Malaya between 1941 and 1942 and to Burma between 1941 and 1945 to help the British fight the Japanese invasion. Sikh soldiers were simultaneously fighting in the Mediterranean theatre, particularly in southern Italy in 1943. Sikhs from villages were also recruited to work in railway construction sites and farms as indentured labour to East Africa, Fiji and West Indies, where many of them eventually worked as supervisors over other indentured labourers. These exposures to different parts of the world led to settlements in new lands. They also brought news of employment opportunities back to Punjab, which drew others from villages to these places. Liberalised immigration policies after the Second World War coincided with the partition of india in 1947, which also led to the division of Punjab. This saw mass migration of people from displaced areas as well as of those who availed the opportunity to move out of villages. Throughout the 1950s and 1960s fresh migrants contributed to their increasing numbers. The events of 1984 led to a new wave of Sikh migration, this time to European countries as well. This has resulted in a large Sikh presence across the world. It is difficult to trace the histories of each of those movements, yet one could try focusing on trajectories, which have led to sizeable communities in places that remain preferred destinations for new immigrants. The main among these are South East Asia, Australia, Canada, US, UK and Europe.

This staggered history of Sikh migration holds stories of different generations having passed through different stages of identity formation leading to a diverse and ever-shifting composition of the community diaspora. The circumstances under which people leave their home countries and those under which they arrive in the host countries determines how they evolve as communities. The diaspora is impacted by the dominant narratives, economic processes and state politics of the lands the displaced communities chose to live in (Brah 1988: 617). This applied to the Sikh community as well. The following discussion is divided into two parts. The first part traces the trajectories of Sikh arrival and their settlement in different parts of the world and the peculiar social, economic and political negotiations these led to. The second part considers the shifting patterns of identity evolving through these and how they are now leading to responses different from earlier ones. To look at the Sikh community settled overseas through these lenses is to understand the need to acknowledge these shifting stances.

Different Trajectories

South East Asia

Perhaps the history of Sikh migration rightfully begins with their movement to South East Asia. The British had trade interests in areas south of China and east of India, and like other European powers, such as the Portuguese and the Dutch, they tried to find footholds in the region. A trading post was founded in Singapore as early as 1819. With the establishment of the Straits Settlements in 1826, the British and the Dutch came to a formal agreement by which clashing trade interests were resolved with division of trading areas. The British came to control Malay, which included areas of Penang, Malacca, Singapore and the island of Labuan with Singapore as the central British post. In 1867, these areas of the East India Company were brought under the control of the Crown. The need to control Chinese gang wars, particularly in Singapore, required a dependable police force. Less expensive than Europeans and more dependable than the Chinese, Sikh forces had already been effectively deployed in Shanghai and Hong Kong. As members of riot squads, mounted police and army troopers, Sikhs had secured British interests in the free-trade zone in Shanghai. They were also employed in police and security forces in Hong Kong. Having seen their effectiveness, the British brought a Sikh police contingent and stationed it at Pearl Hill overlooking China town in 1870. A Sikh temple was built for them at the Pearl Hill Barracks. Sikh policemen were also recruited by the Tanjong Pagar Dock Company in Singapore to form the Dock Police Force, and also at other places in Malaya.

Men from the Straits Settlements Sikh Police contingent were posted at different places in the territories of Penang, Singapore, Hong Kong and Shanghai. This created routes and linkages for Sikh communities settled in the Far East. As travel routes opened to and through the Far East, Sikhs travelled through them to further destinations such as America, Canada and other parts of the Pacific. Some stopped at destinations like Indonesia and the Philippines for break-journeys and decided to settle there permanently. The size of the community increased as kinship networks aided more men from Punjab to come to South East Asia looking for gainful employment in a land which was not too far from home and where the climate was quite comfortable too. Those who could not be absorbed in regular policing became additional police constables to guard government-run opium shops. Others started petty businesses and dairy farming. Some became moneylenders and a few even served as labourers (Arunajeet Kaur 2011: 2). Local needs determined other occupations. Sikhs in the Dutch areas of Jakarta, for instance, gradually started catering to the Dutch need for sports goods.

The major trends in the evolution of the community were however determined by their role as policemen in British territories. It not only gave them a privileged position as the strong arm of the power bearers but also ascertained the survival of their religious identity. Maintaining their Sikh appearance was made mandatory for those in service with the British police and army. This led to a growth of community culture, which can be charted through the establishment of gurdwaras, Singh Sabhas, committees to manage religious and language instruction, libraries, Punjabi classes and even Punjabi schools. These helped in maintaining and solidifying community identity amidst an alien people and culture. Due to the nature of their work, Sikhs were predominantly settled in urban areas. Due to this, they could benefit from the English educational facilities created by

Christian missionaries and the British government as well (Amarjit Kaur 2011: 39–40). The next generation of Sikhs in these areas were literate with a knowledge of English, which provided greater opportunities for occupation all over Malaya. Through it all, Sikhs in these areas kept their links with their native villages active through frequent visits. The partition of Punjab at the end of colonial rule in India in 1947 led to another short spurt in Sikh immigration to South East Asia. Those who arrived at this point were predominantly Sikh business families dislocated from West Pakistan, who came to seek business opportunities in urban centres like Bangkok, Singapore and other South-East Asian cities. They started small businesses, generally in textiles. Despite common religious affiliations, these new immigrants were different from the Jat Sikhs from rural areas and were to develop a new and alternate Sikh community culture centred around family businesses and closed community networks.

If colonisation and their role of auxiliary forces for the British determined their development as a community in South East Asia, the decolonisation of the area was to impact the Sikh community even more. Singapore became a fully sovereign state in 1965. As an ethnic subgroup, Sikhs were not of any particular interest to post-colonial leaders in the Far East. It was left to them to either stay or go back to India. Some from rural backgrounds returned to Punjab not wishing to risk what could turn out to be living under communist regimes. Others stayed hoping for a better deal from future governments for a better future rather than going back to India (Arunajeet Kaur 2011: 5). Meanwhile, stringent rules to regulate immigration from the rest of the world to the South-East Asian countries now stopped new migrants from Punjab as most of them did not have the mandatory educational and professional skills. From the mid-1960s to the 1980s, the thrust of the government was to integrate those from other ethnic identities into the Singaporean identity. Sikhs, like others who had stayed back, were under pressure to proclaim primary loyalty to their host countries rather than to their home countries. This included giving up British passports and taking up local citizenship. The links with Punjab diluted. The new governments also expected their participation in the economic and social institutions of the places they had chosen to live in. The 'nation building ideologies of both Nehruvian India and the new post-colonial South East Asian nation states largely discouraged transnational links and bi-national affiliations' (Dusenbury 2011: 62–63).

The following years saw economic growth of the Sikhs but also a a dilution of their cultural identity. For the generation born in these parts, religious and cultural inheritances dwindled despite the efforts of community leaders to preserve religious tenets and language. 'Sikhs in South East Asia became a closed-off community from Punjab and India and underwent a localising process'(Arunajeet Kaur 2011: 5). This was further influenced by government policies regarding minorities and ethnic groups. In Indonesia, Sikhs have had to accept 'Hindu' as their religious categorisation and their only means to address the state is through patronage. Hence, they do not have adequate control over their communal institutions to fashion them as they wish. In Singapore, Sikhs are legitimised as an ethnic group and can articulate their collective interests through state channels. However, they are also a 'radically depoliticised' people. In Malaysia, with an overall racial structuring in favour of Malay socio-economic interests and policy to protect Islam from religious incursions, non-Muslim religions have limited say. Within the Indian ethnic political party, Sikhs as a community do not have much say and feel stifled by state policies (Dusenbury 2011: 63–64).

The cultural ramifications are evident on the third and fourth generation of Sikhs, who have been influenced by the localising processes of the decolonising phase. The necessity of integrating into local culture has led to assimilation through the adoption of local languages and cuisines and many times, the local way of dressing too. Most Thai Sikhs keep two names—one, a Punjabi one, selected according to Sikh tradition and another, a Thai name, chosen by their parents or themselves. Both are registered officially to facilitate government and business dealings. Many times, the Thai names are selected in consultation with local saints and scriptures. In Indonesia, Sikhs in various parts are linked by Bahasa Indonesia rather than Punjabi. Many who wish to join the police force or other government jobs after university, adopt names like 'Surya Dharma' and 'Mardi Sudarma'(Mani 2014: 162). While local influences have led to hybrid identities, the original culture as observed in private spaces has been static for a long time. Old customs no longer in vogue in Punjab continue to be followed and the language spoken is the one of a century before.

In terms of occupation, there has been significant diversification. The necessity of shifting from their original role as auxiliaries of British forces made Sikhs diverge into other fields. In many of these countries, Sikhs are concentrated in sports and the dairy industry. In Indonesia, Pasar Baru, the area called 'little India', has many small shops run by Sikhs selling electronic goods, home décor articles and carpets, etc. In Thailand, Sikhs have a substantial stake in the tourist industry and tailoring while Singapore has a wide range of businesses including printing presses, tailoring and textiles as some of the more visible ones. In more recent times, the opening up of the economy and globalisation have provided new opportunities—particularly to the Sikhs proficient in English—in transnational corporations and companies. Many from the business community too are shifting to corporate jobs and Sikh women have taken to helping with the businesses. In Malaysia, professional skills and language ease have provided opportunities for the community to move to countries like Australia, New Zealand and Canada. In Singapore, the same advantages have provided Sikhs entry into civil services, law practice, academics, etc. The Sikh business community with its existing Asia-wide connections and ready cash for investment has also taken advantage of the opening up of Chinese, Indian and South Asian economies. 'The occupational profile of the Sikh in post-colonial

South East Asia is varied, ranging from billionaire businessman to having successful law and medical practices, and from civil servants to the street peddler'(Arunajeet Kaur 2014: 10).

Participation in new-age occupations with their transnational networks is giving rise to a cosmopolitan urban culture in South East Asia, particularly in places like Singapore. The trends of the global economy bring in influences from the rest of the world ensuring new cultural influences on the once-closed community culture (Dusenbury 2011: 64–65). There is also a growing interaction of Sikhs in South East Asia with those settled in the rest of the world. Media and online connectivity have opened the doors to a larger Sikh world resulting in growing alliances outside their circles. 'Their social, cultural, economic, religious, and political lives are expanding to include marital networks, business relations, religious contacts, cultural exchanges and political interests that are significantly more transnational than they might have been a generation ago'(67).

The religious identity of the South-East Asian Sikhs and processes of keeping it alive has also been influenced by these new developments. While Sikh gurdwaras and affiliated institutions have kept the community linked to each other and their religion, culture and customs, the growing gap between the old and the new generations at times reduces these institutions to a formal connection rather than a live, vibrant one. With new-age communication facilities and online interactions, these Sikhs can now compare how others across borders are negotiating with similar issues in their adopted homes. This has brought to them an understanding of how they are different from their community in the home country and why they must keep that difference in cognisance while trying to link the future generations to their religious and cultural heritages. For instance, Sikhs in Singapore are constructing pedagogical material more suited to the needs of the Sikh generation that has grown up amidst the local influences. Written information imported from India is being modified to make it accessible to the English-speaking Sikhs and to make it acceptable to the bureaucrats in the state education ministry (Dusenbury 2011: 69). There is also a serious consideration about having *granthi*s from within the local-born Sikhs who are more in tune with the language and cultural orientation of the people they are to connect with.

With changing economic policies and globalisation, new classes of immigrant Sikhs are arriving in South-East Asian countries. On the one hand, there are Sikhs from rural Punjab arriving in search of work visas, especially in Singapore, which could facilitate entry into Australia, New Zealand, US, etc. Most of them work as labour and are transitory settlers. It is the educated Sikhs arriving from Indian metropolises to major urban areas of South-East Asian countries, who are bringing in a new community culture. Places like Singapore and Bangkok are becoming alternatives to the West for these people. They bring with them a Sikh identity that has been influenced by the urban cosmopolitan Indian culture, and that influences their language, cultural bearing and even customs. These transformations set them apart from those among the local Sikhs, who have not been similarly influenced by the growing global culture within their spheres. Many times, the new immigrants find the old communities archaic in terms of their bearing and mindset. This new breed of Sikhs is creating its relational paradigms based on common metropolitan identities. For them, it is class that determines membership to social circles rather than caste, kinship and regional affiliations that were the determinants in earlier times (Arunajeet Kaur 2011: 7).

South East Asia is not only one of the first places where Sikhs arrived and settled but also one that formed an important point for their movement to places beyond its borders. Many moved further to other lands, fully or partially colonised by the British. Their evolution as a group identity has been determined by the social, cultural and political responses from these host countries as much as through their own initiatives. Out of these, the ones that have evolved into major Sikh diasporic sites are Australia, Canada, US and UK. The white population living in the first three were themselves immigrants of an earlier time but now claimed the first right to the resources of these countries. Hence, for them, the arrival of Sikhs as of other immigrants was a cultural and economic incursion. Sikhs, who came to these places, had the privilege of being British passport holders but did not wield the authority of being representatives of the British government as in South East Asia. Most of them had roots in rural Punjab and as a matter of course, they sought work in agriculture-related work or labour. Over time, many of them found niches in farming as in Woolgoolga in Australia, the Yuba valley in the US and British Columbia in Canada. However, over a few generations, many from the community have moved to complete or partial urban lives, where they are joined by new immigrants who are already urban in orientation when they reach these places. In the UK, they started as a community of urban workers on peripheries of towns and have now moved to mainstream urban living. More recently, the Sikhs have started settling in European countries as well. The trajectories of these diasporic communities reveal the many ways their lives have been influenced by their engagement with the places they have adopted as homes.

Australia

Australia had been discovered and its East Coast charted by British cartographer James Cook in 1770. By 1788, Britain had established its first penal colony at Sydney and the first English settlement at Norfolk Island. The idea was to lessen the load of petty criminals in jails back home. By 1829, they were claiming all Australia as a British colony. It was in these circumstances that some Sikhs heard about opportunities for agrarian labour and ventured out as early as 1830. By then, some among the British too had started coming to set up farmlands in the vast untapped interiors of Australia. Most of the Sikhs, who initially reached Australia, found work as cane cutters in the fields of Queensland. Some joined Muslims from Western Punjab, who had preceded them and were working as camel drivers in the dry interiors. The gradual drying out of convict supply from Britain increased labour opportunities for others. Meanwhile, new farms in deep interiors with no access to home supplies were potential markets. Enterprising Sikhs started working as peddlers selling household articles, a job made easy because only British subjects were allowed to take up small businesses. In due course, they purchased carts and took an assorted combination of things including pots, pans, clothes, food items that were small luxuries for people in the interiors.

The gold rush in Victoria in 1851 led to an unprecedented flow of immigrants arriving in Australia. The next few decades saw the population increase dramatically with the Chinese population getting so big that the whites began to be wary of them. In 1901, as Australia was unified, immigration restrictions were imposed to stop the flow of people. Though it was targeting the Chinese and later the Japanese, it impacted others as well. Sikhs in Australia could no longer visit families in Punjab for fear of not being allowed back. It was nearly 30 years later that only grown-up sons could be called to be part of the workforce in Australia. It was the Second World War that provided new opportunities to the Sikh agricultural labourers. As the white men on farms were sent to fight with the Allied forces, there was an acute labour shortage particularly in the banana plantations in the coastal area of Woolgoolga and Coffs Harbour close to Queensland.

Many from the cane fields and some in the peddling business shifted there to do what they were best at. With farming in their blood, they soon created a niche for themselves. They were joined by many from the community who left India amidst the chaos of Partition in 1947. Starting as farm labourers, over the next 30 years these Sikhs bought up to 60 per cent of the banana farms in Woolgoolga. This resulted in the establishment of a close community structure. With the war getting over and immigration policies relaxed, many from the community went to Punjab to marry women from their villages, resulting in close linkages with religious and cultural practices from home. The eventual establishment of gurdwaras led to a further solidifying of community living. Their pride in owning land and having agriculture as their means of livelihood resembled the Jat sentiment back in Punjab. They also ventured into blueberry cultivation, leading to even greater prosperity.

The Second World War gave rise to business ventures too, providing opportunities outside farming for the Sikhs. For example, Sikh forces fighting in British armies across the world ate mutton only if it was slaughtered in a manner called *jhatka* (slaughtering the animal in a way approved by Sikhism). Jagat Singh 'Jhatkai' from Australia began supplying tinned lamb to Sikh forces with each tin can stamped with his name. Some Sikhs found their calling in sports and related activities. Prosperity in farming also made money available for venturing into real estate and businesses. Many among the community acquired shops, motels and rental properties leading to parts of families shifting to look after the new businesses. Those in agriculture, who had made money, also used it to educate their children triggering movement out of Woolgoolga. The shift has been slow. There are many cases of young people coming back to carry on farming even after getting university degrees. Many continue to own farms in Woolgoolga even after they have moved to urban areas for professional reasons. However, the shift becomes permanent in the generations that follow. Many among the new generation have graduated in such fields as medicine, economics, law, information technology, commerce, business administration, medical sciences, psychology and food technology and shifted out of agriculture while others in the family continue with ancestral work.

For those who make the shift, there is a corresponding shift of priorities and pressures. Living in the closed community structure of the earlier life, it was possible to maintain an insularity that prevented dilution of identity due to Anglo-Celtic influence. Close connections with Punjab through marriage ensured Punjabi food habits, religious discipline in terms of observing daily routines and Punjabi as the medium of communication at home. The men too were under societal pressure to maintain their bearded and turbaned identity, particularly because they often returned to Punjab. As Sikhs move out of this close community structure into a multicultural setting, there are new adjustment demands. Less frequent interaction with the village culture in Punjab makes it difficult to maintain the kind of affiliations that their parents or grandparents had with that life. Even the community culture within their Australian homes does not gel with their lives in cities. Desire to better integrate with others in their work and social spheres demand a mellowing down of their very distinctive Punjabi way of life and simultaneous blending with the city culture.

> ...[T]he Australian born children of locals run the risk that higher education, occupational mobility and travel will make them too cosmopolitan to fit into the local community, and they might find themselves caught between the model of their parents and the example provided by Sikh cosmopolitans. (McCarthy 2013: 137)

To understand how Sikhs in urban areas respond to their identity as Australian Sikhs, their lives and attitudes must be contextualised within the shifting stances of the Australian government towards non-white residents. Even the earliest arrivals had known that though their British passport had facilitated their arrival in Australia, as non-whites, they were never truly welcome. Their Asian descent clubbed them with the Chinese and the Japanese whom the locals were wary of. Their turbaned identity also posited them as different from the other Asians. Hence, they were always under pressure to prove their difference from other unwanted immigrants. This position, structured within the shifting stance of the Australian government towards immigrants in general, has impacted the Australian Sikhs in terms of their identity projection. Starting from 1950, Australia has shifted its policies many times. In the first phase, it encouraged assimilation or shedding indigenous cultural baggage in favour of Australian culture.

The second phase endorsed integration in the belief that the children of those integrated would naturally shed off old cultural habits. In either case, the Sikhs were acutely aware of their 'otherness' and difference, which they were reluctant to shed for blending into the local lifestyle. At present, multiculturalism is the new mantra, which claims to celebrate different cultures of the world. The truth is that a shift in policy cannot in one stroke change the ideas ingrained in the minds of the locals. Hence, multiculturalism in theory generally runs parallel to fear of the same in practice. The occasional show of celebrating Sikh or Punjabi culture is often underlined by reiterating the difference of that culture from the mainstream one. It continues to construct the Sikhs as 'others'.

The Australian Sikhs have nevertheless taken advantage of the multicultural thrust using it to establish institutions to increase awareness about Sikh traditions, thus leading to greater awareness about their ethnic roots among the younger generation of Sikhs born and brought up in Australia. At the same time, their affiliation with their Australian identity grows stronger despite the undercurrent of racism that has only got worse since the 9/11 incident in the US. The situation is complicated for the young Sikhs because, while on the one hand, they are being connected to their religious and cultural identity, on the other, they are constantly under pressure to adopt more fluid cosmopolitan identities. The young Sikh Australians thus get caught between 'the shifting ideas of ethnic and cultural pluralism, and a steady flow of "tradition" in what could be called competing discourses of national belonging'(McCarthy 2013: 41). For most of the second or third-generation Sikh Australians, Australia is home despite the 'othering' they encounter. Their rare visits to Punjab only crystallise the difference between their origins and their new identities. The hot weather, too many people, lack of privacy and constant attention from distant relatives create a sense of unease rather than one of homecoming.

New Sikhs from India have consistently joined this urban community in Australia. Facilitation for higher education through Commonwealth links and bilateral understandings, which had started as early as 1950, have contributed to this new Sikh profile in Australia. The liberalisation of immigration policies in Australia in the post-war years also led to a spurt of Sikh migration from Singapore, Malaysia and East African countries. While the student community is one facet of the new immigrants, others among them work as taxi and lorry drivers and health professionals. Globalisation and liberalisation in the 1990s have opened opportunities in the corporate sector too. This has led to new community hubs in places like Melbourne, Sydney, Brisbane, etc. According to the census 2016 data released by the Australian government, the population of Sikhs in Australia has grown by 75 per cent in five years. The cosmopolitan culture adopted by them is becoming the new face of the Sikh Australian identity.

Canada and the US

The Sikh movement to Australia almost coincided with a similar movement to Canada and the US, which in coming years were to host one of the biggest Sikh diasporas. Like Australia, Canada too was a British colony. Sikhs were exposed to it as early as 1897 when Sikh soldiers in the British army were taken to British Columbia as part of the imperial ceremonies for Queen Victoria's Diamond Jubilee celebrations. Some of them went back to Vancouver after retiring from service. Sea routes from South East Asia, which facilitated travel and stories of job opportunities, led others to follow. By 1908, British Columbia's farms and lumber mills had nearly 5,000 Sikhs working in them. By 1911, the first gurdwara had been constructed in Abbotsford indicating that they had no plans of leaving. They simultaneously moved further down to the US West Coast to work in lumber mills in Washington and Oregon. Like in Canada, their increasing numbers and their willingness to work at lower wages created resentment amongst locals. There was pressure upon them from locals at both the places leading to racist persecution. Cultural impingement and fear of reduced employment opportunities were among the main concerns and resulted in racism and xenophobia in both countries. The governments were under pressure to stem immigrations.

Settlement of Sikhs in Canada was fraught with difficulties. Right before World War I, Canadian authorities imposed the *Continuous Journey Regulation* (1908) aimed at stopping more Indians, generally Sikhs, from entering Canada. There was no means of a continuous journey from India to Canada. The Sikh community, already in Canada, agitated and demanded free movement within the empire for those holding British passports. Taking advantage of community presence in South East Asia, in 1914, a ship named *Komagata Maru* was chartered from Hong Kong to travel directly to Canada with 340 Sikhs among its 376 passengers. Only 20 among the passengers were allowed entry into Canada. The ship was denied entry at Vancouver and was forced to return to a bloody end in India after two months. Canadian media portrayed Sikhs as dirty with their long hair infested with lice; their turbans were caricatured to make them look absurd and sometimes dangerous. Following the incident, nearly one-third of Vancouver's Sikhs migrated to the US and settled in Washington, Oregon and California. During the Great Depression years of the early 1930s, many were deported back to India. Those who remained were cut off from their families as there was no way to reach back.

The situation was the same in the US. Sikhs, whether those migrating from Canada or the ones arriving directly from India, were subjected to humiliating physical and oral examinations at Angel Island, the point of arrival in the US. There are documented instances of Sikh labourers in the US being yelled at, cursed, spat upon and having garbage thrown on them. In 1907, Sikhs in Bellingham were dragged out from beds and beaten. Harassment pushed some from the community into agro-based jobs on the outskirts, where they could escape racist discrimination. Many went to the Central, Imperial and Yuba valleys to first work in, and then cultivate their own peach and prune orchards. This too was curtailed as The California Alien Land Law of 1913 prevented all aliens ineligible for citizenship in the state of California from owning agricultural land.

The years between the two world wars saw Sikh migration to the West slow down considerably, except for those who continued coming by illegal means. Strict immigration laws prevented Punjabis living in the United States to marry in India and bring back wives. To this can be traced the many Sikh–Mexican marriages between Jat Sikhs and Mexican women, who came across the border to work in farms after the Mexican civil war. The end of World War II, labour shortage during the post-war industrial boom and lax immigration policies to attract labour coincided with Indian Independence and the partition of Punjab in 1947. This led to the next wave of Sikh migration to the West. As Canada and the US reversed their strict immigration policies, chain migrations began with relatives and families of those already in the West arriving to join the early settlers. The result was that the new arrivals were of the same background as the earlier ones. Many Jat Sikhs, uprooted from their homes in Central Punjab, now in Pakistan, also preferred to shift abroad rather than settle in smaller compensatory landholdings of East Punjab. Sensing a good opportunity, many people from the Doaba and Malwa regions of Punjab pooled family resources, mortgaged their land and migrated through the subsequent years.

In Canada, this led to a significant rise of numbers among the Sikhs. The strong trend to sponsor relatives meant that the new people arriving in Canada too belonged to the same rural backgrounds as the earlier immigrants. However, foundations for a new urban profile were already in the making. Many who had been in Canada had ventured into new works and educated their children, leading to professionals and businessmen among the community. British Columbia, the first Sikh settlement in Canada, largely constructed around farm labour and mill workers, is today marked by an increasingly urbanised Sikh population in Abbotsford, Surrey, Vancouver and Victoria. The blueberry farms still abound, but so do Sikh women working in stores, Jat Sikh men driving taxis and trucks, Gills and Sandhus (subcastes of the Jat Sikh community) in construction and mortgage businesses. There are newspapers published by Sikhs, university departments with Sikh faculty and students, Sikh doctors and other professionals. There is also the much-publicised Sikh presence in the government at both the local and national levels. Sikhs professionals have spread out to urban centres like Toronto, Montreal, Calgary, Ottawa, Edmonton and Winnipeg in varied capacities. There are an increasing number of Sikh students in Canadian universities, from within Canada and from India. Among the latter, for many, university education is a way of getting Canadian citizenship.

In the US too, with the Luce-Celler Act of 1946, immigration and ownership of property became easier for Indians. Chain migrations occurred here too, particularly in Yuba City, California, where Punjabi landowners could now bring wives back from India. Liberalisation in immigration policies in the 1960s facilitated the movement of students and professionals as well. Sikhs were now migrating not just to the West Coast but also the East Coast. This trend increased in the next decade and 'the flow of Sikh migration since the 1960s has corresponded with a demographic shift from largely rural farmers and labourers to a significant number of professionals' (Hawley 2017). In recent years, immigration rules have begun to facilitate the entry of those within the community who are among the brightest, most motivated and who then make their way into the best of colleges and professional courses. In a shift from the earlier patterns of Sikh migration, these immigrants are urban in their occupations, attitudes and preferences. This has meant a spreading out of the Sikh population to other areas like Michigan, Illinois and the East Coast. Meanwhile, the less-welcome labour class continues to arrive as legal and many times illegal immigrants from Punjab villages. Many live in the shadows, among extended families, in crowded basements, exploited through lower wages, always in fear of being caught by immigration agencies. Sunjeev Sahota's novel *The Year of the Runaways* (2015) is a telling commentary of their situation.

Today, Canada is the preferred destination of Sikhs, particularly those from Punjab. The substantial Sikh community settled there and the state's thrust towards multiculturalism are important factors contributing to this. The US remains high on the list too for the many opportunities it offers even though it expects all immigrant identities to merge their religious differences into the 'melting pot'. While racism is more blatant in the US, particularly after the 9/11 attacks, it works in more subtle manners in Canada. Besides the fear of immigrants as potential threats to safety, there is the underlying anger due to appropriation of work opportunities. Sikhs being more visible than other communities, also get targeted more.

The United Kingdom

Sikh connections with the British go back to colonial times and it is obvious why many of them chose to go to the UK. The earliest to arrive in England perhaps were the Bhatras who came in the early 20th century. Most of them were former seamen who came to the UK and worked as peddlers. In the wake of a shortage of unskilled labour at the end of the Second World War, British authorities encouraged recruitment from across the Commonwealth countries, including India. This led to many from rural Punjab seeking work in the British industries. New Sikh arrivals generally worked in foundries and textiles factories in places such as London, Birmingham and West Yorkshire and lived in clusters on outskirts of towns where these factories were established. Many had to compromise on outward religious symbols (turban, hair and beard) to circumvent the racist prejudice in Britain to get work. In the early 1960s, while new immigration was curtailed, chain immigration increased and allowed family members of those already in England to follow. Many Sikhs working in the Hong Kong police force, who had been expelled once the force was nationalised in 1952, also migrated to the UK.

The shift to a more integrated urban profile followed in the 1970s. Kenya and Uganda gained independence from British rule and forced Asians out of these countries. Ramgarhia Sikhs had been recruited in large numbers by the British as labour for railway construction in East Africa in the late 19th and early 20th centuries. They now used their British passports to move to Great Britain in the late 1960s. Having lived as an expatriate community in Africa for over 70 years, they were also usually skilled and employable in contrast to the unskilled labour from Punjab. They, at one time, formed nearly 90 per cent of the Sikh population in East Africa and had grown prosperous over time. They 'brought with them capital, professional skills, and settled in a better class of housing. This led to a gradual shift in subsequent generations from manual factory labour to skilled professional activities' (Hawley 2017). They also began settling in London's suburbs. These Sikhs, as expatriates, were also accustomed to being a highly visible minority in their respective places of residence. They proudly maintained their earlier turbaned identity, changing the way the locals perceived the community.

The arrival of the Ramgarhias was also the beginning of caste differentiation among Sikhs in England. Ramgarhias separated themselves from the common gurdwaras, where Jats held dominance and established their gurdwaras with exclusive Ramgarhia managements. The area around Leeds, in particular, saw Ramgarhia resurgence. Community centres were established, sports centres opened and there was brainstorming over the future trends in Ramgarhia identity. Pictures of Zail Singh, the seventh president of India and a Ramgarhia Sikh are found in most of these centres. The Ramgarhia Board in Leeds accepts all Ramgarhia Sikhs to membership, reinforcing caste identity. Prospective members have to fill a form vowing to look after the interests of the *biradari* (Kalsi 1999: 269).

Such efforts have not only consolidated the Ramgarhia Sikh identity in the UK but also led to a caste paradigm reversal. The Ramgarhias, a class considered lower in caste status to the Jats in Punjab, has built up a Ramgarhia identity superior to that of the Jats in the UK. They attribute their urban experience in East Africa and their absorption of British notions of civility for their refined group profile in contrast to the Jats, whom they construct as rough and aggressive in keeping with the working-class status that brought them to England.

While the intra-community differences have marked community politics, Sikhs as a group defined by a common religion have grappled with the laws of the land to maintain the identity prescribed by that religion. The UK had long made it clear that religion and culture are to be kept within private spheres and in the public sphere all immigrant identities must be primarily British subjects, following British codes and principles. Over the years, Sikhs have struggled for exemptions from this mandate to maintain their religious identity in public spaces. It has involved differentiating themselves from other Asian and Indian identities. This has resulted in protests, representations and legal recourses, leading to landmark concessions by the government over time. These include the right to wear turbans as drivers and conductors in the transport sector, exemption from wearing helmets while riding motorcycles if sporting a *keshdhari* identity (1976), allowing school-going Sikh children to wear turbans (1983), and allowing workers to wear turbans on construction sites (1989). With the observation by the House of Lords in 1983 that Sikhs resembled an ethnic group with a long-shared history and cultural tradition, they were brought within the protection of the Race Relations Act and their religious identity was ethnicised (Shani 2008: 110). While the debate on the merit of allowing these concessions has continued because of the British emphasis on uniformity in dealing with its diverse populations, the focus on the turban and the people fighting for its acceptance in public spheres has differentiated them from other immigrant identities in the minds of the locals.

Europe

The Sikh migration to other European countries is a more recent trend and is passing through all the formative stages of the community identity, already crossed over in the West. Although there have been historical links of the Sikhs to certain European countries due to their presence in the British army, immigrations were few and far between. In the 1970s, a few Sikhs trickled into the European countries. Among them were those who shifted from East Africa after the local regimes ousted Asians from the decolonised African states. Some came from India and disembarked in Europe as a stopgap arrangement to bypass restrictive legislation preventing direct entry to the US, Canada and England. Many among them eventually settled down in countries like Germany, France, Belgium, Netherland, Portugal, Spain and later in Italy too. Large-scale migration to Europe was also initiated by the political instability in India in 1984. Today, the shift is voluntary and inspired by the economic improvement of those who are already settled in these countries. Europe is witnessing much quicker enculturation of the second- and third-generation Sikhs than the settlers further West. There has been greater political stability than in the years of the world wars, which were the background to the early Sikh settlement in the US, UK and Canada. Economic liberalisation, the formation of the European Union and the opening of new routes after the dissolution of the USSR have also made movement easier. Quick information systems and global influences make the transition that much faster.

Today, there is a strong Sikh presence in many European countries. Each country has imparted its colour to the Sikh population. Belgium has a population of about 10,000 Sikhs. Apart from a small community settled since earlier, unskilled Sikhs arrived here in 1984 and began working on fruit farms in Limburg province. The next generation has preferred to shift to cities and set up shops there. Brussels already has many financially successful Sikh families. Their permanent status is reflected in the five gurdwaras constructed around the place. France has about 15,000 Sikhs, most of whom migrated in the1980s, particularly 1984, many of them by illegal means. Mostly Jats and Ravidasias, they cluster in the Bobigny area of Paris. Whether due to illegal entry or lack of residence papers or clandestine work, there is a great deal of interdependence on kinship and caste networks. They came into the international spotlight in 2004, when the French government passed rules to stop religious symbols being worn to schools, thus disallowing turbans for Sikh boys. This led to public protests by Sikhs and the establishment of a Sikh school. Many even left France due to the government's inflexible attitude.

Norway, Sweden and Finland saw Sikh arrival around 1984 and have seen chain migration in the subsequent years. In Spain, migration began in 1990 when Sikhs, mostly from Punjab, arrived in Catalonia and entered the construction and catering business. Greece, has about 20,000 Sikhs, mostly in Megara, Chalkida and Psachna. A recent migrant group, Sikhs here are frequently confused for Pakistanis and Afghans, resulting in attacks on Sikh properties, particularly gurdwaras. Greece has, therefore, become more of a transit point for those migrating to other Western countries. Germany saw Sikh migration not only from India but also from Afghanistan under pressure from the Taliban. Today, there are about 30,000–35,000 Sikhs concentrated in Frankfurt, Koln, Cologne and Stuttgart. There is also a component of local converts to Sikhism. Italy has a large illegal Sikh immigrant population with most of the men working in agriculture and agro-industrial sectors, where they tend to get exploited and are made to work on lower wages. Many have also taken over the cheese-making industry with the children of the locals preferring to move to urban occupations.

Sikh immigrants, who moved to European countries, have found the subsequent generations changing, sometimes in intended directions and sometimes unexpected ones. These changes pertain to their social, economic and cultural lives. A shift in occupational patterns is the most significant of these. There has been a trend in second-generation Sikhs to move from farms to cities. Even those still in the agro and dairy sectors are keen to educate their children to help them move into the urban sector. Meanwhile, bilateral agreements with many European countries have also encouraged fresh migration largely from a growing number of students and highly professional labourers in Information Technology, telecommunications and the healthcare sector (Myrvold 2014: 516). Germany is one such important destination. Here, education is almost free and those who come to study eventually join the local workforce.

Shifting Patterns

The trajectories of Sikh movement, spanning two centuries, to different areas of the world show the circumstances in which they moved out of their home country and settled in new lands. There have been other journeys too that are equally important. These pertain to how they have responded to life in these new places, of how they have coped with the cultural differences to evolve as a people who could straddle both the past and the present. The fact that Sikh migration to foreign lands continues unabated also leads to temporal differences between the many layers of exposures. The struggles of the new immigrants and the changing priorities of the old ones have led to a diverse, staggered Sikh profile that does not have one single identity. It would be difficult to slot it into a neat category. What one can trace instead are broader patterns and the shifts that could provide clues to future trends.

At the most basic level, the Sikh diasporic identity shows a shift from the closed community cultures once established by early immigrants to more open ones. This is a process happening in many staggered phases and has its complexities as well as benefits. The early immigrants, mostly labour class, who were met on arrival with local policies that encouraged assimilation, resisted them through policing of cultural identity enforced through group reiteration. This was passed on to new incumbents most of whom arrived from similar backgrounds through chain migrations. Among such groups, identity within home continues to be constructed on the same premises as in rural Punjab. This includes following the rigid community rules and old caste distinctions. Gender paradigms, dress codes and cultural practices continue to be rooted in a time and place far removed from their current lives. In places like Surrey in British Columbia or the Southall area in London for instance, there are many from the community, who continue to live by cultural paradigms that are very different from the life around them. Their family structures too are rooted in the old community structures of rural Punjab. For the generation born and brought up in countries other than their own but within the cultural influences of that other life, the schism between the outside world and home can be confusing. For boys, the macho identity naturalised at home is at odds with the regulated life outside. With no connect to feudal-identity markers and finding no adequate ones to replace them with, many use anachronistic tropes to enhance stature and power within closed groups. Resistance to the discipline of legal and educational structures is one of the outcomes. With parents who are not educated themselves, or are are too busy making ends meet, it is easy for children to go wayward. It is not unusual to see boys hanging out with aggressive postures and loud Punjabi music blaring through their cars, making others wary of them. There are instances of petty gangs inducting young people based on village and clan affiliations that they do not even understand. In Canada particularly, this has translated into involvement in drug trade, gang wars and trouble with the police.

However, there is a shift in making. Where the younger generation has been integrated into the education system, it has become a means of integration into the local workforce at various levels. This, in turn, has led to movement out of their existing socio-economic constraints and provided them with a choice of non-traditional occupations. This, in turn, has entailed movement away from home, proximity to different social and cultural groups which has had multiple impacts. These people contextualise themselves differently in the wider social setting. At times, this results in life choices which do not go down well with family and community. There are a sizeable number of young Sikh men and women, who are opting for intercultural marriages. Even those marrying within the community disregard caste barriers that were important to their parents. Conservative patriarchal practices are being questioned. The joint-family system is under pressure. Cutting of hair and not wearing a turban, once the biggest taboo, has become an accepted norm. Parents blame different cultural influences for these. What Michael M. Ames and Joy Inglis say of the British Columbian context is true of Sikhs elsewhere too: 'The disputed changes may be to a large extent the unrecognised unintended and unwanted consequences of accepted changes' (1973–1974: 46). While this meets with resistance from some quarters, it is also getting gradual consent from others. This also has other repercussions. As traditional reinforcement for adhering to conservative ideals dissipates, people grapple with connections and disconnections to an earlier sense of self. Through it all, new cultural patterns, which cannot be clubbed into linear models, are formed. 'Alterations in certain ideals and practices interact with and react upon others to produce new structures'(46).

Similar shifts are visible among Sikh women in the diaspora, particularly in Western countries. The thrust of Sikh migration to Western countries has been one of social and financial empowerment. However, there is always the question of who benefits from that empowerment and for whom it leads to disempowerment (Brah 2005: 181). Where Sikh women are placed in context of the benefits accrued from shifts abroad has been a debatable question. Using girls to migrate to Western countries has been a pattern since the earliest times. The second half of the 20th century saw Sikh girls becoming pawns for enabling their men to immigrate. There are cases of girls being sent for adoption to relatives in the hope that on becoming majors, they would sponsor their parents and brothers. This, many times, involved exploitation by guardians who used them as help in businesses and on farms as substitutes for labour. The trend has continued in different forms among the Sikhs from Punjab as it does with Punjabis in general. There are cases where Sikh boys from India marry Sikh girls with foreign citizenship, either to abandon them or to separate with mutual consent once the objective has been achieved. Girls are also married to boys settled abroad in the hope that this will facilitate the rest of the family to migrate.

Many of these marriages are mismatched in terms of educational and financial parity leading to unhealthy and unfeasible partnerships. Marriages arranged to open opportunities for the rest of the family also result in strange combinations of relatives living in small houses, creating a financial burden, lack of privacy and interpersonal problems. The brunt is faced by women. Many from India, who have married abroad, find themselves in restrictive, conservative environments instead of the liberal lifestyle they anticipate in the West. Most are expected to work in factories, etc., yet revert to their roles of dutiful daughters-in-law and wives in claustrophobic homes. The complications of such situations have been sensitively portrayed in Deepa Mehta's movie, *Heaven on Earth*. On the other hand, Sikh girls raised in Western countries have had to contend with the dichotomy of exposure to an education that encourages liberal thinking and a home, where fear of cultural incursions creates an overly conservative atmosphere.

As traditional reinforcements for adhering to conservative ideals dissipate, responses span between resentment and open rebellion. In the case of educated girls equipped with potential for financial independence and others who are entitled to state support in the event of harassment, there are instances of defiance despite family as well as community pressures. In my interaction with young Sikh women in British Columbia, I came across a young mother who rebelled at being told that her husband's physical aggression, unexplained absence from home and drug addiction were not reasons enough for her to walk out of the marriage. There was another who defied her parents by marrying a Sikh boy from a different caste. In both the cases, there was initial opposition from families, which did not stop the women from following their hearts.

Jasbir K. Puar's study on second-generation Sikh women in Great Britain, who 'transgressed' by marrying outside the community, reveals new trends. These women expressed an ability to function well in the two worlds because they have consciously negotiated the contradictions of their situation (Puar 1995: 48). She also found that stories of families disowning their daughters for social transgressions and extreme cases like honour killings are fewer than they once were. They remained in news because they were more likely to be picked up by Western media, which thrived on stories surrounding ethnic behaviours (25). Moreover, in most of the cases, the decision to stand up to community dictates in particular life decisions has not been accompanied by a break with religion, culture or tradition. They only wish to practise all of these from within their present context and the shifts it entails.

Shifts are also visible in other social spheres, particularly those concerning religion and its identification with caste and political polarisations. Caste and group differences were carried into new cultures by the older immigrants as in the case of Jats and Ramgarhias in England. Separate gurdwaras set up by the two groups reiterated the differences and tried to keep the next generation polarised too. New immigrants with more contemporary polarisations in the home country have also carried those to the adopted countries. For example, Ravidasia Sikhs have established separate gurdwaras with diversions from traditional Sikh practices. This, in turn, has created fresh points of deflection and new tensions. An example is the 2009 Vienna incident in which a Ravidasia Sikh leader, Sant Ramanand was killed inside a gurdwara by members of other Sikh groups. Gurdwaras thus have had a history of becoming the sites of exclusionary practices. The result is that religion and caste have got inextricably mixed with each other. The same has also been true of gurdwaras as sites of propagation of fundamentalism. The West has witnessed advocacy of the separatist stance among the Sikh community during the 1980s in reaction to the happenings in India. There was an open endorsement of radical means to attain political gains by leaders of the movement. Gurdwaras being the hubs of Sikh congregations also became centres for political propoganda. While the situation changed in the home country, the remnants of that fundamentalism have sustained for much longer in many of the Western countries.

However, the younger generation of Sikhs, born and brought up with exposure to a more cosmopolitan outlook look for a common stable Sikh identity in an environment already fraught with the many differences they have to contend with in the outside world. Rifts rooted in an unknown past, which they neither understand nor wish to engage with, are giving way to a need for a positive religious and cultural identity. Jasjeet Singh's observations on Sikhs in the UK resonates for those in other parts of the world as well: 'Formal transmission organised by the older generation is generally regarded as being of poor quality and appears to be far too unstable, being subject to personal grudges and factional politics' (Singh 2014: 13). They look for an interpretation of faith and religion through a vocabulary more in tune with their lived reality. While gurdwaras remain very important as a place where they can simply be Sikhs without having to explain their identity, for a non-fundamentalist and more egalitarian interpretation of faith, interactions are shifting from gurdwaras to activity centres, schools and universities. Here, young Sikhs are helped to identify with Sikh values in the spiritual and social contexts rather than political ones. They also meet people, who chose a positive religious identity and therefore serve as better role models for them.

There is also a visible difference in the attitude of the Sikh diaspora in terms of cultural assertion, a clear shift from the earlier practice of attempted assimilation or at least a pretence to it in public spaces. This could also be a result of new policies encouraging multi-culturalism instead of those encouraging assimilation in these countries. The improving economic profile of the Sikhs is contributing to it too. Moreover, there is a growing realisation that to feel at home, they need to connect to their origins within their new surroundings. Cultural camps promoting ideas of 'roots' and 'culture' are proliferating, allowing young people to forge cultural connections with their pasts within the multicultural environment of their new homes. Bhangra tracks and Punjabi music videos have become an industry. An interesting trend is the bhangra and hip-hop fusion, an assertion by the young Sikhs of their ethnic roots even as they claim their place in the broader culture they live amidst. Students are forming clubs and societies focusing on Sikh identity and practices to create awareness among peers. *Sewa* in Barnard College, Columbia University is an example. It has regular langars and turban-tying sessions organised by the Sikh students. The proliferation of Punjabi/Sikh schools across the UK, US, Canada and Europe also shows a trend of consciously connecting the younger generation to their roots. Traditional clothes are making an appearance outside private spaces as ethnic style statements. Also, emerging from within the diaspora is the image of the Sikh woman in a turban making her stand apart from others. Jakobsh feels that in the multicultural diasporic context, it gives the young Sikh women a sense of identity. Instead of being seen as just another immigrant, a turban provides specific cultural contexts. Within the sphere of the white gaze, this is a process of 'identity politics', where Sikh women are 'negotiating their own distinct, ethnoreligious national identity within multicultural, multi-ethnic, multi-religious diasporic contexts' (Jakobsh 2015).

Accompanying these attempted connections to their religious and cultural identities are proactive attempts at integrating them within the broader social spheres outside the community. It is as much an attempt to locate their position outside the once insular community circles, as one to make others more aware of the tenets on which their distinctive Sikh identity is based. One finds Sikh tenets of *sewa* (service) and *wand chhakkna* (sharing) taking new, transcultural meanings and expanding to include people outside the community. In Norway, the Sikh concept of *sewa* is explained as the traditional Norwegian value of *dugnad* or voluntary work for the community. Sikh groups across the world are organising philanthropic services for locals. The Sikh Motorcycle Club in Canada, in partnership with the Canadian Cancer Society, rode 12,000 kilometres to raise $100,000 for donation to the foundation for research and prevention of paediatric cancer and for aiding children undergoing cancer treatment. Sikh community kitchens serve food to people across cultures, during natural disasters and conflict situations. Post 9/11, young Sikh professionals and college students in the US are making concerted efforts to reconstruct the public image of Sikh Americans. There is a concerted attempt at interaction with government officials, participation in interfaith memorial services and attempts to acquaint others about their community. Such 'mobilising practices' go a long way in integrating their identity in the adopted homes (Sokefield 2008: 13).

That the Sikh diaspora is finding ways to explore and establish facets of their identity in the new environments rather than harbouring a romanticised version of a lost life is also an indication of their growing entrenchment in new lives. Tololyan says that as a diasporic identity entrenches into the host culture, it is accompanied by cultural and political reproductions organised, institutionalised and funded by the community (2007: 650). The focus is on rooting better within the new contexts rather than looking backwards. It implies finding anchors within the lives they have shaped, not in ones they have left behind. The Sikh community is seeing many such overtures. Studies on Sikh diasporic identity—its histories and its shifts—are being aided and funded by Sikh organisations through established academic resources of the host countries. The World Sikh Organization of Canada, for instance, financed the first chair for Sikh studies at the University of British Columbia in 1988 followed by several others like the universities of Birmingham, Michigan, California, Berkley and Columbia, etc. Sikhs are also bringing into focus their contributions to the histories of the host nations and 'staking claim' in contemporary political structures (Brah 1988: 624). These stakes take the form of ostensible reiterations of help extended in different times. In Canada, the installation of the sword and the medals of a Sikh soldier of the British army in the British Columbia legislature in Victoria is a step towards entrenchment in the historical spaces of the country. The statue of the air force officer, Mohinder Singh Pujji, who fought in the Battle of Britain in World War II and won *The Flying Cross* at Kent in the UK is another such example. More recently, the sculpture of a Sikh soldier in the British army has been installed at Gurdwara Smethwick in West Midlands near Birmingham to commemorate Sikh contributions in World War I. The Gur Sikh Gurdwara in Abbotsford, British Columbia, given heritage status by the Canadian government, now also runs the Sikh heritage museum that traces the contribution of the community to Canada. It is to be noted that staking such claims to the history of the nations they have adopted has been facilitated by their growing numerical strength and considerable voting power.

An important indication of the shifting community stance is its changing engagement with the legal and political structures of the host countries. This is most clearly indicated in the shift within 'the politics of recognition' that the community has been engaged with since their arrival in foreign lands (Shani 2008: 100). For Sikhs, the assertion of an identity different from the Hindu or the Asian identity had once been necessary to maintain the physical form prescribed by their faith. Over time, the politicisation of that identity in their home country seeped into one in the host countries too. From seeking a right to profess their religion, it extended to a right to seek a separate Sikh state, where Sikhs could be safe from persecution and human right transgressions. In the UK, the Khalistan movement was organised under the aegis of organisations like the Jagjit Singh Chauhan's Khalistan National Council established in 1984. In the US too, the World Sikh Organization came into being in 1984, and its headquarters were established both at New York and Ottawa in Canada. The Council of Khalistan and the Khalistan Affairs centre had been active since 1980.

However, in recent times, there is once again a shift of focus from the fight for a separate homeland to one that Shani calls a movement for 'diasporic political identity'(112). As the Khalistan movement has petered out in India, it has also lost its steam in the West. Many Sikh organisations, though keeping the agenda of a Sikh state alive, are in reality focusing more on participation in the political processes of the countries of settlement. They wish to consolidate their position through entrenchment into the political and legal institutions of their host countries. The Sikh Federation (UK), established in 2003, has been registered as the first Sikh political party in the United Kingdom with the stated aim of giving Sikhs a stronger political voice in UK politics. Apart from aiming to have Sikh MP's and counsellors, it also seeks state-funded Sikh denominational schools, the establishment of Sikh museums, etc. In the US, there is a growing awareness for the need for a consolidated plan of action for acceptance of a distinctive identity. This has gained momentum since the 9/11 attacks with Sikhs being targeted with hate crimes. The Sikh American Legal Defense and Education Fund (SALDEF) reflects the proactive initiatives of the educated Sikh-Americans in creating a blueprint to protect the civil rights of Sikh-Americans and to ensure a fostering environment in the United States for the future Sikh generation. The Sikh Coalition is another well-known organisation working for education, advocacy and protection of Sikhs in the US. In Canada, the Khalistan rhetoric has stayed alive despite the movement petering away, largely because of its potential to influence local politics. Important Sikh leaders, already in a position of importance within the Canadian government, are still being assessed for their position on Khalistan. Their interests are more inclined towards Canadian politics than a Khalistani one. However, playing on the local Sikh population's concern for Sikh victims of 1984 and anger against Operation Blue Star are always successful rallying points for prospective vote banks. For the highly emotive response to both the events to get constructed as a separatist stance is common. For those whom it benefits, remaining non-committal about their exact stand is convenient. Their aim, however, seems to be to make way into the Canadian power corridors through political participation.

In countries, where Sikhs have been expected to blend into the larger Asian identities or the national identity, there is a resurgence of attempts to change the situation. Sikhs in England, for instance, are making concerted efforts for a separate ethnic identity for the 2021 census. A series of representations have been made for separate Sikh identity boxes being provided in the census forms, which, if granted, will also aid in separate state funds for the community. In the US, there is a growing trend of Sikhs calling themselves Sikh-American to emphasise that they are different from *other* Sikhs and *other* Americans. The implication is that 'Sikh' identity cannot be merged into the American 'melting pot'. This also translates into consolidating that different identity as American in the American psyche (Shani 2008: 121–122). There have been repeated representations by Sikh groups to the US census regarding the need for Sikhs to be recognised as a different ethnic group. The US census department has conceded the need for this and a separate code will be provided for the community in the 2020 US census (*Times of India* 2020).

As the process of entrenchment in new countries gathers speed, it simultaneously harks to a changing relationship with the home country. For those settled in the West, the earlier nostalgia and glorified memories of the village life of Punjab is on the wane. The earlier trend of constructing palatial homes in ancestral villages with plans of returning is lessening. Even if houses are constructed, it is to establish a certain reputation within old networks rather than to shift back to. Nostalgia is being replaced by a recognition that home is where their present lives are. Instead of planning a return to Punjab, they have switched to maintaining connections through contributions for improving the lives of those still living there. Monetary aid for education, sanitation and knowledge creation in villages of origin are on the rise. This, moreover, is inextricably entwined with an understanding that they are too comfortably ensconced within the Western structures to go back to that earlier life. Increasingly global in character, Sikhs settled abroad find a greater similarity with others like themselves spread across the world, rather than in the community back home. Their social, economic and intellectual exchanges are increasingly impacted by 'intra-diaspora exchanges within transnational spaces' (Thandi 2014: 549).

While these shifts indicate the broader patterns of Sikh diasporic identity, it is also true that the continuing migration of the community to the rest of the world ensures that there is no simple description for the Sikhs settled beyond Indian borders. The shifts themselves are staggered, situating the people concerned at various points in the continuum, perpetually leading to what Tololyan calls new 'social formations' (2014: 625). Each wave of immigrants arrives with certain new pre-conditionings, negotiates its way through a situation that might not be the same as earlier ones, and grows into mindsets different from the generations that arrived before them. Moreover, as the second and third-generation immigrants cross over to different stages of engagement within the host countries, the new arrivals, different in orientation, grapple with adjustments of the initial phase. What continues is the complex process of simultaneously engaging and disengaging with past identities. The fact that the profile of the Sikh immigrant is shifting too makes a difference to how he responds to the new life. While the flow from the rural and semi-urban areas of Punjab continues unabated, there are also Sikhs from urban areas and a non-agricultural background making the move. Among them are professionals, entrepreneurs, students and business aspirants. Many of them are a floating population, shifting between countries, living transcultural lives. They also bring with them a cosmopolitan culture different from the one brought by earlier immigrants. In turn, they create new dimensions to the community identity.

There is, therefore, no linear description of the Sikh settled abroad. It is an identity mutating with time, formulating itself differently as it responds to its own changing needs within shifting contexts. What Kristina Myrvold says of European Sikhs is true of Sikh diaspora in general: '...[T]he future will most likely entail the shaping of new self-representations and identity constructions that more noticeably than before reflect their multiple belongings' (2014: 520). There is a need to recognise and to assimilate this into the perceptions constructed around the community identity.

References

Ames, Michael M. and Joy Inglis. 'Conflict and Change in British Columbia Sikh Family Life'. In *British Columbia Studies*, Winter 1973–1974, (20).

Bhattacharya, G. 2000. 'The School Adjustment of South Asian Immigrant Children in the United States'. In *Adolescence*, 35 (137).

Brah, Avtar. 1988. 'Border and Transnational Identities'. In *Feminist Post-Colonial Theory, A Reader*, edited by Reina Lewis and Sara Mills. Edinburg: Edinburg University Press.

———. 2005. 'Diaspora, Border and Transnational Identities'. In *Cartographies of Diaspora, Contesting Identities*. London: Routledge.

Cohen, Robert. 2008. 'Four Phases of Diaspora Studies'. In *Global Diasporas, An Introduction*, second edition. USA and Canada: Routledge.

Dusenbury, Verne. 2011. 'Southeast Asian Sikhs in Global Perspective'. In *Sikhs in South East Asia: Negotiating Identity*, edited by A.B. Shamsul and Arunajeet Kaur. Singapore: ISEAS Publishing.

Hawley, M. 2017. 'Migration, Sikh'. In *Sikhism. Encyclopedia of Indian Religions*, edited by A.P.S. Mandair. Dordrecht: Springer. Available at: http://link.springer.com/referenceworkentry/10.10007%2F978-94-024-0846-1_443 (accessed on 20 February 2020).

Jakobsh, Doris. 2015. 'Seeking the Image of "Unmarked" Sikh Women: Text, Sacred Stitches, Turban'. In *Religion and Gender*, 5(1): 35–51. DOI: 18352/rg. 10085.

Kalsi, Sewa Singh. 1999. 'The Sikhs and Caste: The Development of Ramgarhia Identity in Britain'. In *Sikh Identity: Continuity and Change*, edited by Pashaura Singh and N. Gerald Barrier. New Delhi: Manohar Publishers.

Kaur, Amarjit. 2011. 'Sikh Migration and Settlement in South East Asia, 1870s–1950s, Social Transformations, Homeland, and Identity'. In *Sikhs in South East Asia: Negotiating Identity*, edited by Shamsul A.B. and Arunajeet Kaur. Singapore: ISEAS Publishing.

Kaur, Arunajeet. 2011. 'Introduction: Studying Southeast Asia'. In *Sikhs in South East Asia: Negotiating Identity*, edited by Shamsul A.B. and Arunajeet Kaur. Singapore: ISEAS Publishing.

Mani, A. 2011. 'Sikhs in Multi-ethnic Indonesia'. In *Sikhs in South East Asia: Negotiating Identity*, edited by Shamsul A.B. and Arunajeet Kaur. Singapore: ISEAS Publishing.

McCarthy, Rory G. 2013. *The Sikh Diaspora in Australia: Migration, Multiculturalism and Imagining of Home*. Pennsylvania: University of Pittsburg.

Myrvold, Kristina. 2014. 'Sikhs In Mainland European Countries'. In *The Oxford Handbook of Sikh Studies*, edited by Pashaura Singh and Louis E. Fenech, UK: Oxford University Press.

Puar, Jasbir K. 1995. 'Resituating Discourses of "Whiteness" and "Asianness" in Northern England. Second Generation Sikh Women and Constructions of Identity'. In *Socialist Review*, 24 (1& 2). Durham, North Carolina: Centre for Social Research and Education, Duke University Press.

Shani, Giorgio. 2008. 'The Politics of Recognition'. In *Sikh Nationalism and Identity in a Global Age*. USA, Canada: Routledge.

Singh, Jasjeet. 2014. 'An Insight into The British Sikh Community'. In *British Sikh Report*. Available at: http://www.britishsikhreport.org/wp-content/uploads/2014/04/British-Sikh-Report-2014.pdf (accessed on 14 March 2020).

Tatla, Darshan Singh. 2014. 'The Sikh Diaspora'. In *The Oxford Handbook of Sikh Studies*, edited by Pashaura Singh and Louis E. Fenech. UK: Oxford University Press.

Thandi, Surinder Singh. 2014. 'Sikh Migration, Diasporas and Transnational Practices'. In *The Oxford Handbook of Sikh Studies*, edited by Pashaura Singh and Louis Fenech. UK: Oxford University Press.

Times of India. 2020. 'Sikhs to be counted as separate ethnic group in US census for first time'. *Times of India*, World, 16 January. Available at: http://timesofindia.indiatimes.com/articleshow/73283755.cms?utm_source=contentofinterest&utm_medium=text&utm_campaign=cppst (accessed on 21 February 2020).

Tololyan, Khachig. 2007. 'The Contemporary Discourse for Diaspora Studies'. In *Comparative Studies of South Asia, Africa and Middle East*, 27 (3). Available at: https://muse.jhu.edu/article/224587/pdf (accessed on 23 January 2020).

5

Process of Becoming: The Sikh Woman

When we talk of Sikh women, it is easy to lapse into narratives constructed around their religious identity and the reformist intent of the Sikh religion. However, a nuanced understanding of how that tradition has translated into lived reality requires its contextualisation within the broader ethnic culture, its class and caste paradigms, and the historical ruptures which have impacted it. This lived reality also needs to be scanned for how it has been influenced by demographic transitions and the cultural shifts which have marked Sikh history. A close analysis of these placed within broader debates on feminism would perhaps yield a trajectory, which could provide an objective understanding of the Sikh woman's experience. It would also focus on a selectively used Sikh religious and intellectual tradition, with a feminist potential far greater than what it has been used for. As the Sikh woman learns to articulate her experiences, to question the gap between the professed and the performed, she also learns to optimise this legacy, to push the boundaries towards a more empowered self.

A Liberal Religious Tradition

According to Margaret Somers, 'All of us come to be who we are however ephemeral, multiple, and changing, by being located or locating ourselves (usually unconsciously) in social narratives rarely of our own making' (1994: 606). The Sikh woman emerged from a social landscape which had entrenched practices against her gender. North Indian culture had long let go of the dignified and important position given to women within the Vedic social and religious systems. Interpretations of *Manusmriti* and other religious scriptures relegated women among the lowest in the social order. The potential for fertility, which had once been worshipped, was seen as a polluting and dirty biological function that demanded the woman's exclusion from religious spaces and by corollary denied her the possibility of spiritual liberation. Within this broader framework was the specific social milieu in Punjab. Its occupational structures, class and caste positioning and social pressures gave this degradation of female life its peculiar forms.

Though it might not have been an absolute norm, the injunctions of the gurus indicate that women in the existing social order had been subjected to a discriminatory and suffocating social atmosphere. Guru Nanak's objective assessment of the position of women, a realisation of the wrongs it entailed and his clear abrogation of the same must have been iconoclastic for the times he lived in. His focus on several of the issues not only brought them into the open but also questioned the social sanctions underlining them. It was perhaps common to kill daughters at birth. Depending on the strata and occupation, methods of controlling women varied in forms of marriage customs, coercion of widows, cloistering women in purdah, treating them as peripheral beings on the patriarchal chart. Nanak insisted that women and men have the same rights to spiritual liberation and equal potential to achieve it. He spoke against traditions which deprived them equal access to religious spheres. He emphasised that a woman's reproductive cycle and its associated biological functions did not make her impure. He also regarded purdah as an unnecessary restriction. He opposed discrimination against widows and the practice of Sati. Female infanticide was explicitly prohibited. There was great emphasis on fidelity in marriage for men. As the Sikh faith evolved, the subsequent gurus not only institutionalised many of these practices but also brought women from their own families out of purdah into active participation in spheres like the community kitchens. The concept of *sangat* or congregation ensured the same for other women followers too. It is true that the Sikh vision of a better position for women still situated them within the domestic sphere. This does not, however, lessen the significance of the reforms in the given ethnic contexts and the deeply entrenched practices within them. The Sikh gurus were much ahead of the views prevalent in contemporary society.

By the time the tenth guru established the Khalsa, the women in his own family had greater power than could be envisaged for women in an earlier time. Scattered evidence indicates that after the death of Guru Gobind Singh at the beginning of the 18th century, his wives exercised substantial influence. Mata Sundri*ji*, who settled in Delhi, exercised a position of authority and instituted at least nine known *hukumnama*s from 1717 to 1730 to the *sangat*s of Patna and Ghazipur. Another wife, Mata Sahib Devi/Sahib Kaur, also instituted nine *hukumnama*s from 1726 to 1734 addressed to the *sangats* of Patna, Benaras, Pattan Shaikh Farid and Naushehra Pannuan. Both the sets of *hukumnama*s directed Sikhs to send a stipulated amount of money through the bill of exchange (*hundi*) handed over to the authorised messenger for carrying on the work of community kitchens run out of their establishments. Mata Sundri*ji* also settled disputes by nominating arbitrators through *hukumnama*s, as is evident from a *hukumnama* dated 18 October 1723 (Malhotra 2013: 6). These *hukumnama*s indicate that their word held authority among the Sikh *sangat*s everywhere. Even though the authority of the gurus' wives derived from the guru himself, it did set precedents for the possible roles for women within the community.

Class, Caste, Ethnicity and Politics as Determinants of Gender Roles

The martial culture of the Khalsa consolidated by the tenth guru continued after his death with the formation of *misl*s under different Sikh leaders. These eventually led to the formation of small principalities in the middle of the 18th century. Women in these powerful families also seem to have held properties and wielded power in the capacity of spouses, widows or regents of the new rulers and *pattidars*, who were granted shares of the spoils of conquest. The summary settlements and land surveys by the British after their annexation of Ranjit Singh's kingdom reveal that they made many personal contributions to charity in the last quarter of the 18th century. There are records of Sada Kaur's (Maharaja Ranjit Singh's future mother-in-law) grants to the *mahants*. There are also references to politico-administrative activities of elite Sikh women like Ram Kaur and Ratan Kaur—the widows of Baghel Singh and Karora Singhia (Malhotra 2013: 69). Purnima Dhawan gives examples of Mata Fatoh, wife of Alha Singh of Patiala, who assumed administrative charge in the absence of her husband and even initiated diplomatic dialogue with Ahmad Shah Abdali when he attacked Patiala. Patiala again saw women of the royal house assuming charge during the time of the Raja Sahib, a minor, towards the end of the 18th century. Even after he formally assumed royal duties, his sister, Sahib Kaur continued to be powerful and even warded off the Maratha attackers (Dhavan 2010: 77).

Running parallel to this relatively strong position of the Sikh elite woman was the socio-religious discourse, providing conflicting views on the position of women within the Sikh society. It provided interesting insights into the imagined role of Sikh women within familial and social settings. These differing opinions were part of the process of consolidations of Sikh religious identity by people with separate viewpoints deriving from different backgrounds. Some of these views were later given the status of *rehitnamas* or the codes to be followed by Sikhs. Karamjit Kaur refers to the two significant *rehitnamas* of the times, the *Chaupa Singh Rehitnama* and the *Prem Sumarag Granth*, to provide an understanding of the very different stances in these. The first was written by Bhai Chaupa Singh—originally Chaupa Rai—a Chibber Brahmin, who was also a contemporary of the last four Sikh Gurus. A part of his writings was perhaps written in the time of Guru Gobind Singh; however, the *tankha* part (punishment for not accepting edicts), is said to have been added in around 1740. This part of Chaupa Singh's *rehitnama* categorically states that a Sikh who administers *khande ka pahul* (baptism by holy nectar) to a woman, is a defaulter and would have to be put through penance. He also says that women are not to read the Granth Sahib in a general assembly. Married life was regarded as ideal for women and they were expected to be loyal to their husbands. A woman's ideal life, according to him, was one which revolved around her home and the *dharamsal* (the place of congregation for those following the Sikh faith). She was not to believe in anything except the guru, her husband and the *sat sangat* (congregation). She was also to be the cornerstone of social and religious decorum. Chaupa Singh suggests that a Sikh woman was not to sing popular or vulgar songs, only hymns called *suhaag* and *ghorian* composed by the fourth guru (Malhotra 2013: 6). His writing has been extensively analysed by Western scholars like W.H. McLeod and Doris Jakobsh in forming an opinion of the place of women within Sikhism.

Attempts to use Chaupa Singh's *rehitnama* for defining a woman's place in Sikh society would be to overlook other streams of thought and writings existing simultaneously within the Sikh social order. It would also be to ignore the fact that Sikhs were undergoing significant shifts in power structures, which could have determined the relative importance given to any one of them at a particular point. Talking of Chaupa Singh's *rehitnama*, Karamjit Kaur points out that it 'was neither the earliest nor the representative prescriptive text'(Malhotra 2013: 56). She posits Chaupa Singh's *rehitnama* against the *Prem Sumarag Granth* (The True Way to Love), an anonymous work, probably written in early 18th century and re-published by the Sikh History Society in 1953. In a view very different from the earlier writing, the *Prem Sumarag Granth* states that liberation was possible for both men and women if they followed right conduct, and a woman had the choice to join the Khalsa through the prescribed way of baptism. Married and unmarried women were to be treated alike. The choice was open to widows too. It also laid down codes of conduct which dented into social practices discriminating against women. During marriage, not to demand and accept anything from the bride's parents was said to be akin to a million *gurupurab*s and parents on both sides were advised to treat each other as equals within the Khalsa brotherhood (Malhotra 2013: 58). Instructions for widows made crucial departures from the existing social systems in keeping with the Sikh faith. A childless widow could be married to another man within the same family or another, irrespective of his caste, through a process involving his baptism. He also talks of property rights. Instructions regarding the property of a deceased say, 'among brothers and sisters the property should be divided "equally"'(Malhotra 2013: 61). If there was no son, the property would go to the daughter's son. In certain circumstances, the daughter's daughter and son have equal rights over the property after her death. There are also other minor *rehitnama*s said to be from the 18th century, like those by Bhai Prahlad Singh and Bhai Desa Singh, which state that no Sikh was to have any relationship with another Sikh who practised killing of daughters.

The complexity in the somewhat opposing stances of the *rehitnama*s is to be understood in the fact that they were responding to a chronological as well as a social shift. What they reflected was 'a moral system passing through significant socio-political change'(Malhotra 2013: 54). The untimely death of the last guru, the different components of the community with different socio-cultural orientations, the opposing movements of the *sanatan* and *tat* Khalsa traditions running parallel to each other could be some of the factors leading to these different opinions. The shifting focuses of those in power could also have influenced the thought processes. Also, the Khalsa order, when instituted, was a male-centric one focused on creating the ideologies and principles of a warrior class. The focus on women could have come a little later, allowing a greater diversity of opinions. The *rehitnamas* could as well be reflecting conflicting stances of the people within Sikh society, some of whom, while adhering to the spiritual teachings of the gurus, were sceptical of the social changes these called for. These changes would impact their existing kinship structures, which many times extended outside the Sikh faith. For example, the customs among the agricultural Jats were entwined with their economic lives and occupational patterns. Those of the Khatris gave them a higher status in society, which they found difficult to relinquish. What remains significant is that there grew a certain validity around these writings that could be harnessed either way. The 20th century would seek elements from both during attempts to construct a more cohesive Sikh identity. Where that would place the women within the broader identity would continue to be a matter of debate.

Within these social paradigms, the gaining momentum of Sikh political power was also an important factor in determining the future position of women in elite circles, which would also create veritable models for others. As different Sikh chiefs and rulers aggregated strength, the dynamics between them began to determine some of the constituents of the Khalsa identity. Constant skirmishes engendered a culture of feuding and need for a warrior identity. Meanwhile, many of the Sikh rulers, in a bid for social mobility, traced their origins to Rajput Kshatriyas and adopted their customs. Among the consequent changes in the status of a Sikh woman was her new use as an instrument of political alliances through elaborate marriages (Dhavan 2010: 64). Women became symbols of family honours which had to be fiercely protected. On the other hand, like many other warrior cultures, the Khalsa warriors needed to be constructed as fierce fighters, incorruptible by women and far removed from any interest which could be remotely found effeminate. 'Fierceness in the defence of women, yet indifference to womanly wiles were desirable traits for warriors in other cultures as well' (Dhavan 2010: 77). These created new gender paradigms, not belonging to the social life that the gurus had addressed. Hence, with the contemporary shifts in focus, new dictates emerged. From the broader social focus of the gurus, these narrowed down to the warrior Khalsa identity and the need to maintain its hyper-masculine image.

Among these was the construction of the Khalsa identity as a primarily masculine prerogative, where women could be diversions; womanly conduct and interest undesirable; and power in the hands of women a threat. Dhawan talks of the pressure to maintain a 'hyper masculine identity in order to maintain an imperilled social and political status' (Dhavan 2010: 64–65). One of the ways this was done was to curtail the powers vested with women. Despite the resistance of women, new norms of courtly behaviour came into place. By 1820, Sikh queens were being asked to remain in purdah. In 1837, this was followed by rules which barred them from succession and in 1858, they were excluded from Councils of Regency (Dhavan 2010: 78). Elite Sikh women lost power in matters of property and succession; they were no longer in a position to aid in times of need as their predecessors could, and were reduced to a weak position within the structures of power. 'The closing period of Ranjeet Singh's reign was in sharp contrast to … the relative freedom of women among the powerful Jat families of the Sikh chiefs in the period immediately preceding that of Ranjeet Singh' (Malhotra 2002: 20).

While the elite of the society was adapting to these new paradigms, it was in the much broader diffused base of the non-elite that the position of the average Sikh woman was embedded. This came into focus during the British times. The colonial incursion in the late 19th century and the reformist response to it from within North Indian society was to result in the active construction of the Sikh female identity and impact it in many ways. As the colonial gaze fixed upon Punjabi society, particularly its women, it revealed interesting insights into the ground reality of gender equations in the community. It also provided the British with the justification to interfere with and infringe upon social structures of Punjabi society causing concern among the various groups. As facts tumbled out, it was apparent that many among the Sikhs had continued to follow cultural practices prohibited by the gurus. Without implying that the position of women ordained by the gurus had not been assimilated into lived practices at all, it does seem that among a large majority, the earlier trends had continued as late as the 19th century. This, of course, refers to general trends and does not preclude more informed behaviour in forward-looking families.

In keeping with the schisms within the Sikh social structure, the prejudices towards women too varied with group practices. Among the Jats, social practices were centred around control of land, and a son as a successor was infinitely more important than a daughter. Although the woman was used as agricultural labour and hence had economic value, her status was one of subordination. Female infanticide was common and there was a dearth of women. Within this was rooted the practice of accepting a price for the marriage of daughters. Many also purchased girls from other castes for marriage. The Jat woman could be married to a set of brothers in polyandry or would be expected to marry one of the brothers of the husband in case of his death (Malhotra 2002: 21). Also prevalent were practices like *takka* (buying and selling of girls as brides) and *vatta* (exchanging sisters in marriage). Anshu Malhotra uses reports from 1896, 1901, 1911 and 1914 to draw a dark picture of conditions in Jat families which suggests that 'if a girl escaped infanticide and survived neglect, she could be married to someone willing to pay money for her hand' (Malhotra 2010: 107).

Khatri Sikhs continued to follow the upper-caste Hindu practices despite their allegiance to Sikh faith. Control over women and keeping them confined at home was closely entwined with the assertion of a socially superior status. For them 'the very vulnerability of this proud honour nurtured by closeting women, was the stuff that defined an exalted status' (Malhotra 2002: 22). While they professed superior moral codes in keeping with high-class traditions, they often shirked the burdens these translated into in real life. For example, marrying daughters in keeping with the *punn* method (colloquial for *punya*, an act of piety), was the preferred way among rich trading classes. It, however, entailed large expenses in terms of dowry and resulted in considerable financial burden, which made the birth of a daughter unwelcome. The social pressure to seek grooms in families of better social status also held within itself possibilities of humiliation for the denigrated position of the 'girl's side'. On the other hand, leaving a girl unmarried was considered disgraceful. These resulted in covert practices like killing newborn female children. Bedis and Sodhis, both from Khatri sects, were among those who practised it. The upward mobility, which followed their exalted status as families from which the gurus came, meant greater expectations in social terms. Reluctance to suffer the humiliation that marriage of daughters could entail resulted in female infanticide becoming a norm within these families.

Within these group distinctions lay common patterns, which were also part of the larger Punjabi life. Living in joint families with their hierarchical structures, complete financial dependence on the husband and his family, no say in family decisions, were some of these. Role devaluation can be assessed by common terms used for women. A woman could often be shown her place by being called '*paer di jutti*' (a shoe worn on the feet). Hitting a woman, especially in anger, was not unexceptional. For both Jat and non-Jat women, acceptance of a place subordinated to the husband and subservience to the family were parts of a cultural make-up which was accepted as the correct mode of conduct. It would be wrong to assume that there was nothing but persecution in these relationships. Yet, the basic dynamics ensured that a woman's place was a vulnerable one. Adding to it was the pressure of women being constructed as instruments of the family *izzat* (honour). Any transgression of the right code of conduct, in terms of dressing, speaking and conducting themselves within social spheres was a threat to the honour of the men in the family. This restricted them further and often elicited male coercion over their roles as daughters, sisters and wives.

Colonial Gaze, Cautious Shifts and New Identity Constructions

The British came from a different cultural context and saw the situation from outside, which allowed them an objectivity unfettered by a positioning within the system. While they might have had their agendas for focusing on the stilted gender practices in Punjab, it did jolt the complacency with which the locals practised it. The one practice that came into immediate focus was the killing of daughters. Since the British focused more on higher castes, the Bedis—the elite among the Khatris—were among the first to come under the lens. They, along with other important families, were summoned to a public function in 1853, where they were persuaded by British officers to give up killing newborn girls, desist from demanding dowry and incur less expenditure on marriages. Official recognition for what was considered the right conduct or a better caste/class behaviour made a serious impact upon Punjabi society, particularly on higher-caste Sikhs. It also led to a domino effect with varied impacts. The rate of female infanticide came down in the upper castes. It also made them call for reforms among other castes and classes. The Khatris now also called for putting an end to *takka* and *vatta* marriages common among the Jat agriculturists, and for adopting the custom of *punn* marriage as a more respectable way of treating daughters. Ironically, this was to create another social problem with far-reaching effects in times to come. In advocating *punn* marriage, they also initiated a process of one-upmanship. This assumed serious proportions because of an official injunction dividing people into three economic categories, stipulating how much each could spend on such marriages. Spending more on the marriage of a daughter thus slotted one as affluent and became a means to class mobility. To this can be traced the growing prevalence of dowry in Sikh families (Malhotra 2002: 61–62).

Apart from the immediate response to official pressure, and an impulse to structure a more flattering sense of identity through such shifts, the situation also spurred reform movements among the larger Punjabi society, which included both Sikhs and non-Sikhs. Each group tried to prove that they were rational and modern and could retrieve the lost egalitarian position of their women, which they professed, was impacted only because they had lost touch with their roots. Within the Sikh fold, an initial joining of hands with the Hindus soon gave way to the construction of a separate Sikh identity that followed other political requirements. The evolution of the Singh Sabha movement, already in progress, took up the agenda at hand too. This would lead to new identity structures for Sikhs at large, and a distinct identity for Sikh women within that new identity. The intellectuals spearheading this movement would wrest control from the traditional carriers of Sikh traditions and give Sikhism a new form. Just as the position of elite women during Sikh rule was dictated by wider political engagements of elite Sikh men, this time, the position of the ordinary Sikh woman would be determined by the neo-intellectuals among the community.

It is often difficult to distinguish between the religious and social motivations of people leading such movements. The Sikh intelligentsia, which would invoke the words of the gurus and Sikh history to create a thrust for an improved position for Sikh women, would also partially subvert that thrust with their deeply patriarchal orientations. This was to have long-term effects on the image into which the Sikh woman was to evolve. The Hindu reformist movements focused on women from Vedic times as symbols of educated, empowered women. Sikhs like Kahn Singh, eager to further the construction of a separate Sikh identity, encouraged an emulation of women from a more recent Sikh history. The lives of Bibi Nanki, Bibi Bhani, Mata Sahib Devi, Mai Bhago, etc., were posited as the ideals to be followed by Sikh women. The image emanating from this narrative was that of a Sikh woman who was at par with men, who could fight in the battle and who could take part in institutional structures of Sikhism. The gurus were frequently quoted to prove that this position for women had religious sanction in Sikhism. It was also posited as the new ideal for the Sikh women, who the Sabha claimed had fallen back into the cultural morass from where they had been lifted.

While on the one hand, the reformists impressed that Sikhism ordained a position of equality for women, it appears that they were also wary of disrupting existing familial and relational structures. Hence, the tone and tenor of their injunctions were in many cases directed towards ensuring that those were not disturbed. The same was true of the caste structures, which while being ostensibly dismantled, were being constructed in upper-caste codes. Sikhism as a religion advocated a casteless society making the persisting caste prejudices within the community embarrassing for the higher castes, who were leading the change. Yet, relinquishing the higher-class social codes was difficult for them. Since women from all castes were being brought under the movement, structuring their lives within higher-caste codes and traditions became imperative. The Singh Sabha movement was led by upper-caste Khatri intellectuals, who would have wanted to prevent the dilution of high-caste practices in the new inclusive Sikh society. Ordaining a high-caste code of conduct for all the women would ensure that the dilution was limited.

> In a period when the multitudinous pulls of multiple identities, whether demanding loyalty to a caste, community or even a nation, were shaping people's lives, men found it possible to stabilize status through regulating women's conduct. This also released men from owning up to caste based prerogatives. In fact, they could positively shun its advantages, helping them participate in a political discourse that spoke of equality for all. (Malhotra 2002: 45–46)

Within these overtures at creating a modern egalitarian identity for Sikh women and attempts to root it within the tenets of Sikh religion while also not disrupting the existing social structures, was born the blueprint that continues to inform Sikh female identity. The contradictory pulls inherent in the situation were palpable in many of the role constructions that emerged. These were most apparent in the suggested gender equations within conjugal and familial settings. Anshu Malhotra quotes extensively from the Khalsa Tract Society set up in 1894 to promote the objectives of the Singh Sabha movement. The ideal Sikh way of life portrayed in these, by default or design, promoted conservative role models for Sikh women. Many of the stories published in the tracts were clearly to reinforce subordinated behaviour patterns. While the Singh Sabha movement shunned the Vedic symbols of exalted womanhood, it continued to use mythological figures euologising women's commitment to home and husband.

The Khalsa Tract was supplemented by other reformist literature, which too followed the same line. The ideal daughter-in-law in Mohan Singh Vaid's novel, for instance, is Agya Kaur or the obedient one (Malhotra 2002: 138–139). Numerous articles stressed on the three *bhabas* (the three 'b's) as the pillars of a happy married life—*Bhuli ji, Bhala ji, Bhana rab da ji* (My mistake, As you wish, God's will)—were posited as tenets which ensured success in the marital home (Malhotra 2002: 131). The Khalsa Tract Society's successful pamphlet *Patibrat Dharm* ran into more than five editions (Malhotra 2002: 121). Thus, while on one hand the Sikh woman was being structured within the tropes of the brave warrior woman and the one whose service extended to public spheres, on the other hand, she was also being bombarded with messages in print of what an ideal Sikh woman should be like. One of the most enduring images which Sikh women came to associate with their own identity was that of Mata Sahib Kaur, wife of Guru Gobind Singh, adding *patasas* (sugar puffs) to the initiation *amrit*, thus adding sweetness to the martial Khalsa identity. The emphasis was on the ability to somehow influence the public domain from within the precincts of home and family.

An important part of the Singh Sabha movement was to bring women into the ambit of the distinct Sikh religious identity, and to construct them as different from a diffused Punjabi female identity. This was to have a long-term impact upon how the Sikh woman would be perceived in times to come, and how it would place her within mainstream society. It would also give the Sikh woman a unified recognisable identity. All reform movements of the time took steps to wean women away from common cultural practices and to bring them under the ambit of new traditions. Like the Arya Samaj ordained the *Yajnopavit* ceremony for girls, the Sikh reformers reaffirmed practices started in the time of Guru Gobind Singh. Sikh men and women were encouraged to take *amrit*, wear the five 'K's and participate in *amrit sanskar* (baptism) ceremonies performed in gurdwaras. Sikh prayer routines or *nitnem* were prescribed for them. Salwar kameez and dupatta became the Sikh woman's dress code, identifiable across caste and class. Sikh women were now given names chosen from Guru Granth Sahib, which are unisex. They were encouraged to use 'Kaur' against their name instead of caste verifiers.

These changes were not always readily accepted by Sikh women entrenched in the common cultural spaces, which criss-crossed between religions and castes. Many times, they had to be 'coaxed and coerced into identifying with new religious causes' (Malhotra2002: 168–169). Among Khatris, both Hindus and Sikhs had traditionally married their daughters into each other's families. However, with the Singh Sabha movement carving out a distinct Sikh identity, Sikh women were asked to desist from following Hindu rituals. Women resented these injunctions and the shifting expectations within the two communities; *vrat* (fasting), an important part of Hindu female custom, was banned in the new Sikh code of conduct, leading to rifts within families and a forceful implementation of the same by men. Shauna Singh Baldwin's novel *What the Body Remembers* (2000) gives a perceptive account of how a woman in a Sikh home has to give up her Krishna idol and the ritual of *sandhya* when the man of the house decides to proclaim his Sikh identity and has his home purified with *akhand path*. The political undercurrents, which were the impetus for the male members to adopt exclusive identities, were not always cognisable to the women impacted. While some willingly joined the change, the shift was difficult for others.

'Purifying women' was another of the Singh Sabha's projects; it was primarily implemented through attempts at veering Sikh women away from many of the transcultural practices which had marked the life of women in Punjab. While some of these like *siyappa* (wailing rituals on death) were common across groups, others like visiting holy men, particularly Muslim pirs or attending melas at dargahs for *mannat*s, etc. were more common among the rural women. Often, this involved unchaperoned interaction with other men. The Sikh reformists tried to bring Sikhs hitherto separated by their rural and urban lives, caste and class divides, under one common religious identity, which demanded uniformity in social conduct which emulated their own high-caste traditions. The practices of the rural women were not only seen as transgressing the new insular religious identity but also as sites of moral misconduct. It was deemed necessary to provide new codes of conduct. As a corollary, all spaces where women could venture without male supervision were looked upon as indulgences, which the Sikh woman with their high moral codes, were to shun. One of the stories from the Khalsa Tract Society about a woman adamant on continuing with such practices names her Nishang Kaur (unabashed and audacious) (Malhotra 2002: 183). By creating such codes, the Singh Sabha closed in upon spaces which gave women a certain amount of freedom and allowed participation in the fluid, inter-religious practices marking Punjabi culture. These new codes were most resented in rural areas, where women as participants in field labour had had greater liberty to move outside home. There were many instances of clear hostility to what they construed as the constrictive rules of the Singh Sabha leaders.

The Singh Sabha, in the process of establishing its modern stance—particularly one which emanated from Sikh religious identity—did take certain steps which were to have a positive impact despite the checks and balances with which they were initiated. One of these was discarding the purdah (veil) that was seen as a Muslim practice and inconsistent with the image of the brave, battle-ready Sikh woman (Malhotra 2002: 127). However, there were simultaneous measures to prevent the possibility of women abrogating too many liberties and crossing the bounds of acceptable social behaviour. With the modern stance of doing away with the purdah, they also prescribed almost Victorian dress codes for women when they ventured into public spaces. The advised attire consisted of long-sleeved clothes, clothes made from materials which were not transparent, buttoned-up shirts, etc. Sikh women also kept their head covered in public, which although a traditional Punjabi dress code, now became a particularly Sikh one. Yet, freedom from purdah did provide a better access to social spaces.

A momentous decision of the Sabha was to encourage education among girls within Sikh families. This was to have a long-term impact, one of the results being that today Sikhs have one of the highest literacy rates for women. The necessity of allowing education to Sikh girls arose for many reasons. One of these was to thwart British attempts at bringing marginalised women, especially widows, into the sphere of Christian missionary influence largely effected through Christian schools. Like the purdah, this too came with a set of rules meant to keep its impact in check. Schooling for girls, though encouraged, was designed to aid in areas of moral and religious upliftment and to make them experts in running good houses, keeping family accounts, stitching for contributing to family incomes and so on. Although Sikh families started sending girls to schools to show solidarity with the Singh Sabha, education beyond school level was still looked down upon and treated as a precursor to problems in social life. Girls were often persuaded to stop studying after school because elders, particularly grandparents would discourage it. A common adage was '*pyo di chitti pag te daag lag jayega*'(it will stain your father's white turban)—the turban, here, a signifier for respectability could be tarnished by daughters who ventured too far out into the world.

However, once initiated, the process veered into directions not fully anticipated. It led to women demanding greater space and also opened ways for education becoming an instrument of relative empowerment. Sikh women had always been literate in greater numbers because they were taught Gurmukhi at home to read the scriptures. Now, they were equipped with an improved and structured form of language to be used as a tool for expression. While Sikh reformers used the printed word to forward their agendas, these were at times usurped by literate women to question those. An anonymous Sikh woman, for instance, managed to find her way into the widely read publication of the Khalsa Tract Society through her piece *Letter from a Sister*. While reiterating her faith in what the reformers said about the special privileges granted to women in Sikh religion, she questioned why they were not being translated into her lived reality. She also questioned why there could not be a *streebrat dharm* on the same lines as the *patibrat dharm* (Malhotra 2002: 158). More women demanded access to education as a means to economic independence and a change in status. Many younger Sikh men associated with the movement and more open to new ideas joined the chorus. While agreeing to the reformist construction of the ideal woman as one focused on home, they wondered why Sikh women could not be allowed to venture into fields like medicine and teaching where they could be useful to other women from the community. Within these tiny shifts were the seeds of change which could overturn the carefully constructed constraints on women.

The duality in the Singh Sabha's overtures can be understood in terms of a fear of creating a breakdown in family structures, perhaps the only stable units in the existing social, economic and political flux. The success of the movement would also have depended on the Sikh *samaaj*'s acceptance of the new injunctions, which was possible only if fear of a breakdown of existing structures was allayed. In this sense, the changes initiated perhaps cannot be seen only in terms of the Singh Sabha's patriarchal subversions of their public narratives. While they did draw their orientations from the broader Punjabi society, they have to be given their due for moving beyond their own entrenched biases. Retrospectively speaking, the Singh Sabha has had a far-reaching impact on the construction of the Sikh women's identity as we understand it today. From being part of a fluid Punjabi identity, they now clearly represent a particular religious and community identity. The rural and urban divide and its cultural chasms that were sought to be bridged, has resulted in a common recognisable identity for Sikh women across other differences. An overall rational approach and emphasis on belief in one God have dispensed with many of the constricting rituals and superstitions. Sikh men and women have an identical religious discipline and there are no rituals which woman alone need to follow. There are no distinct dress codes or markers that distinguish a married woman from an unmarried woman or even one who has been widowed; this is a radical departure from the underlying discriminations these traditions entailed. A culture of hard work and ethical behaviour has also come to be associated with Sikh women.

Institutionalised Hierarchies and Patterns of Resistance

The narrative of empowerment for women and reforms in the ethnic culture which the movement claimed to have initiated, however, needs to be probed for its validity below the surface. Retrospectively analysed, the many contradictory thrusts which have gone into the construction of the Sikh female identity have produced mixed results. While they have had definite positive bearings, at times, they have also resulted in thwarting the proclaimed shifts due to inbuilt checks to the momentum. The full impact of the reforms has also been thwarted by social and economic practices within which the community has been entrenched and which have been fundamentally detrimental to women. Ethnic identities worm their way through religious affiliations and reform practices. Hence, what has been proposed in theory might not always have been translated into practice. Reading between the lines reveals many areas where contradictions exist, some in blatant contravention to the intent of the religion. Yet, a positive intellectual tradition and a clearly stated religious intent have been important in two manners. These persist as a background causing constant dissonance in case of contradictions, thereby garnering potential to create an embarrassment to those flouting them. It also provides women with a potential for change, the validity of which cannot be denied by the community, even as they try to subvert it. Both have combined to make a difference which has led to visible shifts.

An example of this is the evolving community stance towards education for women. Initiated by the Singh Sabha movement, education eventually became part of community objectives and its organisational structures like the Shiromani Gurdwara Prabandhak Committee (SGPC) and the Khalsa educational trusts. However, education for daughters in Sikh homes was constantly accompanied by a reiteration that personal aspirations must be made subservient to the needs of the home. Underlying it were anxieties of a rupture in the family structure and its supporting power hierarchies if a woman's, especially a daughter-in-law's education got translated into a career. While more and more families wanted an educated daughter-in-law, they did not want a working one. Interestingly, among educated girls, families did not want a girl with a law degree because a girl aware of her legal rights could assert those and demand inconvenient answers at some point. Added to it was the fear that once a woman tasted freedom, she could not be reined into the duties at home. A common adage has been, '*ik waar janani da paer gharon bahar pai gaya, phir paratdi nahi*' (once the woman steps out of home, she will not return). Implicit in it are connotations of keeping her from financial and personal freedom to maintain a status quo in relational dynamics.

The duality in the Sikh approach in its emphasis on education for girls but its subservience to the duties at home has been consistently reflected in the lives of Sikh women. The underlying emphasis on the centrality of home has had a deep bearing on the way she has perceived her options in life. Increase in levels of education prepared a generation of women who were more aware of the outside world than the generation which had been denied that opportunity. However, they could not always translate education into economic independence or personal empowerment. Despite the many changes that have happened within a restructured Sikh identity, old patterns and mindsets have continued, constantly acting as reductive constraints. Yet, they also form links to a gradually shifting stance in the generations that follow.

The following example from lived reality will provide an insight into this duality of approach and its unintended impact. A woman now in her 50s, tells of how she had access to the best education upon her mother's insistence, who herself had to leave college midway for marriage. However, access to higher education was constantly accompanied by the adage that it was up to the family she married into to decide whether she could work or not—which they turned out not to wish for. A letter from her father-in-law, before the marriage, clarified that a Sikh woman's education should foremost make her a repository of cultural and religious knowledge. Speaking of her cultural conditioning, she narrated an incident, where, a few years into her marriage, despite her professional qualifications and work experience before marriage, she could not contradict her father-in-law, when he told visitors that she was purely a housewife with interests focused on home. The future trajectory of the story is important in its positioning between attitudes filtering from the past and the ones in making. Twenty-five years later, the two daughters born to her have been educated to the best of their parent's ability, this time with an emphasis on career and financial independence. The mother's past and her experiences within cultural constraints have helped her shape her daughters' worldview in empowering ways. That she was supported in this by her husband points to a shift in attitude too.

On various points of this continuum, defined by class, strata, education and exposure, lies the average Sikh woman's profile. The collective force of the many reiterations entrenched into her consciousness has dictated the ways in she has responded to the world around her. As the cumulative thrust of change initiated over the decades is aided by new social impetuses, she can perhaps look more objectively at the past and use that understanding to nudge the future into a different direction. A survey in urban India shows that older Sikh women, educated but not financially empowered through that education, have taken a stand to see that their daughters are not only educated but are also focused on developing their financial capability. Those among them who could work have felt the impact it has had on their position within the family hierarchy. Among those who have not studied beyond a point, there is a great urge to see their daughters do so. Education has also exposed Sikh women to opinions outside their cultural contexts, making them aware of the problems within them. As an older woman explains in simple terms, because of education '*dimaag wadh gaie*' (their understanding of things has increased). They are no longer ready to fit into the earlier moulds (Mooney 2010: 166).

In due course of time, the change has gathered its own momentum. Sikh organisations like SGPC and DSGMC are now taking a proactive approach in providing finances and infrastructure for female education. The presence of Sikh women in different fields has created new 'approved' areas as careers. The desire among Sikh boys for double-income families has added to the gathering assent for the profile of the Sikh working woman. This does not always ensure a radical shift in the larger social response but does manage to dent into some of the adages. That new assertions blend with old ones to create mixed patterns is evident in some of the matrimonial advertisements in newspapers. While looking for a professionally qualified girl for their sons, Sikh parents still wish to ensure that her role at home will continue to be one where she preserves traditions and conventions (Kapur and Misra 2010: 203). However, there are an increasing number of families who have moved beyond this, especially when the son supports the wife in her pursuits. It is through this slow shift in the community response, still carrying within it the echoes of the past but also adding new notes in the present, that a move forward is visible.

The Sikh woman's position and participation in the community's religious structures has been defined by a similar trajectory. Although there have not been as many restrictions on Sikh women as on those in some of the other religions, there are areas of contention. Sikh gurus gave equal rights to women in all spheres of life. The Singh Sabha movement too declared equality for men and women in religious institutions. However, the gap between the professed and the practised has been underlined by the same patriarchal trends that have defined other spheres of Sikh life. This is perhaps also true of most religions across the world but demands a special analysis in light of the social philosophy integrated into the religious teachings of the Sikh gurus. Guru Nanak envisaged a society with no discrimination based on gender. However, even within the realm of a religion which sanctions such equality, the inequality has been visible

The discrepancies have ranged from the small, everyday differentiations between men and women to the ones ingrained in the structures built around religious observances. The dynamics within the gurdwaras have never blatantly discriminated between men and women except in almost imperceptible distinctions, many of which could be passed as general social protocols. For instance, in religious congregations, men and women have been sitting on opposite sides in the gurdwara with the Guru Granth Sahib placed midway, but with those doing kirtan almost always facing the men. Within the langars, while both men and women have cooked, cleaned and washed the utensils together, it is men who generally serve the langar. There has also been the issue of considering menstruating women unclean, ironically in direct contravention to a clearly stated negation of such concepts of pollution within *gurbani*. Management of the gurdwaras too has largely been in the hands of men. There have been no women *ragi*s (those trained in classical music for singing hymns from *gurbani*) or *granthi*s (those trained to read and explain the Guru Granth Sahib). Some significant demarcations in the highest centre of Sikh religion have made the issue less than coincidental and evoked questions on the disparity between letter and intent. In Harmandar Sahib, the highest Sikh religious seat, women have never been allowed to participate in important religious rituals like carrying the *palki* (palanquin with Guru Granth Sahib in it) to the sanctum sanctorum in the early morning hours. Similarly, women have been denied entry to the sanctum sanctorum, where weapons of the tenth guru are displayed in Huzoor Sahib, Nanded, one of the five *takhts* or spiritual seats of the Sikhs. The gender imbalance in the highest committees overseeing the management and finances of Sikh religious and social institutions is also clearly in favour of men. Out of the 170 seats for SGPC, 30 per cent are reserved for women as per a ruling in the 1996 elections, and yet there is hardly any representation of women in the management.

Many of these exclusions have been pointed out by academics working on Sikh identity in the West as evidence of the subordinate position of women in Sikhism. It has also been pointed out that Sikh women have rarely contested these disparities, and that it is Western academic light that has initiated any attention being paid to it. That disparities have existed cannot be denied. However, constructing Sikh women as ready to accept a subordinate position within the religion would be simplistic. Power dynamics are many times so enmeshed with what one perceives as tradition that deference to it makes one impervious to the hierarchies inherent in it. Moreover, the Western perception of a feminist stance might not always be the one, which women in other cultural contexts find suitable or effective. There could be less conspicuous and gradual shifts, more easily assimilated within socio-religious structures, which seem more viable to them. Sikh women have, over time, pushed for space. Though not appointed *granthis*, Sikh women have taken turns in the recitation of the Guru Granth Sahib, during *akhand paths* (continuous recitation of the Granth Sahib over three days) not only in homes but in the inner sanctums of gurdwaras, barring only a few places. On important days like *gurupurabs*, women are now taking the stage for kirtan, like their male counterparts. While the most renowned and popular *ragis* are still men, there are catalogued women *kirtani jathas*, (a group trained in a musical rendition of the *gurbani* in classical mode) with their details provided in *jantris* (traditional calendar of *gurupurabs* and other important religious occasions).

There never have been any restrictions on women in most of the gurdwaras. Where there are, the younger generation of girls are forthright in questioning them. Most educated Sikh women do not pass on the cultural references of purity and impurity during menstruation to daughters. An interesting indicator of the changing gender paradigm is currently reflected in the seating arrangements in gurdwaras in India. From strict segregation among men and women, women can now frequently be seen sitting on the men's side, gradually converting the gurdwara space into a gender-neutral one. Traditionally, *ragis* doing kirtan are positioned to face the men. With women appropriating the men's space, they also appropriate direct access to the kirtan in the gurdwaras. It is now a common sight to see Sikh girls distributing langar, a *sewa* once the prerogative of men and boys. Many of them prefer it to working in the cooking areas. While management of gurdwaras is still largely in the hands of men, an interesting usurpation of the role by women is visible in a parallel religious tradition of sorts, fast gaining ground. In a confluence of resistance to social as well as religious traditions, Sikh women get together either in a gurdwara or by turns in homes, to do a group reading of the Sukhmani Sahib (part of the Sikh scripture). In these Sukhmani Sahib groups, women claim not just physical space but also the traditional male prerogatives of managing finances and logistics. Sikh social codes, which approve of Sikh women's space primarily within home, have been subverted using the very dictates which summon her to be the carrier of religion and tradition within those homes. Interestingly, it is the older women who lead the way. These micro-practices of resistance are significant because from their various and differentiated placements within the community, they have gradually created shifts absorbed by the community. Without turning that overture into a battle of sorts, they are managing to change the paradigms bit by bit.

Resistance to the male-centrism inherent in Sikh religious and organisational structures is also becoming increasingly visible. Whichever party they belong to, all women candidates in the SGPC elections have similar priorities (Nibber 2011). They demand a greater voice in decision making and changes in established practices. Voices like that of Kiranjot Kaur, former General Secretary of SGPC who found a place within the religion's power structure, spoke loud and clear repudiating any reasons forwarded for women not being allowed into the space reserved for male *ragis* within the Golden Temple. She says, 'For long, women have been subjugated because of "God's word" and now they are no longer buying this story!'(Kaur 2017). It is interesting to note that in November 2019, days before the worldwide celebrations of 550 years of Guru Nanak's birth, the Punjab Legislative Assembly unanimously passed a resolution urging the *Akal Takht* and the SGPC to allow Sikh women to sing hymns in the sanctum sanctorum of the Golden Temple in Amritsar. Voices of dissent could not sustain as their invocation of *rehit maryada* was countered by clearly stated views of Sikh gurus on gender equality. The move has been endorsed by the Akali Dal, which has substantial influence over the SGPC.

Sikh women are also resisting new male constructions from within radical groups of what their ideal bearing should be. Among these are attempts to portray the turban-wearing Sikh woman as the one proscribing to the real Sikh identity. There has been a trend, beginning from sections of diaspora Sikhs and gaining momentum in the post-1980s resurgence of Sikh identity that aims to construct the 'real' Sikh woman as the one wearing a turban. Splashed across the internet, the Sikh woman in a turban for some time became the new identifiable for those outside the community. In India, the image has over time been appropriated by groups within the community who wish to posit themselves as 'more Sikh' than the others. The image of the Sikh girl in the turban is being floated as an ideal to be reached, an emblem of the correct female Sikh religious identity, even though nowhere in Sikh religion has the turban been prescribed for women as it was for Sikh men. There are women from specific groups like that of Bhai Randhir Singh Jatha, or some others, who have always chosen to wear turbans as part of their group tradition but it has never been the norm among the larger Sikh society. There are some among the younger generation, particularly in the West, who adopt it for reasons other than merely religious. For them, it is an assertion of a specific identity within a faceless immigrant identity, and sometimes appropriation of the male space signified by the turban. However, the urban Sikh woman in the Indian mainstream resists such constructions. She prefers a more cosmopolitan identity, even as she continues to maintain other symbols of her faith. The college-going girl wearing jeans and a kurta, the small-town school teacher with her dupatta flowing from her shoulder, the middle-aged executive wearing trousers and a shirt are all reiterations of the contemporary Sikh woman's identity. As is any of them bowing down in a gurdwara, with her head covered in deference to her faith.

Held Back, Moving Forward

While the Sikh woman persists at these overtures at selfhood, social indicators put a question mark on where the community itself places its women on the value scale. Unfortunately, statistics show that 500 years of adherence to a faith that tried to reform the ills inherent in the society from where the Sikhs emerged has not impacted many of those practices, at least in certain sections, even today. The national census of 2001 shows that the sex ratio of the Sikh population is more skewed than any other community in India. In contrast to the national average of 933 women for 1000 men, Sikhs have 893; even more worrying is the sex ratio for children below six years of age. Among Sikhs, there are 786 girl children for 1000 male children—far below the average for Christians (964), Muslims (950) and Hindus (925). The indication is that the overall ratio among the Sikhs might decline further in the future (Jodhka 2010: 22–23). Female foeticide is rampant. Perhaps, it is so because while Sikh social narrative claims equality between men and women, the inequalities begin early and create a cycle of situations where a woman remains a liability. Within many Sikh families, the continued preference for the male child is rooted in seeing him as security in old age and as heir to carry on the family name. He is also the one to look after family businesses and landed properties, which if shared with daughters, would transfer to their marital homes—an unacceptable option. A *Shodhganga* report indicates that the trend is more rampant in the well-off landed population ('Female Foeticide in Haryana and Punjab: An Empirical Study'). There is pressure to give huge dowries because it is understood that the girls will not be given a share in the property, which poses a financial liability on the parents. The more recent legal pressure to give girls an equal share has only become an added reason to terminate female foetuses in early stages with advancements in technology only making the process simpler. Ironically, many among the community try to wash their hands off the problem saying such misogynistic practices or attitudes are by very nature 'outside Sikhism' (Jakobsh 2010: 22). Many also blame women for perpetuating such trends, conveniently ignoring familial and social pressures on them. With such ontological narratives, men forego responsibility for the regressive attitudes while allowing them to persist (Behl 2010: 72). No one ever seems to question why they do not proactively stand up to them. There are efforts from within Sikh social, political and religious spaces to stop these practices with media being actively harnessed and sops being offered for the girl child. However, entrenched biases within the system make these overtures less than convincing. Besides, till underlying social and economic impetuses persist, so will the prejudice against the girl child. Sex selection and not recognising the inheritance rights of daughters continue to be some of these.

Yet, there are shifts in making. With growing urbanisation, shifting occupations and concomitant advantages like education, attitudes are changing too, even if in small sections. That sex selection is lower among Delhi Sikhs and the Sikhs in Chandigarh might be some indication of the influence of new contexts. Sikh families with two daughters, a rarity in earlier times, are now more common. They might not be representative of the community at large, but they do indicate new trends that dent into existing social patterns. When asked about the family dynamic, many from urban Sikh families, both girls and boys, said that there is no distinction in how they are treated at home, including the resources being spent on their upkeep and education. Girls are encouraged to take up professional courses just like the boys. The only disparity being practised seems to be the late hours allowed to boys, which perhaps has more to do with concern for safety. In rural and semi-urban areas, the percentage of Sikh girls going in for higher education has far exceeded that of boys for long. There is now an increasing willingness to let girls use that for finding work. Many are sending their daughters to study abroad. Even as a means of finding their way to foreign lands, it is infinitely better than the earlier ways.

Poised at a particularly significant juncture are Sikh women who are assuming the role of tellers of their stories. Education and exposure has given many among them the ability to probe, analyse and articulate female experience in the community. Works of literature by Sikh women are cataloguing external as well as internal journeys of the women in the community. Younger Sikh women are using social media for articulating contemporary viewpoints. They are retelling both their own experiences and the community experiences from the female perspective. Sikh women in academics are deconstructing the community stances. By probing the community trajectories and placing their lived experiences within them, these Sikh women are analysing images into which they have been constructed and crystallising how close or far these are from who they really are, or what they would rather be. By understanding their position within the existing network of social and economic relations, they are in the process of determining what they want to change within it. They are raising uncomfortable questions to their advantage. In the process, they are also claiming their place as thinking, questioning, articulating members of the community. They are tracing the continuum of the community history and their shifting presence in it, thereby clarifying for themselves the possibility of moving on from where they are.

For the Sikh woman, the process of becoming continues. The various histories which have built her have also created traditions that have been both empowering and disempowering. Tradition is not something we can consider as something other. It is a part of who we are (Gadamer [1991] quoted by Alcoff 2006: 95). How we perceive the world and act on it, therefore, becomes fundamentally influenced by 'the background, framing assumptions we bring with us to perception and understanding, the congealed experiences that become premises by which we strive to make sense of the world, the range of concepts and categories of description that we have at our disposal' (Gadamer 1991). These determine the complex ways in which we perceive our options. The Sikh woman too has operated within such parameters. On the one hand, she has carried within herself the social constraints coming from her ethnic contexts. On the other hand, she has constantly been aware of a religious philosophy, which offers a way out of those contexts. She has been held back and pushed forward at the same time. As new tools of awareness and empowerment increase her understanding of both, she has been making her way forward, shifting a little as the horizon shifts, moving beyond existing standpoints in search for a better place for herself. Alcoff says, 'being a "woman" is to take up a position within a moving historical context and to be able to choose what we make of this position and how we alter this context' (2006: 149). The Sikh woman seems to be on her way to doing so.

References

Alcoff, Linda Martin. 2006. 'Real Identities'. In *Visible Identities: Race, Gender, and the Self*. New York: Oxford University Press.

———. 2006. 'The Identity Crisis in Feminist Theory'. In *Visible Identities: Race, Gender, and the Self*. New York: Oxford University Press.

Behl, Natasha. 2010. Politics of Equality: Caste and Gender Paradoxes in the Sikh Community. Unpublished PhD Dissertation: Department of Political Science, University of California, Los Angeles.

Dhavan, Purnima. 2010. 'Tracing Gender in the Texts and Practices of the Early Khalsa'. In *Sikhism and Women: History, Texts, and Experience* edited by Doris R. Jakobsh. New Delhi: Oxford University Press.

'Female Foeticide in Haryana and Punjab: An Empirical Study'. Available at: https://shodhganga.inflibnet.ac.in/bitstream/10603/132445/14/14_chapter%206.pdf (accessed on 1 February 2020).

Gadamer, Hans Georg. (2006. [1991)). Quoted by Linda Martin Alcoff. 'Real Identities'. In *Visible Identities: Race, Gender, and the Self*. Oxford University Press.

Jakobsh, Doris R. and Eleanor Nesbitt. 2010. 'Sikhism and Women: Contextualizing Issues'. In *Sikhism and Women: History, Texts, and Experience*, edited by Doris. R. Jakobsh. New Delhi: Oxford University Press.

Jodhka, Surinder S. 2010. 'The Sikhs Today: A Development Profile'. In *Religions and Development, India: Working Paper Series*, 01(02). Indian Institute of Dalit Studies, and Religions and Development Research Programme.

Kapur, Preeti and Girishwar Misra. 2010. 'Changing Identities and Fixed Roles: The Experiences of Sikh Women'. In *Sikhism and Women: History, Texts, and Experience*, edited by Doris. R. Jakobsh. New Delhi: Oxford University Press.

Kaur, Kiranjot. 2017. 'Why Debate Kirtan by Sikh Women in Darbar Sahib? It's Our Indisputable Right'. *The Times of India*, Chandigarh, 14 August. Available at: https://timesofindia.indiatimes.com/city/chandigarh/pb-guest-column/articleshow/60050500.cms (accessed on 26 February 2020).

Malhotra, Anshu. 2002. 'Controlling Women'. In *Gender Caste and Religious Identities: Restructuring Class in Colonial Punjab*. New Delhi: Oxford University Press.

———. 2002. 'Gender, Caste and Religious Identities in Punjab'. In *Gender Caste and Religious Identities: Restructuring Class in Colonial Punjab*. New Delhi: Oxford University Press.

———. 2002. '"Killing", "Gifting" or "Selling" Daughters'. In *Gender Caste and Religious Identities: Restructuring Class in Colonial Punjab*. New Delhi: Oxford University Press.

———. 2002. 'Powerful Men-Fearful Men'. In *Gender Caste and Religious Identities: Restructuring Class in Colonial Punjab*. New Delhi: Oxford University Press.

———. 2010. 'Shameful Continuities'. In *Sikhism and Women: History, Texts, and Experience*, edited by Doris. R. Jakobsh. New Delhi: Oxford University Press.

Malhotra, Karamjit K. 2013. 'Issues of Gender among the Sikhs: Eighteenth-Century Literature'. In *Journal of Punjab Studies*, 20 (1/2): 53–76.

Mooney, Nicola. 2010. 'Lowly Shoes on Lowly Feet'. In *Sikhism and Women: History, Texts, and Experience*, edited by Doris. R. Jakobsh. New Delhi: Oxford University Press.

Nibber, Gurpreet Singh. 2011. 'Women seek right to do kirtan in Golden Temple'. *Hindustan Times*, 13 September. Available at: https://www.hindustantimes.com/chandigarh/women-seek-right-to-do-kirtan-in-golden-temple/story-UDkPukN58n2S5WcfKic78O.html (accessed on 3 March 2020).

Somers, Margaret. 1994. 'The Narrative Constitution of Identity: A Relational and Network Approach'. In *Theory and Society*, October, 23 (5): 605–649. Available at: http://www.jstor.org/stable/658090 (accessed on 21 June 2014).

6

Images and Stereotypes: Exploring the Impetus

The Sikh has long been constructed in stock images placing him in a strange position, where he constantly needs to reiterate other aspects of himself. These images form a lens through which a pre-determined version of him is made available for social consumption. Irrespective of his difference, he is perpetually at risk of being held ransom to the value iterations surrounding these images. Over time, these have evolved into stereotypes, which have infiltrated personal interactions, media representations and the social psyche. As the community negotiates with the many shifts that settling into an urban cosmopolitan setting entails, these images become increasingly awkward and ill-fitting. However, there is no letting go of them, indicating a resistance to the new identities forming through new situations. An analysis of these images, the histories they derive from and the social complexities that they mirror reveal more than the ostensible. It indicates power paradigms and social dynamics resting on deeper control issues. It also reveals exclusions and elisions, which preclude the need to go beyond the image to the reality. It is important to deconstruct these images, operating both within the home country and outside, to understand the impulses underlying them. Common histories ruptured by new identity formations, a minority positioning at odds with its ambitious aspirations and the impasse these have led to from time to time could emerge as some of the underlying factors. Sifting through them could make visible anxieties and attempts to deal with them. It is through an analysis of these that one can hope to understand the impetus that goes into the stereotyping, its impact on the people concerned and the possibility of breaking through it.

Humour, Cinematic Representation, Media Portrayal: The Underlying Impulses in India

The response to the community at home is different from the one outside. In India, Sikhs are integrated well enough and are equal recipients of all common social structures and economic opportunities. As a minority, they have been able to maintain their distinction from the majority while also maintaining an acknowledgement of a common national and cultural identity. Their growing integration into urban living has created many points of convergence with the mainstream. At a social level, Sikhs integrate well with the non-Sikhs, celebrate many of their festivals as their own and share social spaces. Participation in common educational opportunities has opened the same avenues and opportunities to them, leading to similar lifestyles and aspirations. On an individual level, there is a cordiality which marks the community's relationship with the majority with each recognising the common attributes of their identities and respect for the difference. Most of the other communities will talk of Sikhs as a generous people with a great capacity to help others in need. Much is made about their participation in help during times of crises. They have also been identified as brave soldiers, successful agriculturists, people with exceptional enterprise and an upbeat nature.

Yet, within these many positive constructions lie the half-submerged images of the Sikh as a butt of jokes, the Sikh as someone dangerous, the Sikh as a potential anti-national, the Sikh as the 'other'. These images, very much at odds with the more positive ones, reflect underlying emotions, not always clear and crystallised. They are remnants and outgrowths of an uneasy past entwined with social shifts incurred through historical processes and the diffused attitudes they have bequeathed. An attempt to unravel these would perhaps take us back to the legacy of the colonial intervention in terms of the rigid identity constructions which it induced, the many political trails it triggered and the emotional fissures it resulted in. As already discussed, India was a land of diffused cultural identities with overlapping faiths and common ethnicities involving deep connections. Despite the creation of the Khalsa by Guru Gobind Singh, which provided the Sikhs with a distinct religious and martial identity, the cultural and ethnic connections to the others were not snapped. The spiritual teachings of the Sikh gurus were respected by the broader Punjabi milieu and the Hindu traditions continued to filter into Sikh homes and lives. However, the last phase of British rule triggered the demarcation of these identities within rigid boundaries. This was, in a way, both the culmination of the colonial methodology of studying their subjects through Western lens and the new political paradigms where power ensued through numbers. This gradually resulted in the emergence of a distinct Sikh social and political identity, which demanded a clear-cut allegiance to the disciplines of the faith or an ouster from it. That the majority too was undergoing a similar sharpening of community identity complicated the situation further. At its extreme, the radical element within the majority demanded a return of the Sikhs into the Hindu fold to prove their belonging, creating further wedges in a once-shared life. As the leaders on either side built mutually exclusive stances, differences appeared where there had been none. Among the majority, it created a certain hardening of feeling for what was seen as a disregard for shared blood ties, fraternal bonds and kinship through marriages. While the Sikhs emphasised the difference as a means of constructing a separate identity, the majority perceived it as a belligerent tearing away and used this to construct the community as the 'other'. This other was also sketched as a contrast to the norm, the majority identity.

Anxieties underlying these differences have been further reinforced in the post-Independence times with the displaced Sikhs from West Punjab arriving in non-Sikh dominated areas. The necessity of inviting them into the existing social and economic structures while also dealing with the underlying angst was a complicated terrain to navigate. It was further aggravated by the refugee culture which the Sikhs got with them. Loud and aggressive, too busy surviving to be bothered with the self-consciousness required for correct social posturing, they were anomalies especially in the genteel social cultures of places like Delhi they arrived in. Their struggle to reconstruct their lives brought the culture of *jugaad* (finding ways to manage with the given resources), vying for limited resources and utilising them through methods which defied order. Their businesses, many times conducted from roadside *patri*s, dented into the existing market norms and threatened established businesses. The eventual success of the Sikhs despite their disrupted past or the mere two per cent strength in the total population, rankled sections of people, who despite an earlier claim on the resources, could not match up to them. In course of time, as Sikhs broke into the existing markets, constructed houses and flaunted their prosperity through lifestyles verging on flashiness, they added to the existing apprehensions and reservations. With passing time, their considerably ostentatious social and community practices led to resentment too. All this cumulatively led to deep-rooted anxiety in the minds of the non-Sikh majorities (Handoo 1990: 161).

Over time, these many anxieties, working through the complicated interplay of overlapping social and cultural lives, have distilled into micro-practices of 'othering'. For example, 'Sardar*ji*', a term of respect used in the same tone as 'Lala*ji*' in a more congenial past, became sardar with pejorative connotations that constructs the bearer as someone different. It is the same anxiety, which underlies social humour and cinematic representations built around the Sikhs. These have constructed the difference into images and stereotypes verging on the absurd. For more than one can remember now, the Sikh is synonymous with the sardar*ji* and Santa Banta jokes, which have become staples of Indian social life. According to Christie Davies, jokes are a reflection of the social environment. It is not surprising that most of these are constructed around the trader-professional Sikh, not the agriculturist. A Sikh in these jokes is constructed as a social blunder, a person who is at odds with the life around him and one who deals with it in ways that are strange and laughable to others. That these jokes are narrated in common social spaces, including homes, offices and schools, places Sikhs in the awkward position of choosing between risking group alienation by protesting or acting as a good-humoured people who can laugh at themselves. The same holds true for Sikh representation in Indian cinema, which generally constructs a Sikh as a loud and awkward side character providing comic relief.

The pervasiveness and persistence of these images despite their growing incongruity to the average Sikh require an analysis of the impetus behind them. Anxiety over difference leads to 'othering', which at some level is assuring oneself of one's own superior stance. Hobbes, in the 17th century, said that laughter directed at someone is a validation of the self, which by implication involves denigrating the other. This includes experiencing importance by comparing oneself with the weak points of others (Hobbes quoted by Hughes 2003: 1450). Sigmund Freud elaborated this further when he said that by making someone 'small, inferior, despicable or comic, we achieve in a roundabout way the enjoyment of overcoming him which is important because someone else bears witness to it through laughter' (Freud quoted by Hughes 2003: 1450). When this humour arises out of social or cultural anxiety, it involves imposing implications of inferiority or comicality on the ethnicity of the people concerned. By placing them on the cultural boundary, those at the dominant centre emphasise their distance from what is constructed as the cultural norm. Built within this are attempts at drawing comparisons to 'our' way of doing things which are ostensibly the correct and rational ones, against 'their' ways which are constructed as absurd and irrational (Davies 1998: 65). This involves policing socio-cultural boundaries which prevent the bridging of a gap between the two. This 'othering' becomes particularly stringent if the other group threatens disruption of the dominant group's organised social and economic structures. The value-expressive function of such humour rests in proving the behaviour of the targeted people as ridiculous, which is why, work ethic, language and social skills become usual areas of targeting.

Many of these traits are visible in the constructions around Sikhs, whether in humour or cinema. Humour might not be intended to have any specific consequences but it does reflect the social environment which goes into making it. The Sikh in 'sardar jokes' is generally subjected to the majority's superior gaze. His work ethic is projected as one relying more on brawn than on brain. His acumen in fields requiring physical prowess is portrayed from the reverse perspective, as lack of intellectual acumen within modern economic and market systems. This, often, takes the form of contrast between the shrewdness and frugality informing what is constructed as the purposive and organised life of the majority, and the sardar's less calculative, 'obtuse' approach. Humour targeting his language constraints implies the apparent sophistication of the onlooker. The consistent focus on his awkward accent and loud manner of speaking puts him in the category of the lesser 'other'. His blundering use of English, the linguistic marker of elitism in Indian society, firmly places him in the non-elite category. His social skills or the lack of them make him consistently laughable. He is never tuned into the nuances of social etiquette and ends up making hilarious faux pas. He elicits laughter with his attempts at being a part of the mainstream, which he is at odds with, due to his over-the-top enthusiasm and silly antics. The same image gains visual currency in cinema. A male Sikh in Indian cinema is loud and boisterous, his gregariousness a genial indicator of his underdeveloped social etiquette. He is generally the drunken wedding guest, the neighbourhood uncle always in *balle balle* mode, the taxi driver who speaks with an alien and obdurate accent, the fat young adult who is infantilised in his obsession with eating, etc. Even if he is shown as good-hearted, he is either a simpleton or a socially awkward character on the verge of being a caricature. In most cases, his colourful clothes, his strange mannerisms and even a differently structured physical body make him the subject of 'carnivalesque curiosity'(Mehta 2013: 73–95).

These images do not just construct the Sikh in a diminutive manner but also place him on the periphery of a majority culture instead of making him the centre of his own world. Built within the images is a systematic negation of the validity of his cultural difference. His difference is portrayed not as one which needs to be recognised and accorded a place of its own but in terms of a joke or a spectacle. It offers no contextualisation in a distinct, fully formed social and cultural background, which would necessitate his evolution into a complete person. Unlike other characters plotted on different referral points of a real-life continuum, a Sikh in Indian cinema is shown to have a limited underdeveloped response and is generally used as a side character. The incomplete translation of difference in these depictions reflects the reluctance to accept that difference on its terms (Mehta 2013). Running parallel to this negation of a distinct social identity is the dispensability of the Sikh character within the plot. He is present to provide comic relief and is hardly ever crucial to the plot. There is also a tendency to invest his character with lovability only in proportion to his availability for others. Even his historically proven courage is considered for a serious portrayal only when depicted in service of the hero, the people or the nation. It is otherwise reduced to a mock-heroic trope with outlandish outfits and slapstick humour.

Indian cinema continues to display '...a strategic amnesia that continues to manifest an avowed secular narrative of "inclusion" in contemporary cultural production with a consistent refusal to allow a full range of subjectivity for the male Sikh body' (H. Singh 2006: 115–204). The images constructed around the agriculturist Sikh have been less obdurate but as rigid. The various shifts of the community refuse to get incorporated into the images. A Jat Sikh must remain forever stuck in his bhangra regalia, dancing in his mustard fields or looking his dangerous feudal part with a gun in his hand. The images suggest that while the rest of the world moves on into the new global roles, the Sikh remains where he was even within new contexts.

These images need to be deconstructed to reveal how they influence the perception of the listener or the viewer, and why those perpetuating them are so reluctant to let go of them. A stereotype once formed subordinates the person to itself and his behaviour is made to conform to the directives of the image (Allport quoted by Boskin and Dorinson1985: 82). These representations make it seem that a Sikh in every social sphere, every stratum, irrespective of individual difference and background, is essentially a type. He must act under the prescribed image recognisable to the majority. This makes it difficult to envision him as he is, outside these constructs, spread in a huge range of mainstream roles, many times quite different from the traditional ones. This unwillingness to accede space to an evolving identity is underlined by a reluctance to let go of the superior–inferior, centre–periphery, normative and non-normative binaries within which these images are constructed. The image of the Sikh must remain frozen if the hierarchies woven into it are to be sustained. The section of society proscribing to 'iron-bound stereotypes' keeps returning to them. The stereotypes keep becoming more persistent even as the people they caricature move beyond and outside (Boskin and Dorinson 1985: 97). It is not as if the Sikhs or others are unaware of the anomalies within these constructions, or that everyone enjoys the berating inherent in them. The pressure to accede to the diminutive, comic, or awkward, works around the need to belong. 'Humour is a powerful means of pulling people together and, in doing so, automatically shutting other people out.... The laugh makes group boundaries visible and palpable: he who laughs belongs, he who does not laugh is excluded' (Kuipers 1971: 10).

Systematic constructions can become even stronger when these begin to be created or reinforced through knowledge-producing mediums. While jokes and cinematic representations have constructed the Sikh as peripheral and laughable, the news mediums did the more dangerous task of constructing the Sikh as dangerous. The political turmoil of the 1980s and the rise of radical sentiments among a section of Sikhs in Punjab led to unfortunate incidents of terrorism in the state. Bhindranwale's exhortations to the community to build a highly masculinised and defiant Sikh identity also equated this identity with the turban, the beard and the kirpan, which distinguished them from others. However, media used the images without qualification so that the average Sikh using these as basic symbols of his religious identity also got constructed in the same image. While covering acts of aggression by militants before and after Operation Blue Star, images of AK47-wielding turbaned and bearded men introduced as Sikh militants rather than just militants, reinforced the identification. Ordinary Sikhs came to be identified as people who thought and felt differently from others and who in their hearts were fundamentalists. The sentiment grew stronger in the months following Operation Blue Star when Sikhs as a community were attributed with religious fanaticism which ostensibly would lead to dire consequences for the majority community. Indira Gandhi's assassination at the hands of her Sikh bodyguards validated the opinion and infused the images in circulation with greater authenticity. The Sikh was the 'other', the dangerous fundamentalist, the fanatic in search of revenge. That none of these images synchronised with the Sikh living next door seemed to be of little consequence. The events of November 1984 saw the Sikhs in Delhi and other North Indian states suffer the consequences of this image construction.

As an anthropologist collating information while working closely with the Sikh victims of the 1984 genocide, Veena Das came across views, which would be highly surprising for the average Sikh. Das collates the essence of what she discovered in her interactions, in a few succinct points. For the majority,

> A Sikh does not believe in any loyalty except that to his religion.... A Sikh is like a snake. He will bite the very hands that feed him.... Sikhs are naturally aggressive and attracted to violence. They are not capable of observing normal social constraints.... There is a fanaticism bordering on madness in Sikh character. (Das 2007: 133)

The play of perceptions generated through these opinions determined how the majority saw the Sikhs even while the killing, looting and burning was going on. Sikhs taking shelter in gurdwaras were seen as groups collecting weapons to attack the majority community. Those who refused to move to shelter houses for fear of being trapped were painted as zealots awaiting martyrdom. All this eventually built up collective rancour, which failed to distinguish between the image and the individual, between social reality and political rhetoric: '...[T]he simultaneity of events at the level of phenomenal time that are far apart in physical time, make the whole of the past simultaneously available' (Das 2007: 97). The 'othering' passed on from one generation to another and exacerbated by the more recent events became the reason for the backlash which has since sunk into the community psyche. A lot of time has passed since. The militant movement in Punjab has ended as much due to the elimination of various actors of that movement as the wish of the common Sikh to resume a normal life. Sikhs outside Punjab, victims of insane violence, have resumed their lives too. Individual relationships between Sikhs and the people among whom they live have in many cases emerged stronger for many among the majority rose above political rhetoric. Yet, the images constructed around the Sikhs survive at a subconscious level. This is evident in how the submerged image of the Sikh as a fundamentalist makes the Khalistani trope easy to revive as and when convenient.

The Turban as a Signifier: Historical and Cultural Associations Outside India

Outside the home country, the image of the Sikh is that of the man with the turban. The turban here signifies his ideological identity as much as a religious one. The turbaned Sikh image has different connotations in different parts of the world, related to the community's past histories in those lands and how their identity evolved in those contexts. The turban in East and South East Asia has different connotations than in the West where the Sikh diaspora is much bigger and is contextualised within the immigrant phobia and its related anxieties. In Singapore, for instance, the turban is part of the assimilated identity that offers no threat. Even past connotations are not negative. The Bukit Brown cemetery in Singapore has a doctor's grave protected by statues of two turbaned Sikhs in uniform on either side, reflecting the trustworthy status they once enjoyed, particularly with the elite. In Malaysia, Sikhs are only one per cent of the population and are not considered a threat either. Celebrated Malaysian cartoonist Lad shows them as background characters in social situations as lawyers, teachers or police officers (Kaur 2011: 245). The turbaned Sikh in these portrayals is a burly, good-natured man who can, at times, look forbidding.

In China, Sikhs were deployed by the British as a police force, particularly in Shanghai. Cao Yin, from Tsinghua University, says, '… many of them actually served in the colonial police forces while their Indian and Chinese counterparts were indentured laborers, miners, craftsmen, and merchants and so became the subjects being policed' (Yin 2017: 5). In the highly nationalised Chinese narratives, Sikhs are still portrayed as conduits of the British. They continue appearing in movies and comic books as peripheral characters wearing the hated red turbans of the British paramilitary uniform. However, as Cao Yin points out, such images do not always capture the complete picture. What is lost in them is the Sikh presence in the anti-imperial Gadar party within Shanghai, the colonial hub with the greatest Sikhs presence as policemen. Cao Yin says, 'Since the Sikh migrants in Shanghai were subalterns, that they had nothing to do with the elite politics in India or China, their history has largely been distorted and forgotten in both countries' (164). Cao Yin's attempt to 'transcend the limitation of imperial and national historiographies' (164), to construct Sikhs in Shanghai as a people caught in the translocations of the colonised world, is a perspective which could yield interesting insights into the images constructed around the community in other post-colonial societies as well.

In the West, the turban has different connotations resting in the larger immigrant identity. Immigrants have always been perceived as encroachers who poach jobs, lead to cultural incursions, and pose a threat to white political and economic supremacy. The turban is a visible symbol of it all. It is not surprising then that since the earliest days of Sikh presence in the West, it has been associated with a threatening 'otherness'. Sikhs with turbans have been described in pejorative terms like 'ragheads' in US and Canada. The image has been held together by media representations too. For example, during the *Komagata Maru* incident, while the ship was docked in Canadian waters and the passengers—mostly Sikhs—were not being allowed to disembark, Canadian newspapers were actively depicting Sikhs as dangerous and threatening, their turbans caricatured to look alien. The undertones of a cultural incursion were clear and deliberate (Girn 2014). The image later gained more dangerous undertones as the political tumult of the 1980s began to be reflected in Canada. The bombing of the Air India Flight 182 from Montreal to London in 1985 killed 329 people on board, most of who were Canadians. Those responsible for it, who had made public declarations of avenging Operation Blue Star, wore turbans too. Those images got etched in the Western mind through media coverage. Sturla Gunnarsson's short film *Air India 182* (2008) is one example. The threatening connotations of these images were valid and evoked a lasting reaction. It appeared, for example, in the 1990s Canadian outrage against a Sikh being allowed to wear a turban as part of the Royal Canadian Mounted Police. The petition for revoking the order was signed by 200,000 people. Thousands of pins, showing a white man, surrounded among others by a turbaned Sikh, were sold. In Alberta, Herman Bittner brought out a calendar lampooning turbaned Sikhs, which sold 13,000 copies, at six dollars per piece. In more recent times, the Attorney General of New Jersey, Gurbir Singh ended up being called 'Turban Man' on a radio show, despite his rise within the legal-political structures of the country.

In the US, there are more deep-rooted threats associated with the turban. The turban, for Americans, and all of the West has been associated with the mysterious, threatening and different world of the East, which functions on principles alien to the West. It represents an exact opposite of all that the rational white world stands for. The Sikh turban has often been associated with all these connotations. This has impacted the Sikh image in complicated manners, particularly since the 2001 attacks on the World Trade Centre and other places by Arab fundamentalists. Many among the locals have reacted severely and are targeting anyone who could pose a similar threat in the future. The Sikh, because he seems to be flaunting this alien, dangerous identity through his physical bearing, becomes the foremost target of American hatred. To find a turbaned man freely roaming in their land, claiming their resources and doing so with an impunity that refuses to blend that difference in the melting pot, raises heckles and evokes sharp reactions. An example is the 2012 attack on the Oak Creek Gurdwara in Wisconsin, in which six Sikhs were killed. Michael Page, the white supremacist, targeted Sikhs not because they were Sikhs, but because they looked like 'enemies of his twisted version of the American ideal' says Amardeep Singh, an Associate Professor of English at Lehigh

University in Bethlehem, Pennsylvania (2012). The racial hatred against the Sikhs is thus not rising from their religious identity but one rooted in this sense of 'otherness'. It runs so deep that despite the integration of Sikhs in local communities and within political structures, the ordinary Sikh continues to be viewed with scepticism. Although the Mayor of Sacramento, Yuba Valley in California and the Vice Mayor of Manteca in California's Central Valley are both Sikhs, the huge Sikh population in these areas is most prone to racist attacks. Indian classification in the US had once classified Hindus as exotic but safe, Muslims as dangerous and Sikhs as strange. Since 9/11, the Sikhs are being seen as both strange and dangerous (Ahluwalia and Alimchandani 2012).

Moving Beyond Cultural Essentialism

The Sikh, whether in India or abroad, has remained caught in these images of the comic and the dangerous for long. Whether it is the jokes and media representations in India or the image of the 'raghead', the towel head and the camel jockey in the West, the Sikh is caught in tropes of cultural essentialism which do not allow any space for an objective opinion. These images have for long been perpetuated and reinforced through family and group settings too. Listening to family stories about other communities is a child's first exposure to in-group/out-group differentiation. It establishes their perceptions of different ethnicities and also the responses to them. For instance, non-Sikh children cracking '*barah baj gaye*' jokes or referring to a Sikh child as '*oye* sardar' in India, or a white child ridiculing one for wearing a 'beanie' on his head, are probably just mimicking adults. They unconsciously imbibe attitudes from their settings and carry them to the outside world. In-group loyalty enhances these behaviours and perpetuates skewed narratives. It is through these cycles that the images constructed around the Sikhs operate.

Meanwhile, contending with these numerous constructions, at home and abroad, is part of being Sikh. Whether it is the diminutive stereotypes of the Sikh joke, the dangerous image of the Sikh terrorist, the picture of that particular 'other' immigrant identity, each of them makes him a little more alienated, a little more 'othered'. These are also becoming increasingly awkward as he moves beyond the circumstances which generated them. The dangers of allowing these constructions to persist are to acquiesce to the narratives they generate. Social knowledge arising out of prejudicial, ethnocentric social perception and in-group reinforcement can have far-reaching effects. In due course, society begins to view the targeted individuals differently and at some level begins seeing the images woven around them 'as an idea that may hold some truth' (Goffman quoted by Hughes 2003: 1455). Analysing these is important to question that idea. It is also crucial to retrieve the individual behind the image and to bring to light the impulses that hold him ransom to those images. As these images continue to construct the Sikh in particular behavioural and attitudinal fixities, the gap between the reality and the image keeps increasing too.

Fortunately, as the community is transitioning into different directions with urbanisation, globalisation and the changes these bring, there is a certain change in response from particular quarters. Concomitant to these, there is a small but visible shift in representations both from within the community and outside. Among the community, a generation which has moved beyond the disadvantages of the past is also self-reflecting, questioning and resisting. This is bringing a more nuanced understanding of the community, its heterogeneities, its responses to the world around them. In India, while the Sikh jokes persist, cinematic representations are gradually showing a change. The Sikh stereotype is reworking itself too. The last decade has seen a stream in cinema moving beyond using Sikhs as comic relief and focusing on serious experiences which have impacted them as a community. Among these is revisiting the post-traumatic impact of Partition on an entire generation of Sikhs (*Bhag Milkha Bhag* 2013), the ordinary rural Sikh's fractured identity through the course of terrorism in Punjab (*Chauthi Koot* 2015), the continuing trauma of those who survived 1984

(*Amu* 2005) and the deep-rooted patriarchy within the Sikh mindset (*Qiissa* 2014). New portrayals are also bringing Sikhs as mainstream characters who are allowed to emerge as complete human beings creating a new public perspective. Sartaaj Singh as a police officer in *Sacred Games* (2018), a popular television series, is a significant example. As the central character in a fast-moving thriller, he is human, flawed, complex and contextualised. So is Darwan Singh, a Sikh university professor-turned-driving instructor in Manhattan in *Learning to Drive* (2015). Living in a basement like hundreds of others, he is a social being existing within a host of past and present relational, economic and political paradigms, which inform his actions as much as his being a Sikh by religion does. The movie is a refreshing portrayal from the West. In an interview, Kingsley talked of the responsibility of portraying the Sikh honestly and added that he would rather adjust the word 'responsibility', to make it sound less of a burden and more of a joy (Kingsley 2015).

New-age popular culture is emerging as another potent tool for restructuring images surrounding Sikhs. One of these is the unlikely medium of stand-up comedy. As the Sikh in a turban assumes the role of making fun instead of being made fun of, his laughter at himself is not one induced by a lack of options, but one which creates new options. This time, the comic effect is a subversive tool appropriated by him. It is used to overturn the images surrounding him, even as he plays on them in a tongue-in-cheek manner. In doing so, he makes others laugh too, not at himself, but at the absurdity of the images centred around him. Similar overtures are visible in the West too. The younger generation of Sikhs is attempting to create new images, which better represent their shifting stances. An example is the comic series created by Sureet Singh, at one time bullied for his appearance, in his US school. His central character, Deep Singh—a turban-wearing aviator, a sporty, educated, multicultural Sikh, who shares his father's love for Elvis Presley—puts across a young American Sikh's perception of himself, and one which he would like to be identified with. Dalbir Singh's 'Sikh Park', a Sikh version of South Park, with its laid-back approach, tries to diffuse the tensions surrounding the turbaned identity by approaching it through a light-hearted take on Sikhs' harmless perception of the same. An advertisement professional himself, he takes a tongue-in-cheek approach to the everyday lives and cultural practices like food habits, arranged marriages and extended kinships of the Sikhs, constructing the community as a less threatening, more relatable immigrant identity. Sikh superman, Vishavjeet Singh, a Washington-born Sikh artist has adapted the 'Captain America' comic role, created by two Jewish artists at the end of World War II, into 'Captain Sikh America', a superhero who fights all evil. After the Milwaukee incident, Vishavjeet visited public places dressed up as the superhero, tapping into the collective American memory for helping them relate to Sikhs through a positive image.

Despite these overtures, old narratives persist. As a community, the Sikhs have long lived with images, representations, significations which have othered them through the identity mandated by their religion. This has the potential of creating reverse in-group formations, which could become trigger points for pent up hostility. Through these micro-aggressions is also created 'prioritisation of affiliation towards faith over other aspects of identity'(Ahluwalia and Alimchandani 2012: 10). In a world that is increasingly connected through common concerns, it is important to resist insularity of such kind. There is a need from either side to look into the social mirror and to 'reflect on aspects of identity rendered invisible by convention' (Spencer 2006: xix). It is only through this that the people behind images could emerge and connect. For the majority in India, it is important to understand that the Sikhs as a separate identity have moved far beyond the point where their separation was a matter of contention. They have developed into a religious and social identity with established conventions and practices, which in certain aspects are different from those of the majority. Their similarities cannot be denied for they are born of a common culture, yet the difference needs to be acknowledged too and integrated into broader perceptions. For the community too, an objective understanding and acknowledgement of the many points of deflection in the course of building this separate identity are important. It will allow an understanding of the impetus behind the othering and perhaps an effort at bridging it. How the identity constructions shift in other parts of the world will have much to do with how the community projects itself. Meanwhile, small overtures at breaking ill-fitting images might create a momentum for the construction of more relevant ones in future.

References

Ahluwalia, Muninder K. and Anjali Alimchandani. 2012. 'A Call to Integrate Religious Communities Into Practice: The Case of the Sikhs'. In *Counselling Psychologist*, XX(X). Available at: http/tcp.sagepub.com. 31 January 2012 (accessed on January 25 2020).

Boskin, Joseph and Joseph Dorinson. 1985. 'Ethnic Humor: Subversion and Survival'. In *American Humor American Quarterly*, Special Issue, Spring, 37(1). John Hopkins University Press.

Das, Veena. 2007. 'In the Region of Rumor'. In *Life and Words: Violence and the Descent into the Ordinary*. New Delhi: Oxford University Press.

———. 2007. 'Thinking of Time and Subjectivity'. In *Life and Words: Violence and the Descent into the Ordinary*. New Delhi: Oxford University Press.

Davies, Christie. 1998. 'Stupidity and Rationality'. In *Jokes and Their Relation to Society*. Berlin, New York, Mouton de Gruyter: Mouton de Gruyter.

Girg, Naveen. 2014. 'Kum-We-Gotum-Maru'. In 'Racism of Political Cartoons | Komagata Maru'. Posted on 25 July in *The Georgia Straight proudly sponsors Komagata Maru 1914-2014: Generations, Geographies and Echoes*. Available at: https://www.straight.com/blogra/647431/georgia-straight-proudly-sponsors-komagata-maru-1914-2014-generations-geographies-and-echoes (accessed on 19 January 2020).

Handoo, Jawaharlal. 1990. 'Folk Narrative and Ethnic Identity: The "Sardarji Joke Cycle"'. In *Story Telling in Contemporary Societies*, edited by Lutz Rohrich, Sabine Wienker-Piepho. Tubingen: Gunter Narr.

Hughes, Melissa K. 2003. 'Through the Looking Glass: Racial Jokes, Social Context, and The Reasonable Person in Hostile Work Environment Analysis'. In *Southern California Law Review*, 76: 1437–1482.

Kaur, Kiranjit. 2011. 'Perception of Sikhs in Malaysia through a Malaysian Cartoonist's Lens'. In *Sikhs in South East Asia: Negotiating Identity*, edited by A.B. Shamsul and Arunajeet Kaur. Singapore: ISEAS Publishing.

Kingsley, Ben. 2015. 'Interview with Brad Wheeler, Ben Kingsley on Honouring Sikhism: Responsibly as a Lead Character'. In *The Globe and Mail*, 27 August.

Kuipers, Giselinde. 1971. 'Introduction: Jokes Humor and Taste'. In *Good Humor, Bad Humor, A Sociology of the Joke*. Berlin: Mouton de Gruyter.

Mehta, Parvinder. 2013. 'Imagining Sikhs: The Ethics of Representation and the Spectacle of Otherness in Bollywood Cinema'. In *Sikh Formations: Religion, Culture, Theory*. Available at: https://doi.org/10.1080/17448727.2013.774708 (accessed on 1 February 2020).

Singh, Amardeep. 2012. 'Being Sikh in America'. *The New York Times*. Available at: https://india.blogs.nytimes.com/2012/08/07/being-sikh-in-america/ (accessed on I February 2020).

Singh, Harleen. 2006. 'Tur (Banned) Masculinities: Terrorists, Sikhs, and Trauma in Indian Cinema'. In *Sikh Formations: Religion, Culture, Theory*, 2(2):115–204.

Spencer, Stephen. 2006. 'Introduction'. In *Race and Ethnicity: Culture, Identity and Representation*. Routledge: New York.

Yin, Cao. 2017. *From Policemen to Revolutionaries: A Sikh Diaspora in Global Shanghai, 1885–1945*. Brill.

Films

Air India 182. Produced by David York. Directed by Sturla Gunnarson. April 2008.

Amu. Directed by Shonali Bose. 2005, India

Bhag Milkha Bhag. Directed by Rakesh Omprakash Mehra. ROMP Pictures. July 2013, India.

Chauthi Koot. Directed by Gurvinder Singh. May 2015, India.

Learning to Drive. Directed by Isobel Coixet. August 2015, Germany.

Quissa, Indo-German venture. Directed by Anup Singh. 2014 (Germany), 2015 (India).

Sacred Games. Netflix series based on a novel by Vikram Chandra. Directed by Anurag Kashyap, Neeraj Ghaywan and Vikramaditya Motwane. 2018.

Conclusion

Continuity in Change: A Centre that Holds

To see people as a whole, one needs to see them through multiple, shifting and intersecting paradigms without 'imposing a false coherence on that synthesis' (Howard 2000: 388). The Sikh community has evolved through a confluence of heterogeneities and histories that must be taken into account for understanding its diversities. Equally important is the need to look beyond a certain set perception to understand its shifting engagements in the present. With an intrinsic need to improve their condition and an inbuilt spirit of enterprise, Sikhs have constantly moved out of given situations into new ones. They have also been responsive to the demands of new environments and have adjusted and grown within these. The different transitions have added new dimensions to their profile, and continue to do so. It is necessary to bring these into cognisance to build a complete understanding of the Sikh. However, an understanding of this multiplicity and its ever-growing facets would be incomplete unless these are contextualised within the binding potential of the Sikh way of life. While this work has focused on Sikhs as a social rather than a religious category, the two facets are not mutually exclusive. Sikhism is as much about social life as the spiritual one. Its core humanitarian values provide common practices and structures to is adherents, weaving a strong and tenacious thread through their multiplicities. The synthesis it creates is not a superficial one, but one that has the potential to absorb within itself the multiplicities and the shifting facets of the community. As new dimensions of identity gain importance, as the pressure to conform to common cosmopolitan identities increases, this not only helps to hold the centre together but also aids in forging new links, both within and outside the community.

As the community moves out of traditional social and occupational structures, one of the major issues it contends with is the preservation of its unique identity in new environments. Sikhs are moving out of culturally entrenched family and community settings, and thereby from the norms through which the community's social as well as religious identity has evolved and functioned. Pressures of blending into mainstream cultures also impact those living far away from group ratifications. All this creates the possibility of a diluted identity, in terms of religious and cultural practices. However, Sikhs seem to be resisting these pressures well. Wherever in the world they have spread, they have not only sustained these connections but proactively nurtured them. Their religious identity has proved to be the one factor drawing them close despite their internal differences. This could be attributed to the fact that both the Sikh family and the community structures have inbuilt mechanisms of cohesion. The Sikh nuclear family continues to carry its religious codes in its everyday practices. Despite the professional and intercultural connections that the Sikhs forge, their connection to their community stays strong because Sikh social life is intricately entwined with its religious systems. All important life events—including birth, death and marriage—continue to be closely connected, not only to religious traditions but also to *sangat* or congregation. The importance of the congregation automatically leads to the establishment of institutions. Wherever a group of Sikhs go, they find or build a gurdwara, which then becomes the fulcrum drawing people to itself. The well-defined routines in the gurdwaras, the community kitchens that call for participation from community members, the confluence between the family and community through frequent religious gatherings provide Sikhs not only with a well-developed sense of belonging to the religion but also to an entrenched community identity.

It is through this enculturation that the subsequent generations of Sikhs keep connected. Despite questioning many of the traditions, like the young everywhere in the world do, they identify with its core practices. In times of crises, almost all turn to faith. A visit to any of the major gurdwaras, even in bigger cosmopolitan cities, reveals a surprisingly large number of boys and girls, who turn up for *matha tekna* or paying obeisance before or after their working or college hours. Most among them believe that connection to community and religion gives them a sense of belonging. There is complete assent to the sense of homecoming, which religion brings. The sound of kirtan and the smell of *parshad*, the rhythm of *Japji Sahib* and the *Rehraas Sahib* are links to the solidarity they feel towards faith, family and community. This is true not only within the home country. In the West, while the old gurdwara politics constructed around differences in groups and castes is slowly losing favour among the younger generation, the gurdwara itself remains important. It allows a generation struggling with so many shifts to have the one anchor that remains constant. Interestingly, there is a trend among the educated and articulate younger lot among the community, to consciously replace their group and caste referents with 'Singh' and 'Kaur'. These second names, common to all Sikh men and women, not only distinguish them as Sikhs but also provide a common identity cutting across all internal differences.

One area of pertinent concern revolves around some among the younger generation doing away with the physical form by which Sikhs have been known the world over, and which is among the fundamental constructs of the Sikh identity. A turban has been the primary distinguishing marker of Sikh identity. There has always been a strong family and community emphasis on keeping unshorn hair and wearing a turban in the case of men. A turban, for Sikh boys, reflects the primary identity they have grown up with. It is one, which has been maintained by their elders and what they recognise as the norm. For those living away from mainstream Sikh culture, it also becomes the means of connecting to group identity and maintaining a sense of self. Sikhs have preserved this identity as a symbol of faith, solidarity and at times, defiance too. However, the pressure to blend into mainstream identities is also leading a part of the younger section into relinquishing this identity. This trend has been more prevalent among the Jat Sikhs, perhaps because they have experienced greater movement out of traditional structures and have faced difficulties in dealing with 'otherness' and stereotyping. However, in recent times, the trend is catching up with other sections of the community too, which have otherwise followed the Khalsa codes more strictly and emphasised on the *sabat surat* identity.

For the old guard, this is, in no uncertain terms, completely unpardonable, for it strikes at the root of the visible manifestation of the Khalsa identity, which has, over time, become synonymous with Sikh identity. It is also a betrayal of centuries of struggle to sustain that identity and the ideological stances it has generated in that course. The catch lies in the fact that for the younger section choosing to dispense with it, it is less about withdrawing allegiance to the faith or group identity and more about finding easier ways to negotiate with other social contexts they are traversing. Unfortunately, a relinquishing of the most recognisable referent of Sikh identity will entail a dilution of that identity, as we know it today. However, for those who take the step, it seemingly does not entail a break with the faith, which that identity signifies. In fact, they continue to proactively build an affirmative social identity rooted in the core values of that faith. Their connection to their religion is intact though fraught with a wilfulness, which seeks more space and flexibility.

Just as there have been apprehensions about the survival of old religious ethics amidst other cultural pressures, there has also been a curiosity over the future forms that Sikh social identity will take. The heterogeneity within the community has involved fissures. Will these be taken forward within the shifts being experienced? Or, will a common religious identity forge new links, as old social structures crumble? For those from the trader communities, movement out of traditional businesses, the consequent breakdown of joint-family structures, the dilution of the *biradari* have also impacted the pressures all these wielded for adherence to group solidarity and the social rules, which maintained their insularity. For the agriculturists, the shift from villages has involved a disconnect with the social codes and family structures, which once defined a social identity revolving around ownership of land. Over the last few decades, a greater focus on education and new opportunities in the urban contexts have created a shift in priorities. A movement away from environments that fostered earlier identities and a cosmopolitan life which works through prioritizing a homogenous urban culture, has impacted all sections of Sikh life. This, as discussed earlier, has also led to many psychological implications for the cusp generation, who attempt to maintain group insularities within the changed circumstances, thereby passing on the exclusivities to the next generation.

Within these pressures, however, are emerging beginnings of a new kind of community cohesiveness. While the historical differences between the different constituent identities continue to persist, there is the emergence of another section defined by a common Sikh identity, especially among the educated younger generation. Similarities in their everyday lives and the larger global cultures in which they operate are constantly shaping their sense of self. For them, differences based on group and caste identities are losing some of the meaning. Instead, education, profession and similarity in social strata are becoming new sought-after commonalities. Polarisation based on stereotypical notions of intra-community identities, is also losing ground except when there are none of the more contemporary markers to fall back on. The result is a slow coming together of people from different groups in social settings.

Such sociocultural shifts within the shifting framework of urban economics are not new to Punjabi society. Between the 18th and 19th centuries, as the Punjabi urban population increased from 9.8 per cent in 1881 to 13 per cent in 1947, people had moved to new areas in pursuit of education and employment. The concept of caste-based mohallas or neighbourhoods in which the *biradaris* wielded clout had begun to decline. It led to new settlements, where professionals, tradesmen and artisans from all over West Punjab came to settle. Instead of caste-based neighbourhoods, those with people from particular professions and strata sprang up. This led to regrouping, which diluted the strictness of sub-caste distinctions in matters of marriages too. 'This was the beginning of the broadening of the endogamous unit which the scholars are noting today as emblematic of metropolitan cities of modern India' (Malhotra 2002: 38).

A similar social shift seems to be consolidating rather than disrupting the fabric of the Sikh community today. For the contemporary educated and professional Sikh strata in their 20s and 30s for example, the narrative of the Jat-Khatri-Arora differences seems to be toning down. Despite initial parental opposition, there are already increasing instances of marriages between boys and girls from different sub-castes for whom being Sikh suffices. These new constructs are still in the process of evolving. Years of differences make bridging a slow process, but the change seems to be configuring itself out slowly.

Yet another concern centres around how the community will be perceived in times to come. For a long time, Sikhs have been embroiled in political struggles, which have led to images of dissent getting constructed around them. As circumstances have changed, so have the pressures and stances, making possible a more inclusive position for the community. The core practices of a common faith, which bring Sikhs together across caste, class and demographic differences are helping build a new profile for the community. *Vand chhakko* or 'share what you have' and *sewa* or 'service' are the two core socio-religious injunctions that have always driven the social outreach of the community. As the canvas grows bigger, so does the scope of Sikh humanitarian work. In an age of quick dissemination through digital means, their overtures are becoming more visible to the world too.

Images like Sikhs reaching out to those hit by natural calamities, such as floods and earthquakes, Sikhs opening their shrines to victims of terrorism, Sikhs helping rescue people out of riot-hit areas, Sikhs creating an infrastructure for people in need of medical help are only some of these. Among these, langar or the Sikh community kitchen has become the most acknowledged practice at home and abroad; '*langar* has always been a form of outreach, and inter-religious, inter-cultural exchange' (Desjardins and Desjardins 2009). However, its scope in terms of its ability to operate as an institutionalised structure to deal with calamities is gradually becoming more recognisable. It has caught the larger imagination amidst the human tragedy unfolding in a world struck by the pandemic. As India sees migrant labourers reduced to destitution and forced into displacement from major urban hubs, gurdwaras across the country have created one of the most effective non-government food security systems. That the labour, money and produce are all voluntary, that the system recognises no class, caste or religious demarcations, is seeping into broader cognition. Food banks in Canada, free mobile food support in areas of the UK, packaged food for elderly in New York and Australia are parts of the same common impetus. This is not only creating a counter-narrative to the many negatives, which the community has been contending with, but also binding it together in its commitment to the values propounded by a common faith.

As the community diversifies into new profiles, there thus remains a connecting link holding it together. It not only prevents it from falling apart but also provides it with means to forge new cohesions. An understanding of the Sikhs must, therefore, derive from within the confluence of this core identity and many others, which make them the people they are. It also lies in recognizing that they profess their faith and follow the values endorsed by it in dealing with a complex social world, through a mutiplicity which moves beyond a singular identity.

References

Desjardins, Michael and Ellen Desjardins. 2009. 'Food that Builds Community: The Sikh Langar in Canada'. In *Cuizine: The Journal of Canadian Food Culture / Revue des cultures culinaires au Canada*, edited by Nathalie Cooke (editor-in-chief), 1(2). McGill University Library.

Howard, Judith. 2000. 'Social Psychology of Identities'. In *Annual Review of Sociology*, 367–393.

Jodhka, Surinder S. 2009. 'Sikhs in Contemporary Times: Religious Identities and Discourses of Development'. In *Sikh Formations*, 5(1): 1–22. Available at: http://dx.org/10.1080/17448720902935029 (accessed on 12 February 2020).

Malhotra, Anshu. 2002. 'Gender, Caste and Religious Identities in Punjab'. In *Gender Caste and Religious Identities: Restructuring Class in Colonial Punjab*. New Delhi: Oxford University Press.

Glossary

Aarti: A Hindu religious ritual with symbolic representations of air, water, fire and earth. A plate carrying a fire in the form of a lighted lamp is circulated amongst participants accompanied by singing of hymns.

Adi Granth: The First Book; an early compilation of Sikh scriptures by the fifth guru, Guru Arjan Dev*ji* in 1604. More verses were later added to it by the tenth guru.

Akhand path: Non-stop recitation of the Guru Granth Sahib. Among Sikhs *akhand path*s are held for all important life events.

Akhara: A seminary with boarding and lodging for training of sadhus or holy men. Different sects have traditionally had their own *akhara*s.

Amrit: Nectar for initiation

Ardaas: A short Sikh prayer conducted after the completion of the prayer routine. It is also conducted before commencing any important event or work.

Balle balle: A phrase used to depict an upbeat, happy attitude

Bhai (brother): In Sikh parlance, a formal title given to a scholar of *gurmat*

Bandook: Gun

Bania: Dealers in grains, petty shopkeepers, moneylenders

Bhangra: A vigorous dance performed by men in Punjab. It is connected to the harvesting season and is performed to the beats of the dhol or drum.

Biradari (brotherhood): Referring to members of a particular caste or subcaste, eg., Khatri *biradari*. Elders and important members of a *biradari* could gather and take decisions on various issues.

Chamar: One of the groups among the Dalits, now classified as a Scheduled Caste

Dargah: A shrine built on the grave of a respected religious leader. Dargahs are generally related to Sufi saints and follow Muslim practices.

Dasam Granth: A collection of works attributed to Guru Gobind Singh, the tenth Sikh guru. There is a controversy on whether all compositions are by Guru Gobind Singh*ji*, or some are composed by court poets.

Dera: A commune; in Punjab, there has been a tradition of *dera*s, many times started by those who rivalled the claims of Sikh gurus. In more recent times, *deras* have been spaces of Dalit mobilisation. Khalsa Sikhs are against the *dera* tradition.

Gidda: An energetic folk dance performed by women in Punjab. It is accompanied by folk songs and clapping by women.

Granthi: People trained in the reading and explaining of Guru Granth Sahib, the Sikh scripture

Gurupurab: Birth or death anniversary of any of the Sikh gurus

Guru ghar: The guru's abode, gurdwara; also loosely refers to the practices and disciplines, which emerged from the teachings of the gurus.

Hallabol: War cry; Sikhs in Nanded celebrate Sikh martial identity by gathering at an allotted place called the Halla Bol Chowk. There is a display of traditional weapons used in Sikh armies and enactment of war-like situations. People too gather and run on the streets with naked kirpans, the mandatory sword.

Harijan: Children of God; a term given by Mahatma Gandhi to the outcastes of society. The term has been more or less replaced by Dalit.

Hola Mohalla: A day designated by Guru Gobind Singh, the tenth guru, for demonstrating martial skills and mockwar drills. It precedes by one day, the festival of Holi, where people sprinkle colour on each other. The first such drill was held in Anandpur in 1701.

Haveli: Mansion, owned by a rich person

Hukumnama: An order given by the gurus

Jagir: Feudal land grants with tax collection rights

Jagirdar: Those who were granted feudal lands with tax collection rights

Japji: A composition by Guru Nanak, the founder of Sikhism. Guru Granth Sahib starts with Japji Sahib. Japji Sahib is also a part of *nitnem*, the daily religious routine of Sikhs in which five compositions are to be recited.

Jatha: In Sikh parlance, a squad. *Jatha*s have been created for different reasons. There can be an armed *jatha*, a *jatha* to present political demands, a *kirtani jatha*, a pilgrim's *jatha*, etc.

Jatka: A term used by the non-agricultural classes to denote a choice which is rustic, unrefined

Jaloos: Religious procession

Janamsakhi tradition: Literature dealing with the life and teachings of Guru Nanak. It elucidates Guru Nanak's life, teachings, mystic concepts through small interesting narratives. Invaluable for the information it provides though its historical validity is questioned by some.

Jo bole so nihal, Sat sri akal: He who speaks of the timeless God, finds deliverance; clarion call of the Sikhs. It is also used at the end of Sikh prayers.

Kachche Sikh: Not fully formed Sikh

Keshdhari: Sikhs who observe the Khalsa tradition of keeping unshorn hair

Khalsa: Tradition started by Guru Gobind Singh, to initiate Sikhs through 'amrit' or nectar into a life defined by codes of conduct and adoption of the five Ks—Kesh (unshorn hair), Kirpan (sword/dagger), Kada (iron bracelet), Kangha (comb) and Kachcha (breeches used as inner wear).

Khande ka pahul: The word *pahul* means an agent which accelerates the potentialities of a given object. *Khande di Pahul* is a ceremony where water in an iron bowl is stirred with a *khanda*, or a double-edged sword, while reciting Sikh prayers. This is administered to those being baptised into the Khalsa. The ceremony was started by Guru Gobind Singh in 1699, when he first started the Khalsa.

Kirpan: A small dagger or sword carried by *amritdhari* Sikhs. Sikhs were mandated by the tenth guru to adopt five Ks. Kirpan was one of them.

Kirtan: Musical rendition of hymns from Guru Granth Sahib

Kirtaniyas: Those who are trained in rendition of hymns, in the ragas specified in Guru Granth Sahib

Kachcha vehra: Mud-plastered open courtyard

Kurta pyjama: Loose long shirt and loose trousers

Langar: Community kitchen

Langri: Cook in the Sikh community kitchens

Lathait: Literally strongmen carrying *lathi*s or solid sticks. Generally used by the powerful and influential people to have their way through force.

Maafi: Pardon; in text, excused from payment of tax

Mahants: Custodians of a *math*, dera or other religious establishments. They became hereditary controllers of Sikh shrines though they were not initiated as Sikhs. There was corruption and self-aggrandisement among them.

Mahua: An Indian tropical tree. Its bark, leaves and flowers are used for various purposes. *Mahua* is used in making soaps, detergents, fertilisers and an alcoholic drink.

Mannat: A wish, a prayer

Math: A place with lodging and boarding, primarily for students of religion, presided over by a religious teacher

Matha tekna: To bow down in reverence before Guru Granth Sahib, and touch the head to the ground as a mark of deference.

Masand: A representative of the Sikh Guru, who collected *dasvand*, one-tenth of the earnings from the Sikhs, in the name of the guru

Mata*ji*: Respectful nomenclature for mother

Misl: A unit of Sikh warriors, claiming control over territories acquired by them

Morcha: March or rally, generally in protest against a government decision

Nagar kirtan: Religious procession, taken around the town or city

Namghar: Prayer houses where Assamese community gathers for prayers

Nanakpanthis: Followers of Guru Nanak's teachings; in Guru Nanak's time, they came from different backgrounds. There are still many people adhering to this identity without being Sikhs in the way the community is perceived of now. Sindhis are an example of such.

Nihangs: Traditional armed Sikh warriors characterised by their blue clothes and huge adorned turbans. They still wear their traditional clothes, although with time they have lost their old roles in the Sikh community.

Patwari: Village registrar

Panth: In Sikh parlance, it refers to the community which follow the path shown by the Sikh gurus. It also has political connotations in terms of reference to Sikhs as a political identity.

Phulkari: A floral embroidery technique typical to Punjab. Synonymous with the work on thick handwoven rust-colured *chadar*s called *bagh*s and dupattas.

Pind: Village

Pindadaan: A ritual performed for ancestors who are dead. The son performs *pindadaan* to aid the dead person's soul to move to the world beyond, relinquishing his attraction to the people and things he has left behind

Putt chamaran de: Sons of Chamars

Putt Jattan de: Sons of Jats

Ragi: People trained in classical music to sing hymns in different ragas as prescribed in the Guru Granth Sahib

Rehit: Code of conduct

Rehitnama: Collection of codes of conduct for Sikhs

Rehraas: The daily evening prayer of the Sikhs. It has hymns from Guru Granth Sahib and the Dasam Granth.

Sabat surat: Sikhs who keep unshorn hair and maintain all five Ks.

Safai karmchari: Sweepers

Sahukar: Moneylender

Sakhi tradition: In the storytelling tradition; many of these were written after the passing away of the first guru.

Salwar kameez: Long shirt with loose billowy trousers

Sanatan Dharm: The eternal dharma; it refers to traditional Hindu thought as it existed before reformist Hindu movements. It does not have sectarian leanings or ideological divisions. It represents a code of ethical conduct.

Sanatani Sikhs: Sikhs who follow the spiritual teachings of the Sikh gurus and also a wide range of beliefs drawn from Hinduism.

Sandhya: The Hindu evening prayer ritual which generally consists of the lighting of a lamp in the prayer area and performing *aarti*. There could be other variations too.

Sangat: Congregation, group of people meeting for religious purposes.

Sewa: Service

Sewadar: Those who offer services in gurdwaras. Many offer voluntary services. Permanent *sewadar*s are given remuneration.

*Shabad*s: Hymns taken from the Guru Granth Sahib

*Shehri*s: City dwellers

Shraadh: Hindus perform *shraadh* to express gratitude and pay homage to their dead parents.

Sikh *aarti*: A composition by Guru Nanak in which the universe and nature celebrate the presence of God

Sikh *samaaj*: Sikh social and religious community

Sikhi: A way of life which derives from the philosophy and social teachings of the ten Sikh gurus

Suniar: Community of people working as goldsmiths

Sukhmani Sahib: Composition by Guru Arjan Dev*ji*, the fifth Sikh guru. He composed it around 1602, before he compiled the Adi Granth.

Thekedar: Contractor

Udasi: A religious, ascetic sect, started by Guru Nanak's son Sri Chand in 1494. It considers itself a derivative of Sikhism but is pushed to the peripheries by Sikhs.

Var: Chapter

Waheguru: The wondrous God

Zamindars: Land-owning aristocrats who reserved the right to collect taxes on behalf of the imperial classes; now also used for prosperous land-owning classes.

Bibliography

Ahluwalia, Munider K. and Anjali Alimchandani. 2012. 'A Call to Integrate Religious Communities Into Practice: The Case of the Sikhs'. In *Counselling Psychologist*, XX(X). Available at: http/tcp.sagepub.com (accessed on 2 February 2020).

Alcoff, Linda Martin. 2006. 'The Identity Crisis in Feminist Theory'. In *Visible Identities: Race, Gender, and the Self*. New York: Oxford University Press.

Allport, Gordon W. 1985. Quoted by Joseph Boskin and Joseph Dorinson. 'Ethnic Humor: Subversion and Survival'. In *American Quarterly*, Special Issue: American Humor (Spring), 37 (1). John Hopkins University Press.

Ames, Michael M. and Joy Inglis. 'Conflict and Change in British Columbia Sikh Family Life'. In *British Columbia Studies*, Winter 1973–1974, (20).

Armstrong, John. 2007. Quoted by Khachig Tololyan. 2007. 'The Contemporary Discourse for Diaspora Studies'. In *Project Muse, Comparative Studies of South Asia, Africa and Middle East*, 27 (3).

Baldwin, Shauna Singh. ([1999] 2011). *What the Body Remembers*. Canada: Knopf, New Delhi, Rupa Publications.

Banerjee, Himadri. 2007. 'The Other Sikhs'. In *A View from Eastern India*, Vol 1: 225. New Delhi: Manohar Publishers.

———. 2014. 'Sikhs Living Beyond Punjab in India'. In *The Oxford Handbook of Sikh Studies*, edited by Pashaura Singh and Louis E. Fenech. UK: Oxford University Press.

———. 2018. '(Curfew-Read) Lives & Histories of Mazhabi Sikhs of Shillong and Guwahati'. Available at: https://www.raiot.in/curfew-read-lives-histories-of-mazhbi-sikhs-of-shillong-and-guwahati/ (accessed on 4 February 2020).

———. 2018. 'Sikhs and Sikhism in Bihar: Their Distinctiveness and Diversity'. In *Sikh Formations*, 14 (2): 167–187.

Behl, Natasha. 2010. Politics of Equality: Caste and Gender Paradoxes in the Sikh Community. Unpublished PhD Dissertation: Department of Political Science, University of California, Los Angeles.

Berman, Marshall. 2011. Quoted by Nicola Mooney. 'Introduction'. In *Rural Nostalgias and Transnational Dreams: Identity and Modernity Among Jat Sikhs*. Canada: University of Toronto.

Bhattacharya, G. 2000. 'The School Adjustment of South Asian Immigrant Children in the United States'. In *Adolescence*, 35 (137).

Billig, Michael. 2001. 'Humour and Hatred: The Racist Jokes of the Ku Klux Klan'. In *Discourse and Society*, 12 (3).

Boskin, Joseph and Joseph Dorinson. 1985. 'Ethnic Humor: Subversion and Survival'. In *American Humor American Quarterly*, Special Issue, 37(1), Spring, John Hopkins University Press.

Bramadet, Paul. 2010. Quoted by Doris Jakobsh. 'Contextualizing the Issues'. In *Sikhism and Women: History, Texts, and Experience*, edited by Doris. R. Jakobsh, 4. New Delhi: Oxford University Press.

Brass, P R. 2008. Quoted by Giorgio Shani. 'The Territorialisation of the Quam'. In *Sikh Nationalism and Identity in a Global Age*. New York: Routledge.

Brah, Avtar. 1988. 'Border and Transnational Identities'. In *Feminist Post-Colonial Theory, A Reader*, edited by Reina Lewis and Sara Mills. Edinburg: Edinburg University Press.

———. 2005. 'Diaspora, Border and Transnational Identities'. In *Cartographies of Diaspora, Contesting Identities*. London: Routledge.

Cohen, Robert. 2008. 'Four Phases of Diaspora Studies'. In *Global Diasporas, An Introduction*, second edition. USA and Canada: Routledge.

Das, Veena. 2007. *Life and Words: Violence and the Descent into the Ordinary*. New Delhi: Oxford University Press.

Dasgupta, Rana. 2014. '1947'. *Capital: A Portrait of Twenty-First Century Delhi*. Noida: Fourth Estate, Harper Collins.

Davies, Christi. 1998. 'Stupidity and Rationality'. In *Jokes and Their Relation to Society*. Berlin, New York, Mouton de Gruyter: Mouton de Gruyter.

Desjardins, Michael and Ellen Desjardins. 2009. 'Food that Builds Community: The Sikh Langar in Canada'. In *Cuizine: The Journal of Canadian Food Culture / Revue des cultures culinaires au Canada*, edited by Nathalie Cooke (editor-in-chief), 1(2). McGill University Library.

Dhavan, Purnima. 2014. 'Sikhism in the Eighteenth Century'. In *The Oxford Handbook of Sikh Studies*, edited by Pashaura Singh and Louis E. Fenech. UK: Oxford University Press.

Dusenbury, Verne. 2011. 'Southeast Asian Sikhs in Global Perspective'. In *Sikhs in South East Asia: Negotiating Identity*, edited by A.B. Shamsul and Arunajeet Kaur. Singapore: ISEAS Publishing.

Freud, Sigmund. 2003. Quoted by Melissa K. Hughes. 'Through the Looking Glass: Racial Jokes, Social Context, and the Reasonable Person in Hostile Work Environment Analysis'. In *Southern California Law Review*, 76: 1437.

Girg, Naveen. 2014. 'Kum-We-Gotum-Maru'. In 'Racism of Political Cartoons | Komagata Maru'. Posted on 25 July in *The Georgia Straight proudly sponsors Komagata Maru 1914-2014: Generations, Geographies and Echoes*. Available at: https://www.straight.com/blogra/647431/georgia-straight-proudly-sponsors-komagata-maru-1914-2014-generations-geographies-and-echoes (accessed on 19 January 2020).

Goffman, Erving. 2003. Quoted by Melissa K. Hughes. 'Through the Looking Glass: Racial Jokes, Social Context, and the Reasonable Person in Hostile Work Environment Analysis'. In *Southern California Law Review*, 76: 1455.

Gadamer, Hans Georg. (2006 [1991)). Quoted by Linda Martin Alcoff. 'Real Identities'. In *Visible Identities: Race, Gender, and the Self*. Oxford University Press.

Gupta, Dipankar. 2012. 'Whither the Indian Village'. In *Village Society*, edited by Surinder S. Jodhka. Hyderabad: Orient Blackswan.

Hall, Stuart. 2014. Quoted by Priya Khanna Mahajani. 'Introduction'. In *Mobility and Identity: A Study of Jat Sikhs in Chandigarh*. US: Xlibris UK.

Handoo, Jawaharlal. 1990. 'Folk Narrative and Ethnic Identity: The "Sardarji Joke Cycle"'. In *Story Telling in Contemporary Societies*, edited by Lutz Rohrich, Sabine Wienker-Piepho. Tubingen: Gunter Narr.

Hans, Raj Kumar. 2016. 'Making Sense of Dalit History'. In *Dalit Studies*, edited by Ramnarayan S. Rawat and K Satyanarayana. Duke University Press.

Hasenaur, Jim. 1988. 'Using Ethnic Humor to Expose Ethnocentrism'. In *ETC: A Review of General Semantics*, Winter, December, 45 (4).

Hobbes. (2003 [1437]). Quoted by Melissa K. Hughes. In 'Through the Looking Glass: Racial Jokes, Social Context, and the Reasonable Person in Hostile Work Environment Analysis'. In *Southern California Law Review*, 76: 1437.

Howard, Judith. 2000. 'Social Psychology of Identities'. In *Annual Review of Sociology*, 367–393.

Hughes, Melissa K. 2003. 'Through the Looking Glass: Racial Jokes, Social Context, and The Reasonable Person in Hostile Work Environment Analysis'. In *Southern California Law Review*, 76: 1437–1482.

Ibbetson, Denzil. 2002. Quoted by Anshu Malhotra. 'Gender, Caste and Religious Identities in Punjab'. In Gender, Caste, and Religious Identities: Restructuring Class in Colonial Punjab. New Delhi: Oxford University Press.

Jakobsh, Doris R. and Eleanor Nesbitt. 2010. 'Sikhism and Women: Contextualizing Issues'. In *Sikhism and Women: History, Texts, and Experience*, edited by Doris. R. Jakobsh. New Delhi: Oxford University Press.

Jakobsh, Doris. 2015. 'Seeking the Image of "Unmarked" Sikh Women: Text, Sacred Stitches, Turban'. In *Religion and Gender*, 5(1): 35–51. DOI: 18352/rg. 10085.

Jodhka, Surinder S. 2009. 'Sikhs in Contemporary Times: Religious Identities and Discourses of Development'. In *Sikh Formations*, 5(1): 1–22. Available at: http://dx.org/10.1080/17448720902935029 (accessed on 12 February 2020).

———. 2009. 'What Makes Sikhs a Minority'. Available at: http://www.india-seminar.com/2009/602/602_surinder_jodhka.htm (accessed on 4 March).

———. 2010. 'The Sikhs Today: A Development Profile'. In *Religions and Development, India: Working Paper Series*, 01(02). Indian Institute of Dalit Studies, and Religions and Development Research Programme.

———. 2012. 'Whither the Indian Village'. In *Village Society*, edited by Surinder S. Jodhka. Hyderabad: Orient Blackswan.

———. 2014. 'Changing Manifestations of Caste in Sikh Panth'. In *The Oxford Handbook of Sikh Studies*, edited by Pashaura Singh and Louis E. Fenech. Oxford: Oxford University Press.

Kalsi, Sewa Singh. 1999. 'The Sikhs and Caste: The Development of Ramgarhia Identity in Britain'. In *Sikh Identity: Continuity and Change*, edited by Pashaura Singh and N. Gerald Barrier. New Delhi: Manohar Publishers.

Kapur, Preeti and Girishwar Misra. 2010. 'Changing Identities and Fixed Roles: The Experiences of Sikh Women'. In *Sikhism and Women:*

History, Texts, and Experience, edited by Doris. R. Jakobsh. New Delhi: Oxford University Press.

Kaur, Amarjit. 2011.'Sikh Migration and Settlement in South East Asia, 1870s–1950s, Social Transformations, Homeland, and Identity'. In *Sikhs in South East Asia: Negotiating Identity*, edited by Shamsul A.B. and Arunajeet Kaur. Singapore: ISEAS Publishing.

Kaur, Arunajeet. 2011. 'Introduction: Studying Southeast Asia'. In *Sikhs in South East Asia: Negotiating Identity*, edited by Shamsul A.B. and Arunajeet Kaur. Singapore: ISEAS Publishing.

Kaur, Kiranjit. 2011. 'Perception of Sikhs in Malaysia through a Malaysian Cartoonist's Lens'. In *Sikhs in South East Asia: Negotiating Identity*, edited by A.B. Shamsul and Arunajeet Kaur. Singapore: ISEAS Publishing.

Kingsley, Ben. 2015. 'Interview with Brad Wheeler, Ben Kingsley on Honouring Sikhism: Responsibly as a Lead Character'. In *The Globe and Mail*, 27 August.

Kuipers, Giselinde. 1971. 'Introduction: Jokes Humor and Taste'. In *Good Humor, Bad Humor, A Sociology of the Joke*. Berlin: Mouton de Gruyter.

M, Hawley. 2017. 'Migration, Sikh'. In *Encyclopedia of Indian Religions*, edited by Arvind Pal-Singh Mandair. Dordrecht: Springer.

Mahajani, Priya Khanna. 2014. 'Conclusions and Inferences'. In *Mobility and Identity: A Study of Jat Sikhs in Chandigarh*. US: Xlibris UK.

Malhotra, Anshu. 2002. 'Gender, Caste and Religious Identities in Punjab'. In *Gender Caste and Religious Identities: Restructuring Class in Colonial Punjab*. New Delhi: Oxford University Press.

———. 2010. 'Shameful Continuities'. In *Sikhism and Women: History, Texts, and Experience*, edited by Doris. R. Jakobsh. New Delhi: Oxford University Press.

Malhotra, Karamjit K. 2013. 'Issues of Gender among the Sikhs: Eighteenth-Century Literature'. In *Journal of Punjab Studies*, 20 (½).

Mani, A. 2011. 'Sikhs in Multi-ethnic Indonesia'. In *Sikhs in South East Asia: Negotiating Identity*, edited by Shamsul A.B. and Arunajeet Kaur. Singapore: ISEAS Publishing.

McCarthy, Rory G. 2013. *The Sikh Diaspora in Australia: Migration, Multiculturalism and Imagining of Home*. Pennsylvania: University of Pittsburg.

McLeod, W.H. 2000. *Exploring Sikhism: Aspects of Sikh Identity, Culture and Thought*. New Delhi: Oxford University Press.

Mehta, Parvinder. 2013. 'Imagining Sikhs: The Ethics of Representation and the Spectacle of Otherness in Bollywood Cinema'. In *Sikh Formations: Religion, Culture, Theory*. Available at: https://doi.org/10.1080/17448727.2013.774708 (accessed on 1 February 2020).

Mooney, Nicola. 2010. 'Lowly Shoes on Lowly Feet'. In *Sikhism and Women: History, Texts, and Experience*, edited by Doris. R. Jakobsh. New Delhi: Oxford University Press.

Mooney, Nicola. 2011. *Rural Nostalgias and Transnational Dreams: Identity and Modernity Among Jat Sikhs*. Canada: University of Toronto.

Myrvold, Kristina. 2014. 'Sikhs In Mainland European Countries'. In *The Oxford Handbook of Sikh Studies*, edited by Pashaura Singh and Louis E. Fenech, UK: Oxford University Press.

Oberoi, Harjot. 1994. 'Sanatan Tradition and its Transmission'. In *The Construction of Religious Boundaries: Culture, Identity, and Diversity in the Sikh Tradition*. Oxford University Press.

Puar, Jasbir K. 1995. 'Resituating Discourses of "Whiteness" and "Asianness" in Northern England. Second Generation Sikh Women and Constructions of Identity'. In *Socialist Review*, 24 (1& 2). Durham, North Carolina: Centre for Social Research and Education, Duke University Press.

Shani, Giorgio. 2008. 'The Territorialisation of the Quam'. In *Sikh Nationalism and Identity in a Global Age*. New York: Routledge.

Singh, Amardeep. 2012. 'Being Sikh in America'. *The New York Times*. Available at: https://india.blogs.nytimes.com/2012/08/07/being-sikh-in-america/ (accessed on I February 2020).

Singh, Birinder Pal. 2014. 'Sikhs of the Hyderabad Deccan'. In *Economic and Political Weekly*, 26 July, XLIX (30).

———. 2018. 'Dilemmas of Shillong's Dalit Punjabis'. Available at: https://www.raiot.in/dilemmas-of-shillongs-dalit-punjabis/ (accessed on 1 February 2020).

———. 2018. 'In Lieu of Conclusion'. In *Sikhs in the Deccan and North–East India*. Abingdon Oxon: Routledge.

Singh, Harleen. 2006. 'Tur (Banned) Masculinities: Terrorists, Sikhs, and Trauma in Indian Cinema'. In *Sikh Formations: Religion, Culture, Theory*, 2(2):115–204.

Singh, Jasjeet. 2014. 'An Insight into The British Sikh Community'. In *British Sikh Report*. Available at: http://www.britishsikhreport.org/wp-content/uploads/2014/04/British-Sikh-Report-2014.pdf (accessed on 14 March 2020).

Singh, Jaspreet. 2013. *Helium*. Great Britain: Bloomsbury.

Singh, Paramjit and Balwinder Singh. 2014. 'Structure and Pattern of Urbanization in Punjab: A Macro Level Analysis'. In *International Journal of Punjab Studies*, January, 21(1): 69–84.

Singh, Pashaura. 2010. 'Revisiting the "Evolution of the Sikh Community"'. In *Journal of Punjab Studies*, Special Issue, Spring–Fall, *W.H. McLeod: Assessing his Legacy*, 17 (1&2).

Somers, Margaret. 1994. 'The Narrative Constitution of Identity: A Relational and Network Approach'. In *Theory and Society*, October, 23 (5): 605–649. Available at: http://www.jstor.org/stable/658090 (accessed on 21 June 2014).

Sokefield, Martin. 2008. Quoted by Robert Cohen. 'Four Phases of Diaspora Studies'. In *Global Diasporas*. U.S.A and Canada: Routledge.

Spencer, Stephen. 2006. 'Introduction'. In *Race and Ethnicity: Culture, Identity and Representation*. Routledge: New York.

Tatla, Darshan Singh. 2014. 'The Sikh Diaspora'. In *The Oxford Handbook of Sikh Studies*, edited by Pashaura Singh and Louis E. Fenech. UK: Oxford University Press.

Thandi, Surinder Singh. 2014. 'Sikh Migration, Diasporas and Transnational Practices'. In *The Oxford Handbook of Sikh Studies*, edited by Pashaura Singh and Louis Fenech. UK: Oxford University Press.

Tololyan, Khachig. 2007. 'The Contemporary Discourse for Diaspora Studies'. In *Comparative Studies of South Asia, Africa and Middle East*, 27 (3). Available at: https://muse.jhu.edu/article/224587/pdf (accessed on 23 January 2020).

Yin, Cao. 2017. *From Policemen to Revolutionaries: A Sikh Diaspora in Global Shanghai, 1885–1945*. Brill.

Yin, Cao. 2018. 'The Forgotten History of Sikhs in Shanghai'. In interview with Bibek Bhandari. 9 March, Sixth Tone. Available at: https://www.sixthtone.com/news/1001893/the-forgotten-history-of-sikhs-in-shanghai (accessed on 6 March 2020).

Index

A

Abdali, Ahmad Shah, 23, 147
Ad Dharmi, 52, 65
adult franchise, 51
Agrahari sikhs, 74, 76–77, 79–81, 91
agricultural community, 15, 36, 49, 84
agricultural identity, 27
agricultural surpluses, 54
Ahluwalias, 63
Ahluwalia, Muninder K., 189, 192
Air India 182 (2008), 188
Air India flight, bombing of 182, 187
Akal Takht, 169
  demolition of, 40
Akali Dal, 31, 36, 57–58, 169
Akali Morcha, 80
Akali party, 39
Akbar, 19
akhand path, 159, 168
Alcoff, Linda Martin, 13, 173–174
alcoholism, 92
Alimchandani, Anjali, 189, 192
All Assam Gana Sangram, 87
All Assam Student's union, 87
Amar Das, Guru, 18
Ames, Michael M., 131
amrit, 91, 99, 157–158
amrit kund (pond of nectar), 101
amrit sanskar (baptism) ceremony, 158
Amritsar, 19–20, 23, 28–30, 57, 60, 64–65, 85, 169
Amu 2005, 191
Angad, Guru, 18
Anglo-Sikh wars, 26
anti-imperial Gadar party, 187
anti-social behaviour, 43
Arab fundamentalists, 188
ardaas, 96
Arjan Dev, Guru, 19
Aroras, 16. *See also* Khatris; trading community
Arya Samaj, 158
Asa Singh Mastana, 38
Asomiya Sikh, 81–82, 84, 86–87, 90–93
Assam Accord 1985, 93
Assam Sahitya Sabha, 87
Australian Sikhs, 8, 13, 53, 106–107, 112, 114–120
  Anglo-Celtic influence, 117
  close community structure, 116
  community culture, 118
  establishment of gurdwaras, 117
  farms in Woolgoolga, 117
  gold rush in Victoria (1851), 116
  identity projection, 118
  immigration restrictions, 116
  liberalisation of immigration policies, 120
  multiculturalism, 119

opportunities for agrarian labour, 115–116
prosperity in farming, 117
societal pressure, 118
turbaned identity, 118
undercurrent of racism, 119

B

Badi Sangat Gurdwara, 76
Bahris, 17
Baisakhi, 75, 96
Bakshi Ram Singh Haveli, 27
Bal Lila Gurdwara, 75
Baldwin, Shauna Singh, 34, 158
Balmiki, 52
Banda Bahadur, 23, 95
Banerjee, Himadri, 13, 72–74, 76–77, 80, 82–85, 89–90
Bangla Sahib, 38
Banjara sikhs, 97–98, 103
'*barah baj gaye*' jokes, 189
Barkola Sing Gaon, 84
Bedi *got*, 18
Bedi, Khem Singh, 27, 30
Bedi, Sahib Singh, 25, 30
Behl, Natasha, 13, 172
Bezbaroa, Lakshminath, 82
Bhag Milkha Bhag (2013), 190
Bhalla got, 18
Bhangi, 52
bhangra regalia, 183
Bhindranwale, 39, 184. *See also* Gandhi, Indira; Operation Blue Star
Bhuyan, Surya Kumar, 82
Bibi Bhani, 155
Bibi Nanki, 155
Bihari Sikhs, 72–79
dialects of, 78
duality of identity, 78
Guru Nanak's travel to Bihar, 72
origin and evolution, 72
trading professional class, 78
bill of exchange (*hundi*), 146
Bittner, Herman, 188
blundering use of English, 181
Bordoloi, Rajanikanta, 82
Bose, Subhash Chandra, 80
Boskin, Joseph, 14, 183
Brah, Avtar, 13, 107, 131, 137
Brahmo Samaj, 80
British magnanimity, 26
British recruitment of Sikhs in army, 8
Bukit Brown cemetery, Singapore, 186
Bunjahis, 17

C

Canada and the US, Sikhs in, 120–124
agro-based jobs, 121
chain migrations, 122–123
food banks, 201
harassment, 121
liberalisation in immigration policies, 123
physical and oral examinations, 121
preferred destination, 124
racist discrimination, 122
racist persecution, 121
Sikh presence in the government, 123

Sikh students in Canadian universities, 123
Sikh–Mexican marriages, 122
willingness to work at lower wages, 120
xenophobia, 121
Canadian Cancer Society, 136
Caste
abolition of, 51
based mohallas, 200
consciousness, 64
distribution of work and, 50
group differences and, 133
hierarchy, 17, 66
paradigms, 144
resurgence of identity, 68
chaddar pana (Jat custom of marriage), 29
chain migrations, 122, 130
Chamars (leatherworking castes), 52
Chaparmukh Sing Gaon, 84
Chaudhary, Hardatta, 82
Chaupa Singh Rehitnama, 147–148
Chauthi Koot (2015), 190
Chhimbas, 51
Choti Sangat Gurdwara, 76
Churhas (sweepers), 52. *See also* Balmiki; Bhangi; Mazhabi castes
cinematic representation, 177–186, 190
Citizenship Amendment Act 2019, 93
class, caste, ethnicity and politics, 146–154
closed community cultures, 129
Cohen, Robert, 13
colonial gaze, 154–162
colonial intervention, 178
common external symbols of Sikhism, 62
common religious identity, 159, 198
community identity, 2, 6, 8, 15–16, 35, 48, 93, 101, 106, 109, 127, 141, 162, 178, 196
consolidation of, 62
compensatory lands, 32
congregation, importance of, 196
Continuous Journey Regulation, 121
Cook, James, 115
cosmopolitan culture, 120, 141
cosmopolitan identities, 119, 196
Council of Khalistan, 138
Councils of Regency, 151
credit cooperatives, 50
Criminal Tribes Act (1871), 97
cultural camps, 135
cultural essentialism, 189–193
cultural identity, 38, 92–93, 119, 130, 134, 177
diffused, 178
dilution of, 111
cultural practices, 7, 28, 30, 61, 71, 76, 79, 86–87, 130, 152, 158, 192, 196
cultural shifts, 2, 144

D

Dakhani Sikhs, 94–101
ardaas, 96
'correct' Sikh practice, 96
cross-cultural orientation, 101
languages and dialects, 100
local influences, 94
lower rungs of social life, 102
occupational diversification, 102
Dalit Sikh, 5, 63, 65, 67

impact of urbanisation, 63–69
Dandua Droh, 82
Darbar Sahib, desecration of, 40
Das, Veena, 13, 41–43, 185
Dasam Granth, 95–96
Dasgupta, Rana, 44
Davies, Christi, 181
Davies, Christie, 14, 180–181
Delhi Sikh Gurdwara Management Committee (DSGMC), 38, 45, 165
demographic transitions, 71, 144
denotified tribes, 97
Desjardins, Ellen, 201
Desjardins, Michael, 201
Dhavan, Purnima, 13, 20–22, 147, 150–151
Dhubri Sahib, 91
diasporic identity, 13, 129, 136–137, 140
Dock Police Force, 109
domino effect, 154
Dorinson, Joseph, 14, 183
double-income families desire among Sikh boys, 165
dowry, 153–155
dress codes, 130, 162
drug addiction, 43, 92, 133
drug trade, 130
Dumdama Sahib Gurdwara, 82–83
Dumdamiyas, 83
Dusenbury, Verne, 13, 111, 113–114

E

East India Company, 108
East Punjab, 6, 8, 32, 36, 38, 90, 122
economic growth of the Sikhs, 111
economic liberalisation, 7
economic mobility, 66
egalitarianism, 18
ego-enhancing identity, 7–8, 60
elitism, linguistic marker of, 181
employment opportunities, 55, 57, 80, 101, 103, 107, 121
ethnic identity, 139, 163
ethnographical survey of Punjab (1881), 25
Europe, 13, 107, 127–129, 135
  chain migration, 128
  construction and catering business, 128
  illegal Sikh immigrant, 128
  large-scale migration, 127
  shift in occupational patterns, 129
  shift is voluntary, 127

F

female infanticide, 145, 152–154
feudal authority, 56
fidelity in marriage, 145
five 'K's. *See* kakars (the five Ks)
The Flying Cross, 137
frayed community dynamics, 25–29
free mobile food support, 201
Freud, Sigmund, 180
Frontline, 94

G

Gadamer, Hans Georg, 173
Gandhi, Indira, 39, 41, 184
  assassination, 41, 184
gang wars, 108, 130

gatka (martial drill), 96
gender imbalance, 167
gender paradigms, 130
Girg, Naveen, 187
Gobind Ghat Gurdwara, 75
Gobind Rai, Guru, 21
Gobind Singh, Guru, 20–24, 63, 75, 80, 94–97, 103, 146, 148, 157–158
  350th birth anniversary in Patna, 103
  abolished the *masand*, 21
  creation of the Khalsa, 178
  death of, 23, 146
  Khalsa identity, 24
  military culture of, 22
grain and oilseed trade, 77
Granth Sahib, 95, 148, 167–168
Great Depression, 121
Green Revolution, 7, 36–37, 54–55, 65
Gunnarsson, Sturla, 188
Gupta, Dipankar, 50, 67–68
Gur Sikh Gurdwara, 137
gurbani, 167–168
gurdwaras
  litigations over land for, 45
  management of, 167–168
  politics, 197
gurdwara reform movement, 31
Gurmukhi, 77, 161
Gurta Gaddi celebrations (2008), 103
Guru Granth Sahib, 67, 95, 103, 158, 166–168
Guru ka Bagh Gurdwara, 75
Guru Nanak, 17–18, 22, 25, 72–74, 79, 81, 96, 100–101, 145, 166, 169
  association with the peasantry, 18
  celebrations of 550 years of birth, 169
  emphasised the importance of *grihasta* (householder's life), 96
  no discrimination society, 166
  objective assessment, 145
  teachings, 18
  understanding of spirituality, 18
gurupurabs, 92, 149, 168
  show of strength, 44
Guruship in Sikh faith, 18

H

half-submerged images, 177
Handoo, Jawaharlal, 13, 179
Hans, Raj Kumar, 64
Hardatta, 82
Hargobind, Guru, 20, 73, 96
Harmandar Sahib, 41, 64, 75, 79, 167
Hawley, M., 123, 125
Heaven on Earth, 132
Helium, 42
Hindu reformist movements, 155
Hola Mohalla, *hallabol* tradition, 96
homogenous identity, 2
Howard, Judith A., 3, 16, 195
Hughes, Melissa K., 14, 180, 190
hukumnamas, 73–75, 82, 146
humanitarian values, 195
humour, 177–186
Huzoor Sahib, 97, 167
Huzoori Sikhs, 94
  descendants of, 98
  history of the, 95

Huzoori traditions, 96
hyper-masculine image, 151

I

Ibbestson, Denzil, 25
identity entrenchment, 6
'identity politics', 135
'illegal migrant', 94
Indian National Army, 80
Inglis, Joy, 131
institutional structures of Sikhism, 156
institutionalisation of Sikh religion, 13
institutionalised hierarchies, 162–170
intellectual inertia, 4
intellectual tradition, 144
inter-community power paradigms, 9
inter-religious practices, 159
intra-community differences, 5, 126

J

Jack, Surrey, 5
Jakobsh, Doris R., 13, 135, 148, 171
Jamait-i-Sikhan, 98
jantris, 168
Japji Sahib, 197
Jat Boot, 28
Jats, 6–7, 13, 16–31, 37, 43, 51–62, 64–68, 80–81, 91, 110, 122, 125–126, 128, 133, 150, 152, 198
  colonial preference for, 25–29
  differences with Khatri-Arora, 200
  identity revamp process, 60
  influence, 20–22
  intrinsic characteristics, 59
  khud kasht or self-cultivating farmers, 20
  migration as part of the colonial influence, 54
  migration to urban areas, 52–60
  peasantry, 25
  powerful class in Punjab, 58
  resistance to the mixing of castes, 59
  rural identity, 59
  'stereotypical' and 'essentialist characterisations', 27
Jatiachamars, 52
Jatt and Juliet 1 (2012), 43
Jatt and Juliet 2 (2013), 43
jhagra, 28
jhatka (slaughtering the animal in a way approved by Sikhism), 117
Jheers, 51
Jodhka, Surinder S., 3, 13, 50, 54, 66, 171
joint-family system, 131
Jonaki, 82
jugaad culture, 179

K

kakars (the five K's), 76, 99, 158
Kalal community, 62
Kalal, Jassa Singh, 62
Kalsi, Sewa Singh, 125
Kambohs, 51
Kapur, Preeti, 166
Karnataka Sikh Welfare Society (KSWS), 103
'Kaur', 158
Kaur, Agya, 157
Kaur, Amarjit, 110

Kaur, Arunajeet, 13, 109–111, 113–114
Kaur, Harleen, 13
Kaur, Kiranjit, 186
Kaur, Kiranjot, 169
Kaur, Nishang, 159
Kaur, Prakash, 38
Kaur, Ram, 147
Kaur, Ratan, 147
Kaur, Sada, 147
Kaur, Sahib, 147
Kaur, Surinder, 38
Khalistan Affairs centre, 138
Khalistan movement, 138
Khalistan National Council, 138
Khalsa
  brotherhood, 149
  codes, 198
  educational trusts, 163
  egalitarian nature of forces, 60
  identity, 22–24, 30, 75, 91, 150–151, 157, 198
  martial culture of, 146
  Nihangs, 75
  Sikh codes, 77
  soldiers, 52
  warriors, 150
Khalsa Diwan Society, 30
Khalsa Tract Society, 157, 159, 161
khanda, 5
Khasi unions, 91
Khatris, 6, 12, 16–19, 21, 23–25, 27–29, 31, 33, 63, 78, 150, 152, 154, 158
  dominance in the *guru ghar*, 19
  gots of, 18
  influence, 18
  kinship, 22
  leadership role remained in, 19
  pre-dominance, 17–19
  primacy of, 19
  urban culture of, 18
  See also trading community
Khokhran, 17
Kingsley, Ben, 191
kirtani jathas, 168
kirtaniyas, 98
Komagata Maru incident, 187
Kuipers, Giselinde, 14, 184
Kumhars, 51
kutchha vehras, 33

L

Lahore, 17–19, 23–25, 27, 30, 32, 38
Lahore Singh Sabha, 30
Lahori Fauj, 94, 98–100
Lal, Chandu, 98
landholdings, division of, 56
land ownership, 51
langar, 64, 67, 166, 168, 201
Learning to Drive (2015), 191
Letter from a Sister, 161
liberal intellectual tradition, 9
liberal religious foundation, advantage of, 9
liberal religious tradition, 144–147
liberalisation, 45, 123
liberalised economy, benefits of, 55
liberalised immigration policies, 107
Life and Words, 41
'lions of Punjab', 26
Lobanas, 51
Lohars, 51

lower castes, 29, 52, 63–64, 68
Luce-Celler Act of 1946, 123
Lyallpur, 32

M

Mahajani, Priya Khanna, 13, 58
Maharana Pratap, 80
Mahi, Ginni, 67
Mahtons, 51
Mai Bhago, 155
male Sikh in Indian cinema, 182
male-centrism, resistance to, 169
Malhotra, Anshu, 13, 17, 23, 26–29, 147, 152, 155–161, 200
Malhotra, Karamjit K., 13, 148–149
Malwa, 22, 122
Mandair, A.P.S., 13
Mani, A., 112
Manomati, 82, 84
Manusmriti, interpretations of, 145
marginalized identities, 4, 13
martial identity, 15, 23, 60, 96, 178
martial tradition, 73
masand system, 21, 75
  directives of, 21
mass migration, 107
Mata Fatoh, 147
Mata Sahib Devi (Sahib Kaur), 146, 155, 157
matha tekna (paying obeisance), 197
Mazhabi Sikhs, 7, 31, 52, 64, 66, 81, 90–91, 93–94
McCarthy, Rory G., 13, 118–119
McLeod, W.H., 13, 19, 21–22, 60–63, 148
media portrayal, 177–186
media representations, 176, 187, 189
Mehta, Deepa, 132
Mehta, Parvinder, 13, 182
micro-practices of 'othering', 179
micro-practices of resistance, 169
militancy, 40–41, 65
militant movement in Punjab, 45, 185
militarised Sikh sect, 20
military identity, 27
mismatched marriages, 132
misogynistic practices, 171
Misra, Girishwar, 166
mobilising practices, 136
monetary aid, 140
Mooney, Nicola, 13, 27, 37, 60, 165
multi-culturalism, 135
Munrias, 74
Muslim refugees, 34
Myrvold, Gwar Kristina, 13, 129, 141

N

nagar kirtans, 91
  show of strength, 44
Nais, 51, 62
Nanak Jheera Gurdwara, 100–101
Nanakpanthis, 73
nationalistic narratives, 84
new identity constructions, 154–162
Nibber, Gurpreet Singh, 169
Nizam Nasir-ud-daulah, 94
non-rural component, 12
non-rural trader Sikh, 5
non-traditional occupations, 131
normative identity, 2, 72
NRC, 93

O

Oak Creek Gurdwara, 188
Oberoi, Harjot, 13, 24–25, 30
occupational patterns, 49
Operation Blue Star, 39, 41, 139, 184, 187
oral traditions, 79

P

Panesar, Gurdev Singh, 104
panth's membership, 21
Partition in 1947, 116
  losses of, 31–36
  post-traumatic impact of, 190
  refugees, 6
Patibrat Dharm, 157
Patna Sahib Gurdwara, 78
Patna *sangat*, 74–75
Patna Sikhs, 76
patriarchal practices, conservative, 131
patterns of resistance, 162–170
pindadan in Gaya, 76
Pir Jalaluddin, 100
Podum Kunwari, 82
polarisation, 199
political turmoil, period of, 55, 184
Pothwari and Saraiki (Punjabi dialects), 38
power dynamics, 167
Prakash Purab celebrations (2017), 103
Prem Sumarag Granth, 147–148
prosperity, signs of, 66
psychological threshold, 35
psychological trajectories, 106
Puar, Jasbir K., 133
Punjab Land Alienation Act (1900), 26, 64
Punjabi cinema, 43
Punjabi dress code, 160
Punjabi music, 130, 135
Punjabi music-video industry, 59–60
Punjabi Suba, 35–36
punn marriage, 153–154
purdah (veil), 145, 151, 160
'purifying women', 159

Q

Qiissa (2014), 191

R

Race Relations Act, 126
racial hatred, 189
Radcliff Line, 32
radical sentiments, rise of, 184
Rai, Chaupa, 147
Rai, Gobind, 21, 63, 75
Rakabganj Sahib, 38
Ram Rauni fort, 60
Ram, Ronski, 52
Ramanand, Sant, 134
Ramdasias, 52
Ramdaspur, 19
Ramgarhia Sikhs, 7, 26, 60–62, 80, 90, 125–126, 133
Ranghretta, Bir Singh, 64
Ranghrettas, 63
Ranjit Singh, Maharaja, 23–26, 52, 64, 83–84, 94–95, 98, 147
Ravidas, Sant, 67
Ravidasia gurdwaras, 67

Ravidasia Sikhs, 52, 67, 128, 133
Rawalpindi, 17, 27, 31–32, 38
Rayya, Jaswinder, 67
reform movement, 29
refugees, 33, 36, 61, 102
  colonies, 34–35
  relief work, 35
rehit maryada, invocation of, 169
Rehraas Sahib, 197
religious identity, 3, 26, 67, 71, 90, 101, 109, 113, 126, 135, 144, 147, 158–160, 170, 178, 184, 189, 196
religious tourism, 101, 103
religious tradition, 144
reservations and quota policies, 65
right code of conduct, 153
righteousness, 18, 22
roadside *patris*, 179
role devaluation, 153
rural and semi-urban areas, 141, 172

S

sabat surat identity, 198
sabhas, establishment of, 62
Sacred Games (2018), 191
Sahitya Prakash Publishers, 82
Sahota, Sunjeev, 124
Sainis, 51
sakhi tradition, 72, 100
Sanatan Sikh tradition, 30
Sanatani Sikhs, 75–76
sandhya, ritual of, 158
sangat or congregation, 145, 196
Santa Banta jokes, 4, 180
'sardar jokes', 10, 181
Sargodha, 32
Sarins, 17
sati, 145
scavenging, menial tasks of, 66
second and third-generation immigrants, 140
separatist stance, advocacy of, 134
sewa (service), 136
sex ratio of the Sikh population, 171
sex selection, 10, 172
Shani, Giorgio, 13, 36, 126, 137, 139
shifting patterns, 129–141
shifting profiles, 4
Shiromani Gurdwara Prabandhak Committee (SGPC), 31, 38, 57–58, 95, 163, 165, 167, 169
Shodhganga report, 171
Sikh administrative, 21
Sikh American Legal Defense and Education Fund (SALDEF), 138
Sikh coalition, 138
Sikh code of conduct, 90, 158
Sikh concept of sewa, 136
Sikh Federation (UK), 138
Sikh History Society, 148
Sikh identity, 2, 5, 7, 10, 12, 16, 27, 30–31, 37, 71, 74, 77–78, 81, 84, 90–91, 94–95, 101, 104, 114, 126, 134–136, 139, 150, 155, 158–159, 164, 167, 170, 184, 197–199@
  Assamese Sikh identity, 84
  in Australia, 115–120
  Bihari-Sikh identity, 74, 77
  call for, 30
  in Canada, 120–124
  cultural normative, 91
  disparate facets of, 5
  in Europe, 127–129

evolution of, 1
facets of, 95
in foreing lands, 106–141
hallmark of, 78
interest in, 2
Khalsa identity, 198
mapping of, 11
notions of, 2
powerful position of Khatris, 16
Ramgarhia Sikh identity, 126
religious normative, 91
resurgence of, 170
rural, 12
shifting patterns, 129–141
Singh Sabha's role, 81
in South East Asia, 108–115
turban, 197
turbaned, 91
in United Kingdom, 124–127
in United States, 120–124
urban, 12
Sikh intelligentsia, 155
Sikh jokes, 190
Sikh kingdom, rise of, 23
Sikh massacre (1984), 78
Sikh migration, 13, 106–108, 120, 122–123, 127–129, 131
Sikh Motorcycle Club, 136
Sikh movement, core intent of, 104
'Sikh Park', 192
Sikh prayer routines or *nitnem*, 158
Sikh professionals, 38, 63, 136
Sikh reform movement, 67
Sikh social codes, 169
Sikh social identity, 7, 198
Sikh traditions of martyrdom, 36
Sikh victims of the 1984 genocide, 185
Sikh weddings and social gatherings, 44
Sikh woman
in academics, 173
battle-ready, 160
dress code, 158
emphasis on education for girls, 164–165
entrenched in the common cultural spaces, 158
female identity, 151, 157, 162
negotiated their positioning within the community, 9
politico-administrative activities, 147
position and participation in the community, 166
presence in different fields, 165
second-generation Sikh women, 133
social media usage, 173
taught Gurmukhi at home, 161
turban-wearing, 169
who writes Kaur, 5
Sikhs in Assam and Meghalaya, 81–94
'line system legislation', 85
actively participated in the Assam movement, 87
Asomiya Sikh community, 81
challenges, 93
dressing, 86
entrenchment in local customs, 91
evolution of the Sikh community in Assam, 82
ghettoisation of the Sikh community, 85

intermarriages, 86
Janamsakhi tradition, 81
Jat arrival, 90–91
language, 92
mazhabis Sikhs, 81
socio-economic disparity, 92
sweeper Sikhs, 85, 89–90
vulnerable to state persecution, 89
Sikhs in Bengal, 79–81
Bengal's first association with Sikhs, 79
Sikhs as a social group in Bengal, 79
Sikligar community, 96–97, 100
Singh Sabha (Assembly of the Sikhs), 29
Singh Sabha movement, 77–78, 155–158, 161, 163, 166
Singh, Amardeep, 28, 188
Singh, B., 55, 65, 84, 87, 89, 95
Singh, Baghel, 147
Singh, Bhai Chaupa, 147
Singh, Bhai Desa, 149
Singh, Bhai Prahlad, 149
Singh, Bhai Randhir, 170
Singh, Birinder Pal, 13, 83, 91, 93, 95, 98–100, 102
Singh, Chaitanya, 83–84
Singh, Chandan, 87
Singh, Chiranjiv, 104
Singh, Ditt, 30
Singh, Gurbir, 188
Singh, Gurmukh, 30
Singh, H., 183
Singh, Jagat 'Jhatkai', 117
Singh, Jasjeet, 134
Singh, Jaspreet, 42
Singh, Jawahar, 30
Singh, Kahn, 155
Singh, Karan, 87
Singh, Kumedan, 82
Singh, Master Tara, 31–32, 35–36
Singh, P., 17–18, 55, 65
Singh, Pashaura, 13
Singh, Raja Ram, 82
Singh, Sant Fateh, 36
Singh, Sondhe, 28
Singh, Vishavjeet, 192
Singh, Zail, 125
Singha, Chandrakant, 83
Singhia, Karora, 147
Siri Chand, 73
Sisganj Sahib, 38
siyappa (wailing rituals on death), 159
social complexities, 176
social etiquette, 181–182
social identity, 49
social knowledge, 190
social marginalisation, 102
social psyche, 176
social stratification, 50
socio-cultural
boundaries, 181
legacies, 9
orientations, 6, 149
patterns, 17
shifts, 199
structure, 10
socio-economic situations, 48
socio-hierarchical patterns, 49
socio-religious
discourse, 147
structures, 168
Sodhi *got*, 18

Sokefield, Martin, 13, 136
Somers, Margaret, 13, 144
South East Asia migration, 108–115
  cultural ramifications, 111
  fascinating trail of Sikh arrival, 8
  growth of community culture, 109
  legitimised as an ethnic group, 111
  local influences, 112
  occupational profile, 112
  printing presses, 112
  proficiency in English, 112
  radically depoliticised, 111
  religious affiliations, 110
  religious identity, 113
  Sikh appearance, 109
  sports and the dairy industry, 112
  survival of their religious identity, 109
  tourist industry, 112
  urban cosmopolitan, 114
spatial and the cultural differences, 71
Spencer, Stephen, 192
spiritual liberation, 145
state-funded Sikh denominational schools, 138
Straits Settlements in 1826, 108–109
suhaag and *ghorian*, 148
Sujan Singh Haveli, 27
Sukhmani Sahib, 168
Sunar, Pamma, 67
Suniars, 51, 74, 90

T

taboo, 131
Takht Sri Harmandir Sahib, Patna, 75
takka and *vatta* marriages, 154
Talukdar, Daibachandra, 82
Talukdar, Sushant, 94
Tanjong Pagar Dock Company, 109
Tata Steel City, 61
Tatla, Darshan Singh, 13, 106
Tegh Bahadur, Guru, 20, 63, 73–75, 77, 81–83
Thakkarwal, Rajni, 67
Thandi, Surinder Singh, 140
Thoka, Jassa Singh, 60
three 'b's (pillars of a happy married life), 157
Tololyan, Khachig, 13, 136, 140
toshakhana, destruction of, 40
trading community, 16, 31, 36, 38, 41, 44
  contemporary positioning of, 16
  losses of partition and, 31–36
trading markets, 33
trading/professional class, 33, 46
Trehan *got*, 18
turban, 186–189
'turban man', 188

U

Udasi order, 73
unapologetic display of wealth, 44
unemployment, 43
United Kingdom, 124–127, 138
  arrival of the Ramgarhias, 125
  chain immigration, 124
  compromise on outward religious symbols, 124
  intra-community differences, 126
  keshdhari identity, 126
  Ramgarhia Board, Leeds, 125

Ramgarhia Sikh identity, 126
struggled for exemptions, 126
upper-caste social codes, 17–18
urban housing, 56
urban population, growth of, 55
urbanisation, 67, 93

V

Vaid, Mohan Singh, 157
value-expressive function of humour, 181
vand chhakko (*wand chhakkna*) or 'share what you have', 136, 200
Victorian dress codes, 160

W

Waris Shah, 23
West Punjab, 30, 33–34, 36, 90, 179, 200
What the Body Remembers, 34, 158
Williams, Raymond, 40
World Sikh Organization, 137–138
World Trade Centre attacks (2001), 188
World War I, 26, 106, 121, 137
World War II, 107, 116–117, 122, 124, 137, 192

Y

Yajnopavit ceremony for girls, 158
The Year of the Runaways, 124
Yin, Cao, 13, 186–187

About the Author

Dr Manpreet J. Singh has done her PhD in English Literature from University of Mumbai. Most recently, she taught with the Department of English, Mata Sundri College for Women, University of Delhi.

In 2014, the centenary year of the Komagata Maru incident, she was awarded senior fellowship for research on the Sikh community by the Indo-Canadian Studies Centre, University of Mumbai. It was funded by British Columbia province, Canada. Her report on the Sikh diaspora in British Columbia is being published in a forthcoming title by CoHaB, Indian Diaspora Centre, University of Mumbai (2020).

Her interests centre around contemporary literature, gender studies, ethnic identities, popular culture, postcolonial perspectives and their intersections. Her previous works include a collection of poems titled *The Golden Arc* (1991) and *Male Image Female Gaze: Men in the Fiction of Shashi Deshpande* (2012).

She currently resides in Mumbai, India.